Teaching About Culture, Ethnicity, & Diversity

Exercises and Planned Activities

Editor
Theodore M. Singelis

SAGE Publications
International Educational and Professional Publisher
Thousand Oaks   London   New Delhi

For information:

SAGE Publications, Inc.
2455 Teller Road
Thousand Oaks, California 91320
E-mail: order@sagepub.com

SAGE Publications Ltd.
6 Bonhill Street
London EC2A 4PU
United Kingdom

SAGE Publications India Pvt. Ltd.
M-32 Market
Greater Kailash I
New Delhi 110 048 India

Printed in the United States of America

Library of Congress Cataloging-in-Publication Data

Main entry under title:

Teaching about culture, ethnicity, and diversity : exercises and
  planned activities / edited by Theodore M. Singelis.
     p. cm.
   Includes bibliographical references and index.
   ISBN 0-7619-0695-9 (pbk. : alk. paper)
   1. Culture—Study and teaching (Higher)—Activity programs.
   2. Ethnicity—Study and teaching (Higher)—Activity programs.
   3. Multiculturalism—Study and teaching (Higher)—Activity programs.
   4. Intercultural communication—Study and teaching (Higher)—
   Activity programs. 5. Stereotype (Psychology)—Study and teaching
   (Higher)—Activity programs. I. Singelis, Theodore M.
   HM101.T38 1997
   306'.071—dc21   97-21130

This book is printed on acid-free paper.

98 99 00 01 02 03 10 9 8 7 6 5 4 3 2 1

Acquiring Editor:	Jim Nageotte
Editorial Assistant:	Kathleen Derby
Production Editor:	Sherrise M. Purdum
Production Assistant:	Denise Santoyo
Typesetter/Designer:	Danielle Dillahunt
Cover Designer:	Ravi Balasuriya
Print Buyer:	Anna Chin

Contents

PART 2

PART 3

PART 4

Introduction

This book is a resource for teachers. It contains 28 exercises and planned activities that can be used to teach about culture, ethnicity, and diversity. I use the term *teacher* broadly here. The exercises and activities (hereafter simply exercises) are appropriate for graduate, college, and even advanced high school students in a spectrum of classes such as cross-cultural psychology, intercultural communication, sociology, social work, anthropology, ethnic studies, women's studies, and education. However, the contents of this book may be profitably employed by those "teachers" who function outside the traditional classroom, but are no less concerned about issues involving culture, ethnicity, and diversity. Trainers involved in programs to prepare businesspeople for overseas assignments, supervisors who need to prepare health service providers to deal with varied client populations, and workshop leaders whose charge is to enhance productivity and understanding in the increasingly diverse workplace will all find the contents of this book applicable to their audiences.

In addition to being a source of exercises, this book also provides summaries of a variety of research-based concepts that are key to understanding the influences that culture, ethnicity, and diversity have on human thinking, feeling, and behavior. Each chapter begins with a brief essay presenting the main concepts that are illustrated or emphasized in the exercise. The essays provide a solid, literature-based grounding for the exercises. These concept summaries will be useful for teachers either as a refresher or an introduction to the concepts. The concept summaries cite appropriate research literature, and a reference section that can be used by both teachers and students who wish to pursue their study of particular areas is provided. Some teachers may want to use this book as a student workbook, assigning the concept sections and then working through the exercises. Others may wish to tie the exercises to concepts covered in texts or lectures. In either case, the concept summaries provide an undeniable academic substance to the exercises. Therefore, teachers who wish to focus on content rather than personal growth will find these exercises of value, although many will find their students experience personal growth as well (see Monges, Chapter 1, for an exercise that will help to clarify the values of teaching a multicultural course).

Why Use Exercises?

Although many teachers may be leery of using exercises because they have a reputation for being "soft," "touchy-feely," or "time wasters," there is, at least on my campus, an increasing emphasis on "student-centered learning," which actively involves the student in the learning process. Active learning is a pedagogically sound teaching method in any course. It can (a) increase student interest in the material, (b) make the material more meaningful, (c) allow students to refine and elaborate their understanding of the material, and (d) provide opportunities to relate the material to broader contextualized settings. Svinicki (1991) argues that, based on cognitive theory, each of these aspects of the learning process increases the actual learning that takes place.

In courses that deal with culture, ethnicity, or diversity, exercises may be essential. Many students in these courses have had little contact with members of other cultures and therefore do not have an existing cognitive framework into which the relevant material can be placed (Brislin, 1997). In Chapter 2, Casmir provides further rationale for the use of experiential learning in regard to culture and intercultural interactions.

Exercises, then, can provide the experientially based cognitive structure necessary to successfully integrate new material. As mentioned above, each of the exercises presented here has roots in the academic literature. Teachers can be very clear with themselves, and others (such as chairs and deans), what the pedagogical objectives of the exercise are. They may also assess, through testing and assignments, the learning outcomes of the exercises because the concepts are delineated at the outset. Although no experimental studies have assessed the efficacy of the exercises presented here, there is every reason to believe that they are as, or more, effective teaching tools than a conventional lecture alone.

Structure and Content of the Book

Although there is a wide variety of topics covered in the book, it is roughly divided into four parts. I will not detail each chapter here but rather provide an overview of each part with some selected examples. It should be noted that each chapter follows the same format. As mentioned above, at the beginning a concept or concepts are introduced and summarized in a brief essay. Next, the time and materials required are specified. Then, instructions for conducting the exercise are given and possible variations are delineated. Following these, suggestions for discussion are presented and a list of references and further reading is provided. Finally, where appropriate, material to be handed out to students is included at the end of the chapter. The similarity in structure and inclusion of materials is intended to make this book extremely easy to use. Still, each teacher will need to look over the contents of the chapters in deciding what may be appropriate for his or her class.

With the exception of Monges's chapter on teacher values, Part I contains exercises that require a period of time longer than a single class session. These exercises vary in their focus from ethnography (Kluver, Chapter 4) to time (Levine, Chapter 5). This section also contains an exercise (Seymour, Chapter 6) that focuses on disability and the perspective that comes from being in a wheelchair.

Part II might be titled "Culture and Behavior." The exercises here focus on the behavioral outcomes of cultural differences or cultural contacts. Chapter 9 (Singelis and Brislin) relates the individualism-collectivism dimension to the allocation of resources. In Chapter 11, Smith provides an excellent method for combining video presentation with a structure that ensures students will be attentive to the processes of acculturation. A key process in successful intercultural interactions, attribution, is the center of Chapter 12 (Shwayder and Bhawuk).

Identity, stereotypes, and person perception are central to the exercises presented in Part III. Yamada (Chapter 17) provides an exercise, based on a measurement instrument, to aid students in assessing their own level of ethnic identification, and Yeh (Chapter 20) focuses on the development of identity. Both chapters will be especially useful in heterogeneous groups. Exercises on stereotypes (Goto and Abe-Kim, Chapter 18) and accuracy of person perception (Cissna, Chapter 21) are also included in this part.

Part IV might be described as exercises that highlight the cultural construction of reality. Renfro and Hardwick (Chapter 24) use maps to demonstrate the influence of personal and cultural experience on our perception of the world. Likewise, Gourvès-Hayward (Chapter 25) uses color to show how culture and language intertwine to influence our perception. Religious beliefs (Brown and Fraser, Chapter 26) and emotions (Simmons, Chapter 28) are also central features of exercises in this part.

Choosing Exercises

In selecting exercises, one must be cognizant of several factors. Certainly time and content are important considerations. The concepts central to an exercise should also be important aspects of the course or training being done. An exercise that is not supported through reading and/or lecture may not be as effective as it could be. Perhaps more important than the exercise itself is the discussion that follows or accompanies it. If sufficient time to process and discuss an exercise is not used, its effectiveness may be diminished or lost entirely. Please do not rush through these exercises. They are rich in content and opportunity. Often the reactions and observations of the participants are better sources of insight and understanding than any lecture or text.

Finally, use only those exercises with which you feel comfortable. Although none of the exercises presented here is especially evocative, any exercise may bring up varying levels of self-disclosure and emotion in both yourself and your students. Depending on your willingness to deal with emotions, your relationship with the students, and the students themselves, you may decide that a particular exercise is not appropriate. Nonetheless, I am confident that all teachers will find a number of useful and interesting exercises in the pages that follow.

TED SINGELIS
CALIFORNIA STATE UNIVERSITY, CHICO

References

Brislin, R. W. (1997). Introducing active exercises in the college classroom for intercultural and cross-cultural courses. In K. Cushner & R. Brislin (Eds.), *Improving intercultural interactions: Modules for cross-cultural training programs* (Vol. 2). Thousand Oaks, CA: Sage.

Svinicki, M. D. (1991). Practical implications of cognitive theories. *New Directions for Teaching and Learning, 45*, 27-37.

PART 1

Beyond the Melting Pot

A Values Clarification Exercise for Teachers and Human Service Professionals

MIRIAM MA'AT-KA-RE MONGES

Concepts

Those who seek to infuse their curriculum and human service practice with multiculturalism must first clarify the significance of multiculturalism. This is important, because when the value of multiculturalism is clear, one will exert the additional effort needed to infuse it into the traditional curriculum or practice. The theory of multiculturalism is "becoming more thorough, complex, and comprehensive, while its practice in K-12 and college classrooms continues to be rather questionable, simplistic, and fragmentary" (Gay, 1995, p. 4). For multiculturalism to be firmly grounded into the curriculum, those who teach or infuse the theory into their human service practice have to have well-defined reasons.

The ultimate goal of multicultural education and practice is "at least at the infusion and preferably the transformation level" (Gay, 1995, p. 7). However, most educators do not have "the background information or pedagogical skills or personal confidence" (p. 7) to function at the infusion or transformational level.

It is also confusing for many professionals to read so many conflicting scholarly views of the value of multiculturalism. There are those, such as Ronald Takaki (1993), who assert that America has been defined too narrowly.

Diversity, in his perspective, is not a recent phenomenon. America as a concept and country has been diverse since its beginnings. Thus, Takaki maintains, we need to expand the definition of America by infusing into the curriculum information about the various ethnic groups that compose America. This information must be centered in a history that places them as actors, not merely victims (Takaki, 1993).

Other scholars are bothered by the notion that America is a tapestry whose history is woven together by many different but equally colorful threads. Arthur Schlesinger, Jr. (1996) is one scholar who is "troubled by the implication that American history was formed equally by three cultures in convergence—European, African and Amerindian." He asserts that "the formative American political ideas . . . are peculiarly European in origin" (p. A-11).

Teachers and human service professionals are frontline participants in social changes. For example, in California, ethnic minorities enjoy a numerical edge in 115 cites (Tien, 1994). Consequently, many teachers and human service professionals are aware that "the ethical, educational, economic, and political realities of this decade demand that we strive to diversify" (Tien, 1994, p. 238).

The activity in this chapter is to be used as an individual and group exercise that will allow the participants to discuss and begin the process of clarifying the value of multicultural education. It will begin to assist professionals with achieving the transformational level they must reach, before they can seek to help others reach it.

Time

This exercise requires 60 to 90 minutes, depending on discussion time and number of participants.

Requirements

The handout included here is needed. Also, a chalkboard or flip chart to play the Name Game, and to tally and discuss the final results.

Instructions

The instructor briefly discusses the concept that multiculturalism is important, relevant, propitious, and essential for successful practice, in the current and future world. The instructor introduces the Name Game, and then begins by writing his or her full name on the board and illuminating his or her own ethnic history through discussing the family history of the names. The instructor then requests the participants to write their names on the board and tell the group anything they may know about the cultural history of their names. The instructor can then repeat the declaration that America is indeed multicultural, and the present group is a good indication of the diversity of America.

The instructor divides the group (no more than five persons in each group is ideal) and gives the participants five goal statements concerning some purposes of education in a society composed of diverse racial and cultural groups. The participants should place these five objectives of multiculturalism in sequential order. They must first work alone, then try to reach a consensus with other group members. They choose one member of the group to share their decisions with the large group.

Variations

This is an exercise that can also be used with students during the first sessions of a multicultural education class. It can be administered again at the end of the semester and be used as part of an evaluation process.

A role play can also be added to this exercise. One participant affirms the value of each of the goals and the other must contest the goal. Each of the goals can be a separate role play. The larger group can then discuss the arguments given during the role play.

Discussion Suggestions

An excellent discussion branch is to ask what would be needed to practice each of the listed goals. What steps would individuals have to take to practice them, and what policy implementations would the various goals require? The next branch of questions would be to examine whether the group feels it would be worth the extra time and effort to implement the policy and/or personal practices to their logical conclusion.

Discussions could be held on methods of incorporating each of the goals in the classroom. Brainstorming on each goal can stimulate a multiplicity of ideas. The facilitator breaks the participants into groups of no more than five and asks them to elect a recorder and a spokesperson. They are given one goal and asked to call out ideas of how it can be incorporated into the classroom. The recorder writes the ideas on a flip chart. The key is that no one is to comment on the ideas. Neither approval nor disapproval can be expressed. The groups then brainstorm on the next goal, until all five goals have been discussed. The facilitator collects the ideas and the total group discusses them. This creative interaction will produce an extensive variety of resourceful ideas.

References and Further Reading

Banks, J. A. (1995). The historical reconstruction of knowledge about race: Implications for transformation teaching. *Educational Researcher, 24,* 15-25.

Gay, G. (1995, Fall). Bridging multicultural theory and practice. *Multicultural Education,* pp. 4-9.

Nieto, S. (1992). *Affirming diversity: The sociopolitical context of multicultural education.* New York: Longman.

Schlesinger, A. (1996, May 3). History as therapy: A dangerous idea. *New York Times,* p. A-11.

Sleeter, C. E. (Ed.). (1991). *Empowerment through multicultural education.* Albany: State University of New York Press.

Takaki, R. (1993). *A different mirror: A history of multicultural America.* Boston: Little, Brown.

Tien, C. (1994). Diversity and excellence in higher education. In N. Mills (Ed.), *Debating affirmative action: Race, gender, ethnicity, and the politics of inclusion* (pp. 237-245). New York: Delta.

MULTICULTURAL VALUES CLARIFICATION EXERCISE

The five goal statements listed below are various objectives of multiculturalism. Once we are clear about the value of multiculturalism, our ability to communicate its value is enhanced. Although all the goals have merit, please place in order the following objectives of multiculturalism. Work alone first, then try to reach a harmonious decision with other members of your group. You will have about 30 minutes. One member of your group must be elected to be your spokesperson.

Should other distinct goals emerge in your thinking or discussions, please list them separately and be prepared to explain how they fit in the order of the goals presented here.

_____ 1. To maintain cultural history, advance ethnic identity, and transform negative conceptions about cultural awareness.

_____ 2. To promote intercultural proficiency and the ability to interpret differing verbal and nonverbal cultural communication styles.

_____ 3. To develop the cultural expertise, knowledge, and values that will transcend boundaries and contribute to social and economic success in the 21st century.

_____ 4. To abolish ethnic and racial prejudice.

_____ 5. To assist marginal ethnic groups to become a part of the mainstream culture.

The statement we believe identifies the most significant goal of a multicultural curriculum is

_____

_____

Our reasons are the following:

1. _____

2. _____

3. _____

The goal that we value the least is _____

_____

Our reasons are the following:

1. _____

2. _____

The Transferability
of Knowledge

FRED L. CASMIR

Concepts

The concept of learning presents important and perplexing problems to teachers and trainers, and as a result also to those who are being instructed by them. Anderson (1993) identifies the roots of that challenge for those of us who are preparing individuals in one culture to function in another, by pointing out that "learning is separate from performance, and goals trigger the conversion of what has been learned into performance" (p. 37). Pittenger and Gooding (1971) remind us that learning theorists such as Thorndike were concerned several decades ago with the "nature of learning" and that for him it was best explained by the "strengthening of a connection between a stimulus and response" (p. 81). Based on the same model, Pittenger and Gooding insist that the best way to "maximize transfer of what is learned to new situations is to build up a very large repertoire of responses in an organism" (p. 85). What such comments indicate is that how we learn what we learn is of considerable importance.

The transferability of information becomes a real challenge when we move from one situation (the classroom) to "real life" situations, including moves from one culture to another. Bird, Heinbuch, Dunbar, and McNulty (1993) tell us that evidence exists that facts, data, examples, and categories provided in teaching sessions for trainees being prepared to enter an overseas culture, but whose learning experiences did not include interactions with representatives of the cultures studied, do not readily transfer to practical, meaningful applications.

In earlier reactions by those who were challenged by the complexity of intercultural communication, Pedersen and Howell (1986) point out that "unless persons recognize their own culture-based values, feelings and attitudes, are able to communicate them to others, and experientially learn the logic of other culture systems, practical information about another culture will be of little use" (p. xi). Casmir (1991) indicates that there is a very basic problem with learning in our U.S. culture: "Western cultural studies have taught us that our students have frequently been unable or unwilling to use what they have learned in our classrooms. Merely teaching racial or ethnic facts is not enough" (p. 233).

Both the general culture in which a student grew up and the specific cultural setting of his or her learning environment thus have a significant impact on learning, retention, and the transfer of information. Additionally, social scientists have pointed to the fact that "interaction skills are more effectively learned through guided experience in the behavior itself" (Borg, Gall, Kelley, & Langer, 1970, p. 405) and that such learning is even more effective if the learner can immediately apply what he or she has learned (p. 409).

Returning to the specific challenges faced by educators and trainers in intercultural communication, Bennett (1986) has attempted to respond to the teaching, knowledge-obtaining, transferring-of-information conundrum by suggesting the building of a program that balances content with process, culture specific with culture general, and the cognitive with the affective, to model new ways of learning. In that way, it is hoped that the concern of many, including Martin (1989), that students preparing for intercultural efforts are unable to draw on more traditional academic learning to prepare them for intercultural interactions can be dealt with. In training for business and industrial work in other countries, similar suggestions have been made by Gallois (1996) and Odenwald (1993), among others.

Examples, or models that show how such challenges have been met in specific teaching and training programs, include a Canadian State Commission of Education and Sino-Canadian educational and training effort, which incorporated extensive interactions and experiences in both cultures (Dan, 1989), and the interactional program developed by the Los Angeles Police Department and that city's Mexican consulate, which took police officers to Mexico for language and cultural-sensitivity training ("Only in America," 1995).

What can be done to encourage the active understanding, including the development of an attitude of acceptance, respect, and tolerance for cultural differences called for by Noyekawa and Sikenna (1987)? It seems clear, as these authors point out, that relatively little involvement at the emotional level results from our traditional teaching methods and settings with the culture under study. The concerns sketched out above have led to the development of one learning approach that has shown promise as far as transferability of knowledge is concerned, if not generalizability of information to individuals in all the cultures one may encounter.

Time

The project takes place over one semester or quarter.

Requirements

a. International students must be available on campus. The support of an International Students Office can be enlisted. Instructors will provide contacts and/or information about resources at the institution or in the community and possibly make an initial contact on behalf of a specific student or team. However, students will be asked to make the actual, personal, face-to-face contacts for arranging their projects on their own.

b. Students or trainees must negotiate with their partners what their relationships or interactions will be, and they should make clear that they are integrating this experience into a college or training course for which it is a requirement.

c. Various ethnic or racial groups in the community must be available and accessible, providing specific service-learning opportunities with the assistance and support of community groups or agencies. Such opportunities can either be used in addition to international students on a given campus or as the primary focal point of the students' or trainees' experiences.

d. Some practical aspects include availability of transportation and decisions concerning whether to carry out the project in teams, during the first experience. Reinforcement, the opportunity to compare notes, and the presence of a fellow student or trainee could make this a desirable arrangement.

e. The project must be integrated, as a requirement, into a course in intercultural communication or a similar training program. Principles, concepts, and techniques learned in the course or program must be related in the students' reports of their experiences.

f. The concept and application of the principles of service-learning (which goes beyond mere internships or "experiential learning") call for additional preparation of instructors. This would include familiarization with goals, examples, literature, workshops, and other available resources whenever such an approach appears to be desirable. The most significant aspects of service-learning, as it relates to intercultural communication studies, should be clarified for the students or trainees. The approach encourages students and trainees to avoid seeing such an experience, and human beings from another culture, as mere "resources" available for exploitation in the process of achieving their own ends or goals. Rather, the experience should be of some benefit to all involved, which requires openness in discussion and negotiation related to needs, purposes, goals, and benefits.

g. Openness, exploration, and critical assessment can be identified as factors that will help make the project meaningful to the student or trainee. These aspects encourage learning that may lead to greater retention and transferability to similar situations:

1. Actual involvement in a variety of intercultural communication processes
2. Immediate application of and reactions to concepts learned in the classroom
3. Direct and personal understanding of the psychological implications and reactions related to intercultural interactions
4. Real-world experience of success and failure, made possible in a supportive learning environment
5. Deeper understanding of actual benefits of interactive, interdependent, mutually beneficial communication processes
6. Satisfaction that comes from making a meaningful contribution to another human being's life

Instructions

a. Students will be required to keep a detailed diary of their experiences. This diary will be turned in to the instructor for reactions toward the end of the teaching or training period. Students will be required to select one individual from another culture, such as an international student who is a newcomer to the school (in the case of many cultures, someone of the opposite gender may *not* make a desirable partner in the project), or possibly an agency or a small group in the community. That selection should follow a discussion of the proposed interactions and justification of the choice of a partner or partners in cooperation with an instructor.

The students or trainees should develop interactions with their partners that

1. Provide opportunities for learning about each other's cultures
2. Provide opportunities for understanding cultural as well as individual differences
3. Provide opportunities for shared experiences such as meals, cultural events, and visits in each other's homes and with each other's families
4. Are responsive to specific needs in specific circumstances (e.g., information, experiential learning, specific problems with agencies or customs) including those of the student or trainee partner
5. Allow them to serve as intercultural informants for each other

Specific number and types of interactional experiences should be agreed on in a meeting between the instructor and the student or trainee. Students are required to keep a detailed diary of every interaction. To make that process meaningful, instructors will arrange individual meetings with students participating in the project to assure them of strict privacy; that is, the diary will be read only by the instructor, no copies of the material will be made, and the diary will be returned in person to the student, with comments or reactions by the instructor. Reasonable length, formats suitable to the instructor's goals in the course or program, and completion dates can be individually designed. Students should provide more than descriptive accounts; they should also analyze and deal with personal reactions related to their own feelings, the situation, and the specific factors they have learned and can relate to their classroom learning experiences.

b. Two oral reports, one about midterm and one toward the end of the course or training period, should be required. These will be presented to the students' peers in a classroom setting. Anonymity of specific persons should be ensured, but information about specific ethnic, racial, and cultural factors should be precise and authentic. These two reports are intended to share important insights, general cultural and communication-related information (*but not personal identification of partners*), and relevant relationships to the material covered in the course or training process.

Discussion Suggestions

Discussions could beneficially center around the following themes:

1. Culture shock or self-shock
2. Perceptions and expectations, including stereotyping and attributions
3. The role of culture and individual differences
4. The W-shaped curve and intercultural communication experiences
5. Applicability and adequacy of models like those developed by Hall (1959), Triandis (1995), and Hofstede (1980), among others

Comparisons and general discussion with and specific suggestions from peers and the instructor would be part of the report environment.

References and Further Reading

Anderson, J. R. (1993, January). Problem solving and learning. *American Psychologist, 48,* 35-44.

Bennett, M. J. (1986). Modes of cross-cultural training: Conceptualizing cross-cultural training as education. *International Journal of Intercultural Relations, 10,* 117-132.

Bird, A., Heinbuch, S., Dunbar, R., & McNulty, M. (1993, Fall). A conceptual model of effects of area studies training and preliminary investigation of the model's hypothesized relationships. *International Journal of Intercultural Relations, 17,* 415-435.

Borg, W. R., Gall, M. D., Kelley, M. L., & Langer, P. (1970). *The minicourse: A microteaching approach to teacher education.* New York: Macmillan Educational Services.

Casmir, F. L. (1991, July). Introduction: Culture, communication, and education. *Communication Education, 40,* 229-234.

Dan, Y. (1989). Canada helps in management training. *Beijing Review, 32,* 35, 36.

Gallois, C. (1996, June). Book review: Intercultural communication: Training: An introduction. *Journal of Occupational and Organizational Psychology,* p. 213.

Hall, E. T. (1959). *The silent language.* Greenwich, CT: Fawcett Premier.

Hofstede, G. (1980). *Culture's consequences.* Beverly Hills, CA: Sage.

Martin, J. (1989). Predeparture orientation: Preparing college sojourners for intercultural interaction. *Communication Education, 38,* 249-257.

Noyekawa, A., & Sikenna, M. (1987). *World priorities.* Yarmouth, ME: Intercultural.

Odenwald, S. (1993, July). A guide for global training. *Training and Development, 47*(7), 22-31.

Only in America. (1995, February 6). Los Angeles Ca. police officers being sent to Mexico for Hispanic sensitivity training. *Fortune, 131*(2), 142.

Pedersen, P., & Howell, W., (1986). Pros and cons of using structured exercises in intercultural groups. In W. H. Weeks, P. Pedersen, & R. W. Brislin (Eds.), *A manual of structured experiences for cross-cultural learning* (pp. ix-xvi). Yarmouth, ME: Intercultural.

Pittenger, O. E., & Gooding, C. T. (1971). *Learning theories in educational practice: An integration of psychological theory and educational philosophy.* New York: John Wiley.

Triandis, H. C. (1995). *Individualism and collectivism.* Boulder, CO: Westview.

Adventures in Cyberspace

A Cross-Cultural Scavenger Hunt

HARRY GARDINER

Concepts

This exercise has several practical purposes. The first is to provide an introduction to the Internet and the World Wide Web, also known as WWW, W3, or simply the Web (see Abraham, Jas, & Russell, 1995; Kehoe, 1996; Maran, 1995; Turlington, 1995). The Internet is a global network connecting thousands of computers throughout the world. It allows access to all kinds of information including professional databases, teaching materials, e-mail, free software, university and library databases, research documents, and other information. By using a Web browser, for example, Netscape, MacWeb, or Internet Explorer (to name a few), it is possible to connect to the World Wide Web by means of URLs, or uniform resource locators (addresses used to reach Web sites), and link to hundreds of thousands of pages of additional information, which include not only text but also graphics (pictures, videos, or animation) and sound. A URL address begins with the type of Internet tool needed to access the server, for example, http, ftp, or gopher, followed by a colon and two forward slashes and the server address. As an example, take a look at some of the exhibits at the Library of Congress by using its URL (http://www.loc.gov) and selecting the link for exhibits.

A second purpose is to familiarize students and teachers with the diversity of useful information available on the Internet in a wide variety of disciplines including psychology, sociology, ethnic studies, counseling, intercultural communication, social work, business, health care, and other areas (see Berge & Collins, 1995a, 1995b; Collins & Berge, 1995; Gilster, 1996; Linden & Kienholz, 1995; Manrique & Gardiner, 1995; McKim, 1996; Tennant, 1996). In this regard, the Web can be a particularly useful and powerful culture learning tool. At the same time, however, no one person can know about all cultures, so the ability to find and make use of information is a lifelong challenge used well by those who are interculturally successful.

Finally, this exercise is (in part) aimed at those who may feel they are "computer illiterate" or anxious "surfing the net" (see Fristrup, 1996; Kantor, 1995; Krol, 1995; Place, Dimmler, & Powell, 1996; Polyson, Saltzberg, & Godwin-Jones, 1996; Wehmeyer, 1996). Use of these exercises should be an enjoyable learning experience for the novice as well as the most sophisticated "internaut."

Time

Thirty to 60 minutes are needed to complete each of the scavenger hunts, depending on participants' expertise and success in locating information on the Internet. In-class discussion time may vary, but an additional 30 to 45 minutes should allow each student to comment on the experience and what was learned from it.

Requirements

The exercise requires access to the World Wide Web and some knowledge about how to navigate within it. It is helpful if the instructor is sufficiently familiar with the Internet and the workings of the Web to explain basic concepts and methods for accessing information as well as to respond to student questions. If not, arrangements can usually be made for a hands-on presentation by a technical staff person from the campus computer center. If the center has relevant handouts, students should be provided with copies for easy reference while carrying out the exercise.

Instructions

After introducing students to the Internet and World Wide Web (many may already be familiar with it) and how to locate different types of information, the instructor might introduce the exercise in this way: "The Internet and World Wide Web are powerful tools in the search for information. To give you an idea of the variety of information available in cyberspace, and to have fun while looking for it, we are going on a scavenger hunt." You may want to suggest that students work in groups of two or three to reduce the time needed to complete the exercise, which can be done as an out-of-class assignment. You should also stress that although the Internet and World Wide Web can provide (complete or partial) answers to many questions, a great deal of information is not, and probably never will be, located in cyberspace, but is available at the campus or public library. This includes many government documents, census records, reference books, and other materials. Although much of what is "out there in cyberspace" is accurate, scientific, well-documented research, a great deal of it consists of personal experience and opinion. Therefore, because anyone with knowledge and tools can create a Web page and place any type of information on it (scientific or otherwise), students need to be cautioned to critically evaluate what they find on the Internet and on Web pages and frequently check it against other sources before accepting its authenticity.

Variations

Two short versions of this exercise are provided as handouts at the end of this chapter. Either or both can be assigned or modified according to the instructor's needs. Students can work individually or in teams of two or more participants. Prizes, such as tickets to an ethnic or cultural event on campus (international banquet, film presentation, guest speaker, or other event), can be awarded to the first-, second-, and third-place winners based on criteria established by the instructor.

When assigning this exercise, the instructor should be aware that new Web sites are being made available all the time, old Web sites disappear, URLs change, and information stored at individual sites is continually being added or deleted. It is highly recommended that the instructor complete each step in the scavenger hunt handouts (or any variation of them) to make sure everything works before asking students to do the task. With some "surfing" of the Web, it should be relatively easy to construct any number of variations of the scavenger hunt, using lecture material, readings, discussion points, and other topics to make it particularly relevant to one's own class or needs.

Although instructors will eventually find their favorite Web sites, let me get you started with my own list of "Harry's Top 9 Favorite Culture Web Sites." You can connect to any of these pages by typing an address into your Web browser or by accessing my personal home page (http://cslab.uwlax.edu/~gardiner) where each of these is listed.

Here they are.

Web of Culture

http://www.worldculture.com/

This is my favorite culture site, listing lots of interesting information including world capitals, consulates and embassies, cuisine, currency exchange rates, job opportunities, holidays, and many other resources.

Electric Library

http://www.elibrary.com

Conduct real research over the Internet by searching more than 150 full-text newspapers, 800 full-text magazines, two international news wire services, 2,000 classic books, maps, photographs, and so on.

The Character of Culture

http://www.wcpworld.com/future/tcoc.htm

This site contains several categories including Future Culture, links to other countries, letters from members of the Peace Corps, traits of culture, and a quiz focusing on world cultures.

Intercultural Communication

http://www.uark.edu/depts/comminfo/www/intercultural.html

This Web site covers everything from Aboriginal studies to world scripture and many interesting cultural topics in between.

Intercultural E-Mail Classroom Connections

http://www.stolaf.edu/network/iecc/

For several years, I have set up e-mail connections among students in my classes and those in countries around the world. This Web site makes the task easier by making available mailing lists to help teachers and classes link with partners in other countries and cultures for e-mail classroom pen-pal and project exchanges. It includes separate lists for higher education, K-12, projects, surveys, and discussion.

The Human Language Page

http://www.june29.com/hlp/

If you want to know more about foreign languages, this page is for you. It begins with Aboriginal languages and ends with Welsh. Among the many kinds of information are audio tutorials on Arabic, phrases in Croatian, a beginner's course in Dutch, and numerous foreign language lessons for travelers.

Subway Navigator

http://metro.jussieu.fr:10001/bin/cities/english

If you like to travel underground, this site allows you to find routes in subway systems in dozens of cities around the world including Buenos Aires, Toronto, Paris, Hong Kong, Tokyo, Madrid, London, Boston, and Chicago.

Gestures and Body Language

http://www.worldculture.com/gestures.htm

Based on Roger Axtell's book *Gestures: Do's and Taboos of Body Language Around the World,* this site provides an informative and often amusing examination of body language and gestures. The information here may be especially useful for those planning to travel abroad or those who interact with individuals from a variety of international backgrounds.

Ethnic and Cultural Studies Resources

http://www.educationindex.com

This site serves as an annotated guide to the best education-related sites on the Web, conveniently sorted by subject, including ethnic and cultural studies, health and medicine, communications, psychology, sociology, business, marketing, and education. Visitors can stop at the Coffee Shop and chat interactively with others who are researching similar topics or go to the Lifestyle section and select sites covering the lifespan from infancy through preschool, primary and secondary education, to graduate and continuing education, as well as parenting and careers.

Discussion Suggestions

Due to the variety of topics covered in each of the attached scavenger hunts, this exercise should easily provoke lively discussion about the kinds of information available on the Internet and World Wide Web and the many ways in which it might be used. One example centers on the first question in Scavenger Hunt 1 and the search of the World Factbook. Imagine a student looks up Sierra Leone and Kyrgyzstan. What facts might he or she find and what conclusions might be drawn from them? Discussion could focus on how much one can learn about a country based on a few simple statistics. For example, although their populations are nearly identical, Sierra Leone, due to higher growth and fertility rates, will soon pass Kyrgyzstan. These figures might also say something about cultural values regarding family size. In countries where agriculture is important, families are generally larger than in countries where technology is more advanced. Significant differences in overall literacy rates (as well as individual male-to-female rates) provide some insight into the general quality of education in each country as well as sex role status as indicated by who is better educated, men or women. In Kyrgyzstan, female literacy is 96% and male literacy is 99%, whereas in Sierra Leone female literacy is only 11% compared to 31% for males. It can also be pointed out that a comparison of infant mortality rates and life expectancy can be good indicators of the quality of each country's health care system, medical facilities, and possible level of prenatal care, as well as possible use of birth control. For example, in Sierra Leone there are 138.8 deaths/1,000 live births versus 45.8 deaths/1,000 live births in Kyrgyzstan. Life expectancy is greater for both sexes in Kyrgyzstan than in Sierra Leone (males = 63 years vs. 44 years; females = 72 years vs. 49 years). Other items on the scavenger hunt may result in discussions about cultural differences, availability of disability information, cross-cultural research sources, and other matters.

References and Further Reading

Abraham, R., Jas, F., & Russell, W. (1995). *The WEB empowerment book: An introduction and connection guide to the Internet and the World-Wide Web.* Santa Clara, CA: TELOS (Springer-Verlag).

Berge, Z. L., & Collins, M. P. (Eds.). (1995a). *Computer mediated communication and the online classroom: Vol. 1. Overview and perspectives.* Cresskill, NJ: Hampton.

Berge, Z. L., & Collins, M. P. (Eds.). (1995b). *Computer mediated communication and the online classroom: Vol. 3. Distance learning.* Cresskill, NJ: Hampton.

Collins, M., & Berge, Z. L. (Eds.). (1995). *Computer mediated communication and the online classroom: Vol. 2. Higher education.* Cresskill, NJ: Hampton.

Fristrup, J. A. (1996). *The essential Web surfer survival guide.* Upper Saddle River, NJ: Prentice Hall.

Gilster, P. (1996). *Finding it on the Internet: The Internet navigator's guide to research tools and techniques* (2nd ed.). New York: John Wiley.

Kantor, A. (1995). *60 minute guide to the Internet: Including the World-Wide Web.* Foster City, CA: IDG Books Worldwide.

Kehoe, B. P. (1996). *Zen and the art of the Internet: A beginner's guide* (4th ed.). Upper Saddle River, NJ: Prentice Hall.

Krol, E. (1995). *The whole Internet for Windows 95: User's guide & catalog.* Sebastopol, CA: O'Reilly.

Linden, T., & Kienholz, M. L. (1995). *Dr. Tom Linden's guide to online medicine.* New York: McGraw-Hill.

Manrique, C. G., & Gardiner, H. W. (1995). Computer-mediated communications: Applications in selected psychology and political science courses. In M. Collins & Z. L. Berge (Eds.), *Computer mediated communication and the online classroom* (Vol. 2, pp. 123-136). Cresskill, NJ: Hampton.

Maran, R. (1995). *Internet and World Wide Web simplified.* Foster City, CA: IDG Books Worldwide.

McKim, G. W. (1996). *Internet research companion.* Indianapolis, IN: Que E&T.

Place, R., Dimmler, K., & Powell, T. (1996). *Educator's Internet yellow pages.* Upper Saddle River, NJ: Prentice Hall.

Polyson, S., Saltzberg, S., & Godwin-Jones, R. (1996, September). A practical guide to teaching with the World Wide Web. *Syllabus, 10*(2), 12-16. (See also http://www.syllabus.com)

Tennant, R. (1996, February). The best tools for searching the Internet. *Syllabus, 9*(5), 36-38. (See also http://www.syllabus.com)

Turlington, S. R. (1995). *Walking the World Wide Web: Your personal guide to the best of the Web.* Chapel Hill, NC: Ventana.

Wehmeyer, L. B. (1996, September). Teaching online search techniques your students can use. *Syllabus, 10*(2), 52-56. (See also http://www.syllabus.com)

Note to instructors: To receive *Syllabus*—the definitive education technology magazine—free each month during the academic year, contact *Syllabus* Magazine, Subscription Services, 1307 S. Mary Avenue, Suite 211, Sunnyvale, CA 94087-3018, and ask to be placed on the mailing list or subscribe online at the SyllabusWeb site (http://www.syllabus.com).

CYBERSPACE SCAVENGER HUNT 1

You are about to embark on a worldwide mission surfing the Internet for answers to some puzzling questions. If you thought Indiana Jones had some interesting adventures, hold on to your hats!

1. Do a net search for the World Factbook 1995. Select two countries (preferably from different geographical parts of the world), copy down the following information about each: name of country, population, population growth rate, birth rate, infant mortality rate, life expectancy at birth (for both males and females), total fertility rate, and literacy. What conclusions can you possibly draw about government policies regarding education, health care, birth control, and other issues from these figures? Compare and contrast the two cultures.

2. Go to the Web site for Web of Culture

   (http://www.worldculture.com), click on Cross-Cultural Quizzes, play one of the previous quizzes listed there and (without looking at the answers just below the questions), indicate how well you did. What did you learn about these cultures?

3. While caught in the "web of culture," find the recipe for Nicaraguan Chicken Tamales and print a copy. (If you want to try the recipe and leave some tamales in my mailbox, that would be fine.)

4. Search for the International Association for Cross-Cultural Psychology (IACCP). Find the March 1995 issue of the *Cross-Cultural Psychology Bulletin*. Write down the title and author of the book review in this issue. While there, print the list of Related Web Resources. If you have some spare time, you may want to explore some of these.

5. I want to buy a Native American T-shirt. Find a company that sells such T-shirts, write down the toll-free number (if there is one), and tell me how much I will have to pay for one of these shirts. Also tell me the name of the company and where it is located.

CYBERSPACE SCAVENGER HUNT 2

Here's another opportunity to surf the Internet for answers to some more puzzling questions. Like James Bond, Agent 007, you have a license, not to kill but to search the World Wide Web. Good luck and have fun!

1. Visit a restaurant in another country and write down its name, address, phone number, and one item from the menu.

2. Select a topic that you would like to know more about, for example, cultural differences in wedding practices, gestures, intercultural communication, culture shock, Japanese business practices, or African health care systems. Search the WWW for information and print one item you found related to the topic. Be prepared to present a brief summary of your findings to the class.

3. Go to the Special Education page at the University of Kansas (http://www.sped.ukans.edu/) and select Internet Resources on Disabilities. Find one of the organizations that serve women with disabilities and prepare a 5-minute presentation for the class on the information you found there.

4. Visit the city net Web site (http://www.city.net), select one city in the United States and another in a foreign country, and find the current temperature and weather forecast for each. Supply any additional information you find of interest about each of these cities.

5. Go to the Public Broadcasting Service (PBS) television page (http://www.pbs.org) and print a copy of the programs to be broadcast this week. Are there any that might be related to topics being discussed in this class? If so, make a list and bring it to class.

Grocery Store Ethnography

RANDY KLUVER

Recent theoretical studies in anthropology and communication have discarded artificial conceptions of culture as being primarily artifacts, an abstract set of religious and philosophical ideas, or behavioral patterns, in favor of an understanding of culture as a symbolic representation of worldview, or a communicative definition of culture (Clifford, 1988; Geertz, 1973; Leach, 1976; Schneider, 1976). To students operating from these static definitions, learning a culture is primarily a matter of learning of artifacts or doctrines that have little value in real interpersonal interaction. Culture is more accurately understood as a "web of significance," or the interaction of meanings that we attach to the patterns and artifacts around us (Geertz, 1973, p. 5). Learning about culture, according to this definition, is an interpretive science in search of meaning. Geertz proposes that the most appropriate means of teaching (and learning) about culture is through "thick description," or sorting out the structures of signification present in the symbolic actions of how people order their worlds.

Thick description should focus not on the exotic but rather on the normal aspects of daily life. Through close, interpretive observation, we can begin to unravel the levels of meaning present in daily activity, or the "informal logic of actual life" (Geertz, 1973, p. 17). To attempt to analyze culture apart from these daily events is to divorce culture from its application and leave analysis meaningless. Geertz argues that "cultural analysis is (or should be) guessing at meanings, assessing the guesses, and drawing explanatory conclusions from the better guesses" (p. 20). Through this process, students not only gain a better understanding of culture but also are able to attain some degree of cultural competence.

This understanding of culture has direct implications for how teachers teach about culture. First, culture is best taught through examining the informal aspects of daily life, rather than the artifacts and ideas that are often the focus of cultural studies and that only serve as a limited portion of the real symbolic interaction of which culture is composed. Second, students should engage the culture through interpretive analysis and attempt to understand the intricate relationships between worldview, values, and behavior. Finally, students should be encouraged to fully immerse themselves in the daily life patterns of another culture in an attempt to "try on" a new culture as they probe for meanings not easily perceived at a surface level.

The focus of analysis for this type of learning consists of the myriad elements of daily life; those things that are considered "typical" as well as special events, celebrations, or gatherings. Schneider (1976) argues that "it is the analysis of what people do that is our aim " (p. 198). In fact, the normal elements of life, such as work and family interaction, housing, and shopping, can be more revealing of cultural assumptions and values than special events, since they are typically not bolstered up to present an attractive image. In other words, a shopping mall is probably a better unit of analysis than a holiday or festival, precisely for the reason that a shopping mall is not seen as a "preserver of culture."

This exercise is designed to encourage this type of ethnographic interpretation by exposing students to the cultural dimensions of the normal routines of daily life. The exercise forces students to engage in thick description of a culture, attempting to discover the hidden symbolic webs of which it is composed. In addition, it teaches students how to do ethnographic research in an everyday context and helps them to begin to articulate the relationships between cultural values, the informal logic of a culture, and the symbolic expression of culture.

Time

This exercise requires 1 to 2 hours, with previous explanation of the symbolic and cultural dimensions of elements such as space, artifacts, and so on.

Requirements

Students and the instructor will need to travel to a local food store that caters primarily to members of identifiable ethnic or minority groups. Most cities have at least a small African American, Asian, or Middle Eastern grocery. If desired, the teacher can provide a set of questions that will direct the attention of the students to certain areas of the store or focus their attention on certain issues. Some sample questions are included (to be given to students before the assignment; the handout is optional). Students should also have a small notebook with which to note questions and observations.

Instructions

Before traveling to the store, students should be briefed on some basic dimensions of symbolic culture. Some helpful concepts might be the use of space, nonverbal behavior, resource allocation, priorities and values, appropriateness, politeness, and so forth. After this discussion, the teacher should demonstrate to the students that all of the symbolic dimensions of a culture will be manifested in the activities of daily life. Students should particularly be encouraged to think of the grocery store as not merely a store, but rather as a repository of cultural values, attitudes, and beliefs.

At the store, students should work either individually or in couples, slowly going through the store. Any more than two students together usually prevents close analysis. Students should note what products are available, what products are not available, how the store is arranged, the behavior of shoppers and shopkeepers, the variety of specific items, such as alcoholic beverages or fish, purchasing procedures, and so on. Students should be asked to record their thoughts as they notice subtle differences between this store and those to which they are accustomed. It is important that they note any unfulfilled expectations they had of the store. Students should be left to spend about twice the time in the store than they would normally spend to guarantee their close observation.

After the store observation, the class should regroup immediately and the instructor should ask the students about their observations. Students should be encouraged to begin to guess at the meaning of their observations, such as why there was only one type of beer, but many types of fish available. The instructor should probe some of the same areas mentioned above, such as the layout of the store, expected behaviors, and standards of politeness. Students should be encouraged to dialogue about these issues to demonstrate the complexity of culture and prevent oversimplified interpretations.

Variations

Besides grocery stores, there are a variety of places to do this sort of analysis. Ethnically defined neighborhoods, entertainment centers, and bookstores, for example, all provide useful alternatives. Grocery stores, however, are typically much easier to find and provide a rich environment for analysis. The trainer will want to guarantee that the location chosen for analysis is representative of community life for the culture or subculture, rather than a "tourist site."

Another variation might be to have students go into the store to plan a week's worth of meals with only what they find in the store. This is much easier than trying to encourage in-depth analysis, but it will move students into interaction and will bring some of their areas of frustration into the open.

Discussion Suggestions

One starting point for the discussion is to begin asking what was different about this store from other grocery stores, in terms of available products, layout, behavioral propriety, and so on. Discussion about these issues should lead into a deeper analysis of cultural values and priorities. Asking students about their comfort level in the store should uncover many concerns about cultural differences. This will also allow students to measure their own tolerance of ambiguity, varying health standards, and deep-seated beliefs about "the way things ought to be." Students and participants should interact about what they observed and what they learned. Finally, ask students whether there are any cultural variables or explanations that can begin to account for the differences they have observed.

References and Further Reading

Clifford, J. (1988). *The predicament of culture: Twentieth-century ethnography, literature, and art.* Cambridge, MA: Harvard University Press.

Geertz, C. (1973). *The interpretation of cultures.* New York: Basic Books.

Hall, E. (1959). *The silent language.* New York: Doubleday.

Hall, E. (1969). *The hidden dimension.* New York: Anchor.

Hall, E. (1976). *Beyond culture.* New York: Anchor.

Leach, E. (1976). *Culture & communication: The logic by which symbols are connected.* Cambridge, UK: Cambridge University Press.

Schneider, D. (1976). Notes toward a theory of culture. In K. Basso & H. Selby (Eds.), *Meaning in anthropology* (pp. 197-220). Albuquerque: University of New Mexico Press.

GROCERY STORE ETHNOGRAPHY EXERCISE

In preparation:

In what ways do you think that culture is reflected in the components of everyday life, such as stores?

During the observation:

1. In what ways is the store organized differently from what you expected?

2. Are food items categorized in a way that makes sense to you? Is it easy for you to find the things you are looking for?

3. Are the food items packaged in a way that seems attractive to you? What differences do you notice in how products are presented?

4. Did you find items that you did not expect? Did you expect to find items that were not available? How do you think the store managers decide what should be offered?

5. Does the store seem to have comparable standards of freshness and quality as those in which you normally shop? Do you think that there might be any cultural reasons for this?

6. From your observation, who does the typical shopper seem to be? Young, old, male, female? Is this what you would expect?

7. Do there seem to be different rules or norms for issues such as politeness, appropriateness, and so forth?

8. To what extent does the store seem to be identified with a certain culture or subculture?

9. What does the type of food and product selection tell you about this culture?

10. Do people seem to interact in the same way as in stores with which you are more familiar?

11. Note any other areas in which this store seems to be different from other stores. Do you think these differences can be attributed to culture?

Postactivity discussion questions:

1. In what ways did the store differ from what you expected or what you are familiar with?

2. Are some of these differences cultural, or merely organizational?

3. What did you learn about this culture from this activity?

4. Were you comfortable as you observed this store? If not, what was the source of your discomfort?

5. Reflect on grocery stores from your own culture. Do you think that the organization of these stores might reflect cultural values?

Measuring the Silent Language of Time

ROBERT V. LEVINE

Concepts

Every culture has its own unique set of temporal fingerprints. To know a people is to know the time values they live by.

Jeremy Rifkin, *Time Wars* (1987, p. 1)

No beliefs are more ingrained and subsequently hidden by our cultural upbringings than those about time. Almost 40 years ago, anthropologist Edward Hall (1959) labeled culture's rules of social time the "silent language." The world over, children simply "pick up" their society's conceptions of early and late, of waiting and rushing, of the past, the present, and the future.

Adjusting to an alien sense of time can pose as many difficulties as learning the foreign language itself. In one particularly telling study of the roots of culture shock, Spradley and Phillips (1972) asked a group of returning Peace Corps volunteers to rank 33 items as to the amount of cultural adjustment each had required of them. The list included a wide range of items familiar to travel paranoids, such as "the type of food eaten," "the personal cleanliness of most people," "the number of people of your own race," and "the general standard of living." But aside from mastering the foreign language, the two greatest difficulties for the Peace Corps volunteers concerned social time: "the general pace of life," followed by one of its most significant components, "how punctual most people are."

The exercise in this chapter suggests a method for measuring this particularly salient aspect of social time—the general pace of life. The pace of life has been defined as the rate (Lauer, 1981), speed (Amato, 1983), and "relative rapidity or density of experiences, meanings, perceptions and activities" (Werner, Altman, & Oxley, 1985, p. 14). There is evidence of clear and consistent differences between the pace of life of different cultures, and understanding these differences provides a useful tool for interpreting the basic values of culture itself. In this exercise, the participant will measure three different aspects of the pace of life: (a) walking speed, (b) an indicator of work speed, and (c) an indicator of people's concern with clock time. The times for these activities in one's home city may then be compared with those that our research group has found in other studies for large cities around the world (Levine & Norenzayan, 1996).

The exercise rests on the assumption that places, like people, have their own personalities. Strauss (1976) wrote that "the entire complex of urban life can be thought of as a person rather than a distinctive place, and the city can be endowed with a personality of its own." Places are marked by their own cultures and subcultures—each with its unique set of temporal fingerprints. There is, in fact, evidence that it is meaningful to generalize about the overall pace of life of geographically defined areas. Levine and Bartlett (1984), for example, found correlations ranging from .52 to .82 across 12 cities from 6 different countries between the 3 diverse measures of the pace of life described in this exercise—walking speed, work speed among postal clerks, and accuracy of bank clocks.

Time

An individual experimenter should allow 1 full day to gather the field data. If more than one experimenter is sharing the data collection, the time will be decreased accordingly.

Equipment

1. A stopwatch or watch with a good second hand
2. A 60-foot-long tape measure or roll of string
3. For the post office measure, you will need transportation to get around town
4. The handouts

Instructions to Experimenters

Experimenters will be observing three measures of the pace of life: walking speed, post office transactions, and the accuracy of bank clocks. Measurements should be taken during main business hours. To validly compare the times of your city to those in our previous studies, it is preferable that the data be collected on a warm day.

1. Walking Speed

You will be measuring how long it takes pedestrians to walk 60 feet in downtown locations during main business hours. It should not be raining, as this might affect walking speed.

a. *The locations.* Choose streets with relatively heavy (or as heavy as is available) pedestrian traffic in the main downtown area. Downtown is defined as the main business and shopping area of the city. Your goal is to identify locations with the highest concentrations of businesspeople and shoppers. The sidewalk must be flat, unobstructed, and sufficiently broad and uncrowded so as to allow for potentially maximum walking speeds. Choose locations where people tend to walk a full 60 feet without stopping; pedestrians who do stop (to windowshop, talk with friends, etc.) should not be included. To minimize the peculiarities of any particular location, measure walking speed in at least two locations in each city.

b. *Subjects.* Try to time at least 35 men and 35 women in each city. If pedestrian traffic is particularly slow in a city, you can time a minimum of 25 men and 25 women. You don't need to have an equal number of men and women. Do not time children, very old people, people with disabilities, or anyone whose physical makeup might interfere with their walking speed. If someone stops in the middle of their walk to windowshop or talk or whatever, exclude that person from your sample. Only time pedestrians who are walking alone. This will control for the effects of socializing.

c. *Selecting subjects.* Be sure to use some means of "blindly" selecting subjects. You may want to use any of several methods, depending on the location you have chosen. In some cases, you can decide to use the first person to come around the corner. In other cases, you might look at your starting line on the ground and decide to time the second, or third, or first pair of feet that cross the line. It is important that you do not know who your subjects are before they cross whatever imaginary line you set. This will control for experimenter bias in subject selection.

2. Speed of Post Office Transactions

In each city, you will measure the time it takes postal workers to sell you a standard-sized postage stamp (in the United States, a 32-cent stamp at the time of this writing). To control for experimenter effects, this transaction will be done nonverbally. You need to clearly write out a note requesting the standard priced stamp. In the United States, for example, the note will currently read: "I WANT ONE 32-CENT STAMP, PLEASE."

You will hand the note to the postal clerk, along with a single bill of money that requires the clerk to give you a moderate amount of change (both paper and coins, if possible). In the United States, use a $5 bill. If doing this experiment in other countries, try to use the equivalent of a $5 bill from the country. If clerks ask you any questions, do not respond verbally—just point to the note.

Use either a stopwatch or your wristwatch to inconspicuously measure the amount of time that elapses between your passing the note and money to the clerk and the moment they hand you your stamp and change.

Try to measure the speeds of at least 12 postal clerks. In smaller cities, where this is not possible, measure at least a bare minimum of eight clerks.

In most cases, you will be able to time only one clerk in each post office. In big post offices, though, you may be able to inconspicuously move to a second (or even third) line after testing the first clerk—so long as you weren't noticed by the second clerk while you were at the first line. You are aiming for 12 postal clerks—so doing more than one clerk in a post office will save you time.

3. Accuracy of Bank Clocks

As an indicator of concern with clock time, you will measure the accuracy of clocks in banks in the downtown area. Set your watch to the exact time of day (you can usually get it from the phone company). Walk into banks, look at the clock or clocks on their walls, and record, as accurately as possible, how far off they are from the exact time of day (e.g., –1 minute, +2 ½ minutes, + ¼ minute, 0 minutes). Try to measure 15 bank clocks in each city. At a minimum, measure 12 clocks.

Variations

The study can be conducted with many variations. One possibility is to vary the measures of pace of life. The group might use only some of the three measures and/or can develop measures of their own. The only drawback to developing new measures is that the group will not be able to compare its findings to those from earlier studies.

Another group of possible variations concerns the subject sample. Participants might wish to compare the times of different ethnic or socioeconomic groups within the same city, or to compare gender differences. When convenient, participants might wish to time more than one city—perhaps a small and a large city—and compare these results.

Other possible variations include measuring different times of day, or days of the week, or times of the year.

Discussion Suggestions

1. Discussion might begin by having experimenters compare their observed times to those recently observed by Levine and Norenzayan (1996) in large cities in 31 countries from around the world (see Handout 2). Participants could speculate about the meaningfulness of these differences—how they might affect day-to-day life.

2. What other characteristics of cities might predict their speed of life? Levine and Norenzayan (1996) found that scores on the three pace of life measures

were highly related to a country's climate (hotter places were slower); its economic vitality (places with higher GDPs and other measures of economic health were faster); population size (bigger places were faster); and cultural values (collectivistic cultures were slower than individualistic cultures).

3. What are the consequences of the pace of life? How might it affect physical and psychological well-being? Levine and Norenzayan (1996) found evidence that the pace of life has important consequences for well-being: People in faster places were found to have higher rates of death from coronary heart disease and higher cigarette smoking rates, but they also tended to be more satisfied with their lives.

4. How can we explain these (above) apparently paradoxical findings? If a fast pace of life creates the stress that leads to coronary heart disease, should not this same stress make people less happy? Answering this question may lead to discussion about the central role that the pace of life plays in the broader web of community characteristics in which these findings are embedded. Levine and Norenzayan (1996) suggest that some of the same variables that successfully predict the pace of life are themselves the product of the pace of life that they create. Perhaps the two best examples of this are economic vitality and individualism-collectivism. Economic needs are primary forces in creating a sense of time urgency, and that sense of time urgency in turn leads to a productive economy. Similarly, a focus on individualism thrives on a rapid pace of life, which in turn creates pressure for further individualism. Levine and Norenzayan argue that these forces—economic vitality and individualism—have both positive and negative consequences. On the one hand, the focus on making every minute count and being productive creates the stressors that lead to cigarette smoking and coronary heart disease. On the other hand, they provide material comforts and a general standard of living that enhance the quality of life. Productivity and individualism—which in themselves are very difficult to separate from one another—have double-edged consequences.

5. What are the consequences of a rapid pace of life for the social well-being of communities? Levine and Norenzayan (1996) predicted that people in fast cities should be less likely to offer help to a stranger in need. However, they found only marginal support for this prediction. Discussion might focus on what other variables might intervene between pace of life and people's willingness to take the time for social responsibilities. In other words, why is a slow pace of life in itself not an assurance that people will be more helpful to others?

6. What aspects of the pace of life are these three measures missing? Discussion here might focus on questions such as the number of hours that people work, as opposed to simply how fast they move during work hours. Also, how well do people relax when they are not working? It is interesting to speculate about different countries on these questions—to compare, for example, Japan and the United States to the nations of Western Europe.

References and Further Reading

Amato, P. R. (1983). The effects of urbanization on interpersonal behavior. *Journal of Cross-Cultural Psychology, 14*, 353-367.

Bornstein, M. H. (1979). The pace of life: Revisited. *International Journal of Psychology, 14*, 83-90.

Hall, E. T. (1959). *The silent language*. Garden City, NY: Doubleday.

Lauer, R. H. (1981). *Temporal man: The meaning and uses of social time*. New York: Praeger.

Levine, R. (1990, September-October). The pace of life and coronary heart disease. *American Scientist, 78*, 450-459.

Levine, R. (1997). *A geography of time*. New York: Basic Books.

Levine, R., & Bartlett, K. (1984). Pace of life, punctuality and coronary heart disease in six countries. *Journal of Cross-Cultural Psychology, 15*, 233-255.

Levine, R., Lynch, K., Miyake, K., & Lucia, M. (1990). The type A city: Coronary heart disease and the pace of life. *Journal of Behavioral Medicine, 12*, 509-524.

Levine, R., & Norenzayan, A. (1996). *The pace of life in 31 countries*. Manuscript submitted for publication.

Rifkin, J. (1987). *Time wars*. New York: Henry Holt.

Spradley, J. P., & Phillips, M. (1972). Culture and stress: A quantitative analysis. *American Anthropologist, 74*, 518-529.

Strauss, A. L. (1976). *Images of the American city*. New Brunswick, NJ: Transaction Books.

Werner, C. M., Altman, I., & Oxley, D. (1985). Temporal aspects of homes: A transactional perspective. In I. Altman & C. M. Werner (Eds.), *Home environments: Human behavior and environment: Vol. 8. Advances in theory and research* (pp. 1-32). New York: Plenum.

HANDOUT 1: SCORING SHEETS

Walking Speed

City _____ Experimenter _____

Date _____ Time of day _____

Location(s) measured _____

Climate (check one): Uncomfortably warm _____ Pleasant _____

Uncomfortably cold _____

Men		*Women*	
1 _____	19 _____	1 _____	19 _____
2 _____	20 _____	2 _____	20 _____
3 _____	21 _____	3 _____	21 _____
4 _____	22 _____	4 _____	22 _____
5 _____	23 _____	5 _____	23 _____
6 _____	24 _____	6 _____	24 _____
7 _____	25 _____	7 _____	25 _____
8 _____	26 _____	8 _____	26 _____
9 _____	27 _____	9 _____	27 _____
10 _____	28 _____	10 _____	28 _____
11 _____	29 _____	11 _____	29 _____
12 _____	30 _____	12 _____	30 _____
13 _____	31 _____	13 _____	31 _____
14 _____	32 _____	14 _____	32 _____
15 _____	33 _____	15 _____	33 _____
16 _____	34 _____	16 _____	34 _____
17 _____	35 _____	17 _____	35 _____
18 _____		18 _____	

Any particular problems or notes?

Post Office

City _____ Experimenter _____

Date _____ Time of day _____

Location(s) measured _____

Post office teller no.	Elapsed time
1	_____
2	_____
3	_____
4	_____
5	_____
6	_____
7	_____
8	_____
9	_____
10	_____
11	_____
12	_____

Any particular problems or notes?

Accuracy of Clocks

City _____

Locations _____

Clock no.	*Deviation from exact time*
1	_____
2	_____
3	_____
4	_____
5	_____
6	_____
7	_____
8	_____
9	_____
10	_____
11	_____
12	_____
13	_____
14	_____
15	_____

Any particular problems or notes?

HANDOUT 2: TABLE OF MEANS AND RANKS ON PACE MEASURES BY COUNTRY

Country	Overall pace[a] index Mean	Rank	Walking speed Mean	Rank	Postal speed Mean	Rank	Clock accuracy Mean	Rank
Switzerland	−3.43	1	11.80	3	16.91	2	19.29	1
Ireland	−3.02	2	11.13	1	17.49	3	51.42	11
Germany	−3.00	3	12.01	5	13.46	1	43.00	8
Japan	−2.68	4	12.11	7	18.61	4	35.00	6
Italy	−2.13	5	12.75	10	23.00	12	24.17	2
England	−2.09	6	12.00	4	20.78	9	53.72	13
Sweden	−1.96	7	12.92	13	19.10	5	40.20	7
Austria	−1.43	8	14.08	23	20.60	8	25.00	3
Netherland	−1.43	9	11.45	2	24.42	14	82.33	25
Hong Kong	−1.39	10	13.10	14	20.10	6	54.83	14
France	−1.36	11	12.34	8	27.84	18	49.00	10
Poland	−1.32	12	12.90	12	25.83	15	43.00	8
Costa Rica	−1.13	13	13.33	16	21.13	10	55.38	15
Taiwan	−.73	14	13.58	18	20.22	7	68.00	21
Singapore	−.65	15	14.75	25	22.42	11	32.00	4
United States	−.30	16	12.0	36	36.99	23	67.87	20
Canada	−.26	17	12.86	11	30.50	21	70.00	22
South Korea	−.02	18	13.76	20	29.75	20	58.00	16
Hungary	.01	19	13.75	19	28.45	19	64.17	18
Czech Republic	.28	20	13.80	21	27.73	17	76.07	23
Greece	.54	21	13.10	14	24.33	13	117.0	9
Kenya	.78	22	12.58	9	42.50	30	77.14	24
China	1.032	31	4.26	24	39.63	25	51.82	12
Bulgaria	1.59	24	15.57	27	33.67	22	60.00	17
Romania	2.42	25	16.72	30	42.25	29	32.46	5
Jordan	2.44	26	15.79	28	39.92	27	66.16	19
Syria	3.26	27	15.95	29	40.02	28	94.52	27
El Salvador	3.63	28	14.04	22	25.88	16	210.0	31
Brazil	3.98	29	16.76	31	38.17	24	108.0	28
Indonesia	4.14	30	14.82	26	39.64	26	161.5	30
Mexico	4.23	31	13.56	17	70.00	31	92.31	26

SOURCE: R. Levine & A. Norenzayan. (1996). *The pace of life in 31 countries.* Manuscript submitted for publication.

a. Overall pace index means are the average of the z scores for each measure. For the other measures, smaller numbers represent faster walking speeds, faster postal times, and smaller clock deviations (all in seconds). Times were recorded in one or more of the largest cities in each country.

Perspective Shifting
on Wheels

RUTH SEYMOUR

Concepts

$\mathcal{E}$ffective communication in pluralistic settings begins with the assumption that the same interaction will be experienced differently by individuals of varying social groups or cultures. But this understanding is easier gained cognitively than intuitively. Thus, one challenge for an instructor of intercultural and intergroup communication is to help students actually *experience* their own internal centrism—their own deep and unspoken assumption of their perception as the norm—even when they can already cognitively acknowledge the existence of other perspectives and perceptions.

Perspective Shifting on Wheels was designed for advanced journalism undergraduates who are steeped in the ideal and attempted professional practice of "objective observation." It is meant to experientially contrast objectivism and relativism through a forced shift in personal perspective (time spent alone in public in a wheelchair), followed by the introduction of two theoretical frames that accommodate the freshly felt multiperspectivist or relativistic view. When students climb out of their wheelchairs, they generally realize that both (conflicting) ways of seeing their surroundings—on wheels and on foot—were simultaneously true, equally "objective." The primary learning goal is that relativism (and subsequently, in this lesson, ethnorelativism) is more useful in intercultural communication than any hoped-for objectivism, or, in this case, invisible ethnocentrism. The relationship between appreciated difference, relativism, and intercultural behavioral competence has been accepted widely among intercultural communication scholars (Ramsey, 1994).

Two theoretical frames undergird this exercise: Einstein's special theory of relativity and Milton Bennett's developmental scale from ethnocentrism to "ethnorelativism."

The special theory of relativity maintains that everyone *has* a perspective—a location and speed in space/time—that is as physically "actual" as any other. The theory of relativity asserts that observers moving at different speeds will see events in quite different ways. What looks like simultaneous events to one observer might appear like two quite distinct events to another (Briggs, 1984, p. 58). Who is right? Neither. Both. There is no central, compromising, or "eagle's eye" position from which to mediate these conflicting viewpoints. (Because even the eagle, the "neutral" observer, is moving in space/time.)

This understanding of reality as profoundly elastic due to its dependence on the perspective of the observer has, over the decades, seeped into the softer sciences. Many consider this fundamental relativism to be the very foundation of intercultural communication theory. As Whorf wrote in the first half of this century:

> We are thus introduced to a new principle of relativity, which holds that all observers are not led by the same physical evidence to the same picture of the universe, unless their linguistic backgrounds are similar, or can in some way be calibrated. (quoted in Briggs, 1984, p. 214)

The strongest such calibration, of course, operates intraculturally and within subgroups of cultures. We each belong to many different social groups, from which we draw our identities and perceptual calibrations or assumptions (see, among many others, Brislin, 1993; Gudykunst & Kim, 1992). These social groups are major components of our social perspective—the space/time location from which we fantasize ourselves to be neutral observers of all others.

In his categorization of skills and attitudinal development in intercultural competence, Bennett (1993) describes three stages of "centrism" and three more advanced stages of "relativism." Progressing along this scale, one becomes with each step more aware that one's own perspective is but one of many possible; one also becomes increasingly able to differentiate finely among elements of various cultures and groups (see Figure 6.1).

Bennett's developmental model in some ways resembles Hoopes's (1981) four-stage model and Perry's (1970) scheme of ethical development. It maintains that individuals grow toward (ethno)relativism from within a frame of (ethno)centrism in three stages: from *denial* (total segregation and obliviousness to other ways of human being) to *defense* (hostility toward now-acknowledged "others") to *minimization* (tolerating "others" as, after all, quite similar to ourselves). These stages are followed by three subsequent stages of (ethno)relative facility: from *acceptance* (respect for behavioral and value differences) to *adaptation* (empathy and an ability to shift behaviors according to context) to *integration* (an absorption of some aspects of the "other" into one's own sense of self, or personal perspective).

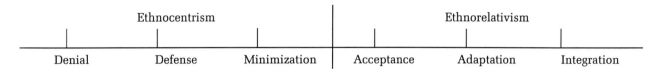

Figure 6.1. Bennett's Developmental Model of Intercultural Sensitivity
SOURCE: M. J. Bennett (1993).

The two early stages of centrism in this model, and particularly the second, *defense,* are recognizable as old-fashioned Archie Bunker bigotry.[1] In interracial contexts, this explicit sense of superiority has been termed "intense racism" (Brislin, 1993) and "dominative" racism (Gaertner & Dovidio, 1986). But, ironically, the final prerelativistic stage, *minimization,* has long been posited as an American social ideal. From this stance, people wonder things like, "Why can't we understand we are just all the same, under the skin?" "Aren't we all children of one God?" The problem with this ideal, per Bennett's model, is that such "understandings" involve the minimizing assumption that suggests that everyone is the same as *"me,"* and that we are all children of *my* God, not yours. Thus, relativism—the ability to hold at least two valid Gods and multiple social differences in mind (and still chew gum)—proves a more effective communicative stance.

As abundant research and theorizing have suggested, human prejudices about social differences take root in unchallenged perceptions of ourselves as the norm. Perspective Shifting on Wheels—coupled forcefully with simple theoretical lectures on relativity as multiperspectivism in physics and the social science of intercultural communication—has proved effective in freeing students, at least momentarily, from what Barnlund (1988) calls the prison of our own frames of reference.

Time

The wheelchair exercise requires 3 hours of off-campus effort as students visit shopping malls. The postexercise debriefing, lecture, and discussion require a couple of hours of class time. I usually space it over two classes: one to initially probe at the notion of objectivity and to allow students to share with each other the essays about their experiences in wheelchairs; the second class to revisit the idea of objectivity and provide the afore-described theoretical "containers" (Einstein and Bennett) for the students' powerful experiences with sudden shifts in personal perspective.

Equipment

Wheelchairs, or means of transportation to shopping centers that offer the public free use of wheelchairs while shopping; a sculpture, or other unusual three-dimensional object; and the student instruction sheet are required.

Instructions

I introduce the wheelchair assignment to students without fanfare or preparation. Because we are a commuter campus, I give them the next class period to conduct their venture. This permits easy scheduling among students who may not share any other blocks of free time during the week. I encourage them to partner with classmates who live near them and to jointly choose a shopping mall to visit. Thus, the class of students scatters to various supermarkets and malls throughout the metropolitan area. (To minimize any appearance of deception and to ensure that rightful users of public wheelchairs have access, it may be best for students to make prior arrangements with stores and malls for educational use of the equipment.)

It is valuable to further emphasize to students that in no way does this exercise attempt to vicariously create the experience of having a disability. That physical situation is large, profound, and inimitable. What we *are* doing, however, is intimately experiencing a public space from the level of a wheelchair and in the process experiencing some shifts in personal ability, mobility, and concept of self.

Variations

At a residential campus, it might be better for students to perform the exercise in pairs, on their own time, outside of class. Alternatively, the wheelchairs can be brought to campus by contacting a medical supply company and providing a modest rental. (Renting the chairs, recently, cost $5/chair, including delivery. It may be that the medical supply company was keeping the price low as a public service.) Although students experienced some greater degree of self-consciousness by appearing suddenly disabled among their peers, this also provided powerful reminders of the physical and psychological barriers present right in their most familiar learning environment, and in some ways, this can be a preferred exercise. The shopping mall option is now my choice because of the difficulties of transporting and protecting a dozen wheelchairs (expensive merchandise!) en route to, from, and on the walkways of our campus.

Discussion Suggestions

At the first class meeting after the wheelchair outings, I continue the experiential tone as a transition to theory. In the center of the classroom, as students enter, is a sculpture chosen because it is very different from its front, side, and back. As the students settle into chairs arranged in a horseshoe, they involuntarily place themselves so as to see one of these three dominant views. I open the class by asking them to take a couple of minutes of silence to record a "purely objective" description of the sculpture. One or two ask permission to walk a circle around the sculpture, and I tell them they must remain where they are seated. (The fact that we do live our lives glued to our personal perspectives becomes a teaching point, later.)

We either read aloud or talk these descriptions through. Naturally, they differ depending on where the person is sitting. We all begin to listen to these dramatically different, yet clinical descriptions until someone says: "Well, it doesn't look like that from here!" Or, "It really depends on your perspective." Then we begin to wind up the sculpture descriptions and move into the reading of personal essays about how it felt to be in a wheelchair.

This miniexercise works very well to position the wheelchair essays in the context of perspective.

After about 15-20 minutes of the wheelchair essays—these tend to be very personal and powerful and the room is so quiet you can hear a paper clip fall—I pose the question: "So. As a news reporter assigned to cover disabled individuals, were you 'more objective' in the chair or out?"

This discussion gets wild pretty quickly, with strong disagreements. It takes a while for these advanced students of "neutral and objective" journalism to glimpse the essential orthogonality of "objectivity" and "perspective"—that these are not contradictory terms; that description from any perspective can be more or less objective, but that it takes multiple perspectives to do justice to a description of the sculpture. We briefly discuss components of our social perspective (gender, race, class, sexual orientation, culture, etc.) that help determine the seat from which we view "reality."

In the third hour, usually in a subsequent class meeting, we embark on a discussion of Einsteinian relativity (Briggs's explanation and cartoon illustration of the theory are very teachable and accessible to students). Then I introduce the Bennett ethnorelativism model. It is important to help them explicitly link Einstein's writing at the dawn of this century to the creep of relativism into the social sciences and related ways of thinking (e.g., Bennett) and how all of this applies to our future as citizens and journalists in a multicultural and otherwise diverse society. These two lectures take about 45 minutes all together, plus break.

For disciplines other than social sciences and journalism, the discussion lesson could be recast in several directions. For instance, courses in social work, health care, or education could recast this in terms of strategic empathy (Bennett, 1979; Davis, 1983; Katz, 1963). Interpersonal communication courses might prefer to apply new insights about perspective to one-on-one interviewing or processes of attribution.

Note

1. Archie Bunker was a narrow-minded, bigoted character in the television show *All in the Family* in the 1970s.

References and Further Reading

Allport, G. W. (1954). *The nature of prejudice*. Reading, MA: Addison-Wesley.
Barnlund, D. (1988). Communication in a global village. In L. A. Samovar & R. E. Porter (Eds.), *Intercultural communication: A reader* (pp. 5-14). Belmont, CA: Wadsworth.

Bennett, M. J. (1979). Overcoming the golden rule: Sympathy and empathy. In D. Nimmo (Ed.), *Communication yearbook 3* (pp. 407-421). Washington, DC: International Communication Association.

Bennett, M. J. (1993). Towards ethnorelativism: A developmental model of intercultural sensitivity. In R. M. Paige (Ed.), *Education for the intercultural experience* (pp. 21-71). Yarmouth, ME: Intercultural.

Briggs, J. (1984). *Looking glass universe: The emerging science of wholeness.* New York: Simon & Schuster.

Brislin, R. (1993). *Understanding culture's influence on behavior.* New York: Harcourt Brace Jovanovich.

Davis, M. H. (1983). Measuring individual differences in empathy: Evidence for a multidimensional approach. *Journal of Personality and Social Psychology, 44,* 113-126.

Gaertner, S. L., & Dovidio, J. F. (1986). The aversive form of racism. In J. F. Dovidio & S. L. Gaertner (Eds.), *Prejudice, discrimination, and racism* (pp. 61-89). San Diego, CA: Academic Press.

Gudykunst, W. B., & Kim, Y. Y. (1992). *Communicating with strangers* (2nd ed.). New York: McGraw-Hill.

Hall, E. T. (1973). *The silent language.* New York: Doubleday.

Hoopes, D. S. (1981). Intercultural communication concepts and the psychology of intercultural experience. In M. D. Pusch (Ed.), *Multicultural education: A cross-cultural training approach* (pp. 10-38). Yarmouth, ME: Intercultural.

Katz, R. L. (1963). *Empathy, its nature and uses.* New York: Free Press of Glencoe.

Perry, W. G., Jr. (1970). *Forms of intellectual and ethical development in the college years.* New York: Holt, Rinehart & Winston.

Ramsey, S. J. (1994). *Riding the waves of culture: Intercultural communication at the end of the 20th century* (No. 7). Chiba, Japan: Intercultural Communication Institute, Kanda University of International Studies.

Samovar, L. A., & Porter, R. E. (1989). *Intercultural communication: A reader.* Belmont, CA: Wadsworth.

Samovar, L. A., & Porter, R. E. (1991). *Communication between cultures.* Belmont, CA: Wadsworth.

Stewart, E. C. (1972). *American cultural patterns: A cross-cultural perspective.* Yarmouth, ME: Intercultural.

Whorf, B. (1940, April). Science and linguistics. Reprinted from *Technology Review, 42,* 229-231, 247-248. Cambridge: Alumni Association, Massachusetts Institute of Technology.

PERSPECTIVE SHIFTING:
DISABILITY

Student Instruction Sheet

Working with a partner from class, meet next week during class time at a department or grocery store that offers a wheelchair for its customers. (If at all possible, meet at a store that has multiple wheelchairs available so that you will not seriously inconvenience shoppers who rely on the chair. You can find this out easily with a 2-minute advance visit.)

Your assignment is to use the wheelchair (for no less than 1 hour each) while shopping in the store. As much as possible, avoid explaining the class assignment to anyone. Just do what you can to experience the department or grocery store from a wheelchair perspective.

For a half hour, you will be assisted by your partner, who will push you and converse with you as you learn to maneuver the chair through the aisles.

For the next half hour, you will navigate alone while doing some shopping. During your half-hour solo time, you should also attempt to use a public restroom marked for handicapped accessibility.

This assignment works best if your partner meets you at your car with the wheelchair so that you don't have to walk in an able-bodied fashion into the store to claim a chair. (It is also instructive to attempt to get in and out of a car with minimal use of your legs and to personally test the curbs and traffic lanes for accessibility and safety.) If you want to be even more socially graceful about it, you could each complete your assignment in different stores. I can think of neighborhoods, for example, that have a grocery store and a Kmart within a mile of each other; both stores offer wheelchairs.

The learning goal. Clearly, a brief exercise like this does not attempt or pretend to show able-bodied persons among us how it would feel to have disabilities. We can, however, carefully note our own reactions and feelings as we try to negotiate a bit of daily life in the chair. We can notice our perceptions of the reactions of strangers, both as we push the chair and as we sit in the chair. We can also report journalistically, noticing what aspects of the stores seem convenient for our disabled readers and what aspects seem inconvenient. How truly accessible is the store?

Your written assignment. Next week, bring to class a reaction and thought-piece (about 500 words) about the experience. It may be written in any style you prefer, and it will be shared with the class. It may work well for you to use the half hour that your partner is off alone in the chair to record your thoughts, observations, anxieties, and experiences. You could use these notes later for your homework assignment.

Multicultural
Literacy Assignment

ESTELLE DISCH

This exercise was designed for an internship course titled Seminar in Urban Social Service. It is grounded in the assumption that people working in human services and most other work settings in the United States will be encountering people different from themselves throughout their lives. Furthermore, it assumes that most people will need to effectively understand and work with a wide range of people. The exercise responds to the reality of changing demographics by encouraging students to become multiculturally literate. By multicultural literacy I mean the ability to learn enough about another culture to begin to know the history of a particular cultural group; to understand some of the common and not-so-common experiences of people in that culture; to understand the widely shared values of the culture; and to understand the place of the group within the wider context of U.S. society. The exercise as presented requires students to begin this process in relation to a group to which they do not belong and about which they know very little. They are required to quickly learn about the group and report what they learn both orally and in writing during the fifth week of the semester.

The need for multicultural literacy has been particularly emphasized in education, business, and human services. Writers in counseling and other human service fields call for culturally sensitive counselors (Lee & Richardson, 1991; McGoldrick, Pearce, & Giordano, 1982; Ponterotto, Casas, Suzuki, & Alexander, 1995). Those in education argue for better-educated students who will be prepared to actively engage both with each other now and with life in

U.S. society in the 21st century (Friedman, Kolmar, Flint, & Rothenberg, 1996; Thompson & Tyagi, 1993). Writers and cultural critics call for similar understanding and competency (Simonson & Walker, 1988), as do those in business (Fine, 1995). Finally, educators committed to reforming general education in universities are increasingly convinced that students need to leave college able to *do* things such as be able to find resources in this era of exploding information, to be able to apply their knowledge and skills in real-life contexts, and to see themselves as lifelong learners (Gaff, 1991).

This exercise attempts to move students toward the goal of multicultural literacy and the practice of skills necessary for lifelong learning. It demands work in the library followed by application of that learning to a hypothetical person in need of service. It requires that students practice multicultural communication in at least a rudimentary way by interviewing someone who belongs to the group they are studying. This exercise also requires students to work in learning teams as they divide up the work of the assignment, share information with each other, and decide how to present their findings. It engages the students in active learning beginning in the second week of the semester and helps to build a sense of community among team members and the class as a whole.

Time

The in-class time required for the exercise includes, first, about an hour meeting in learning teams—approximately 20 minutes each week for three consecutive weeks. During this time, students ask clarifying questions, decide who will address each question posed in the assignment, and decide how to present their findings. Second, about 8 minutes per student will be needed for presentation time (5 minute oral report, plus time for questions and answers addressed to the whole group). Outside of class time varies according to what individual students put into the assignment.

Because I assigned light reading during the 3 weeks while the students were working on this assignment, I lost "coverage" that I might have used for other topics and especially student reading that I have ordinarily included in this part of the course. On the positive side, I covered a few short but very important readings in depth. And, based on student evaluations of this exercise, I am convinced that they will remember a lot more of what they learned on their own than they would have remembered of what I would otherwise have assigned.

Requirements

1. Movable chairs or break-out space so that the learning teams can meet together during class time
2. Library access
3. Access to a multicultural community for the interview
4. The Description of the Assignment—Student Version handout, and the student data sheet. The student data sheet should include (a) information related

to reaching people including name, address, e-mail, and phone numbers; (b) a statement granting the teacher permission to include (or not) parts of the above information on a list to be circulated in class; (c) the student's racial and ethnic background; (d) a list of cultures/races studied or learned about in other contexts; and (e) a list of racial and ethnic groups. Students should indicate their interests/preferences as to which groups they would most like to study. You might encourage them to check groups that they expect to encounter.

Instructions

Week 1. Hand out the description of the exercise and the student data sheet. Have the students fill out the data sheet in class and return it that day. Analyze the data sheets prior to the next class and assign students to groups to which they do not belong and about which they have little knowledge. When possible, assign them according to their interests (but inform students in advance that they might not get their first choice). There should be at least four students in each group. I suggest a maximum group size of six persons.

Week 2. Provide a list of group members, including phone numbers, to each student (providing that students have agreed to have their phone numbers circulated). Give groups 20 minutes or so to decide who will handle each research question and to request clarification of any confusing aspects of the assignment.

Weeks 3 and 4. Give groups 20 minutes or so to check in with each other and to ask questions.

Week 5—Oral reports. These might go into Week 6, depending on the size of the class, length of the reports, number of questions, and ability of the teacher and group members to set clear time limits on presentations.

Troubleshooting

1. Someone will need to be an assertive timekeeper. I found that the students wanted to talk longer than 5 minutes and that the class frequently had many questions for each group.
2. Students will need some preparation regarding stereotypes. They will probably need to be coached as to how to present widely shared cultural values without assuming that each person in the culture shares them. The sequence of interviewing someone after doing substantial reading helps here because the students can assess to what extent their interviewees fit what they have been reading about the group in general.
3. The class will need to be prepared for the fact that other class members and the teacher (who are possibly members of the group being presented) will be asking them questions after their presentations so that they are not surprised by that process. This aspect makes some students nervous.
4. The paper assignment demands complex thinking that students will need support and encouragement to accomplish. Some might forget to apply the library research to the hypothetical case and the person interviewed. Some might forget to cite sources appropriately, running the risk of writing a paper full of undocumented stereotypes.

Variations

1. In locations lacking a multicultural community, perhaps students could watch relevant films instead of doing an interview. Or groups could be chosen based on people available in the local community. Social class, gender, sexual orientation, religion, ethnicity, age, (dis)ability, and other differences could be emphasized in this case.

2. The energy generated by this exercise was so powerful that I am thinking of adapting it to fit other courses. The idea of sending students off to do research in teams at the very beginning of the semester could be adapted to other topics, as could a case approach.

Discussion Suggestions

The energy generated by this assignment convinced me to build on what the students had learned. I decided to use the same hypothetical cases included in this assignment as the basis for their analysis of various intervention strategies in their next paper. In this way, they were able to build on their initial expertise while applying new ideas to the hypothetical person in need of service.

References and Further Reading

Fine, M. G. (1995). *Building successful multicultural organizations: Challenges and opportunities*. Westport, CT: Quorum.

Friedman, E. G., Kolmar, W. K., Flint, C. B., & Rothenberg, P. (Eds.). (1996). *Creating an inclusive college curriculum: A teaching sourcebook from the New Jersey Project*. New York: Teachers College Press.

Gaff, J. G. (1991). *New life for the college curriculum: Assessing achievements and furthering progress in the reform of general education*. San Francisco: Jossey-Bass.

Lee, C. C., & Richardson, B. L. (Eds.). (1991). *Multicultural issues in counseling: New approaches to diversity*. Alexandria, VA: American Counseling Association.

McGoldrick, M., Pearce, J., & Giordano, J. (Eds.). (1982). *Ethnicity and family therapy*. New York: Guilford.

Ponterotto, J. G., Casas, J. M., Suzuki, L. A., & Alexander, C. M. (Eds.). (1995). *Handbook of multicultural counseling*. Thousand Oaks, CA: Sage.

Simonson, R., & Walker, S. (Eds.). (1988). *The Graywolf Annual Five: Multicultural literacy*. St. Paul, MN: Graywolf.

Thompson, B. W., & Tyagi, S. (Eds.). (1993). *Beyond a dream deferred: Multicultural education and the politics of excellence*. Minneapolis: University of Minnesota Press.

In addition to the McGoldrick et al. and the Ponterotto et al. books, the following were placed on reserve in the campus library:

Green, J. W. (1995). *Cultural awareness in the human services: A multi-ethnic approach* (2nd ed.). Boston: Allyn & Bacon.

Takaki, R. T. (1993). *A different mirror: A history of multicultural America*. Boston: Little, Brown.

Thernstrom, S. (Ed.). (1980). *Harvard encyclopedia of American ethnic groups*. Cambridge, MA: Belknap Press of Harvard University.

Zinn, H. (1995). *A people's history of the United States*. New York: Harper.

DESCRIPTION OF THE ASSIGNMENT— STUDENT VERSION

The goal of this assignment is to help you learn how to learn about people different from yourself. You will be working with three or four other students in this class focusing on one cultural or racial group in the United States other than your own that you have not already studied or learned about in another context. You will need to use the library, interview someone who is part of the group, and possibly visit a community agency that serves the group. I will provide a hypothetical case of a person from that group in need of social services. The task of your study group will be to learn as much as possible to figure out how best to help the person.

Obviously, there is no way to learn everything about any group. My goal here is to provide a structure in which you will learn as much as you can in a short period of time using resources that are readily available in the library. With lots of time, you could, of course, do a much more complete job. In your paper, you will have an opportunity to name resources that you found but didn't have time to examine, such as books, journal articles, and community agencies. Near the end of your library research, you should interview one member of the group (see guidelines below). Your group will be scheduled to make a presentation in class about what you learned. The presentation should focus on how the information you gathered helps you to understand the hypothetical member of the group you are studying.

Research Focus

Please divide the work so that each person investigates *one* of the following four topics, so that each topic is covered:

1. *History: How and why did the group become part of the United States?* Have they always been here (e.g., Native Americans or Chicanos whose homeland was incorporated into the United States as a result of the treaty of Guadalupe Hidalgo)? Were they brought as slaves or indentured servants (e.g., some African Americans)? Did they immigrate by choice (e.g., came here to study and decided to stay)? Were they refugees of a U.S.-supported war abroad (e.g., people from Vietnam or some countries in Latin America)? Are or were they refugees unrelated to U.S. wars? Did they come in various ways? What kinds of experiences did various group members experience in their home countries? Include here a brief history of how U.S. law has treated the group, including such things as permission to immigrate, citizenship, voting rights status, treaties signed and either kept or broken, and so forth.

2. *Values: What are the widely shared and/or widely understood values in this group?* Consider what is expected of women and men, how girl and boy chil-

dren are supposed to behave, treatment of elders, religious/spiritual beliefs and practices, use of leisure time, expectations about leaving home, work and careers, sexuality, and so on. What happens to people who do not conform to shared values within the group? Consider people who are gay, lesbian, or bisexual; people with disabilities; people who marry outside the group; people who fail to follow expected religious practices; women who refuse to follow prescribed female roles; and so on.

3. *The situation of the group in the United States now.* What are the major trends in the size of the group over time? What explains increases and decreases in their numbers? How many people are here now? What languages do they speak? Where do they tend to live? In what kinds of jobs do they tend to work? What are their incomes? What kind of political power does the group seem to have? To what religions do they belong? How old (or young) is this population? Which generations of immigrants do they represent? To what extent has the group intermarried/mixed with other groups in the United States? What kinds of conflict do they experience among themselves (e.g., generation gaps, religious conflict, ethnic conflict within the larger group)? What are the major issues or problems that members of this group currently face in the United States? If you were providing services to members of this population, with what kinds of issues might they need support? How are human service agencies, educational institutions, and government agencies responding to the challenges that the group faces? How do attitudes toward the group by major institutions and the public tend to help or hinder their lives here? What strengths do the members of the group tend to bring to the solving of their problems and surviving in the United States? Note: The person who addresses this topic should gather information from at least one agency or institution that serves members of this group.

4. *Attitudes and prejudices.* What are the attitudes toward this group held by the dominant culture? What are the attitudes toward this group held by other groups? How does this group think/feel toward other groups? What kinds of power does this group have and what explains its power or disempowerment? Is this group in conflict with other empowered or disempowered groups? If so, who benefits, if anyone does, from this conflict? What keeps this group from building coalitions with other groups?

Interview

Find someone who belongs to the group and prepare a set of questions you would like answered based on your reading and, if relevant, based on your community research. Ask about some of the person's experiences growing up and living as a member of that group. Find out to what extent the person fits or doesn't fit the descriptions of the group that you have read about or learned about in other ways. Finally, ask what he or she might recommend to help the person(s) in your hypothetical case. Be sure to explain the purpose of the interview and to tell the person that you will not use his or her name or other identifying information in any reports of the interview in any context.

Paper Guidelines

Your paper should be 6-7 doubled-spaced typed pages, plus endnotes, references, and appendixes. In addition to a short introduction and short conclusion, it should contain the following: (a) a summary of what you learned in the library and on any field visits along with an analysis of how what you learned might be useful in understanding how to assist the hypothetical person you have been assigned to help, and (b) findings from your interview. Briefly report who you interviewed and how you located the person. Do not include the person's name, but describe what you know about the person's demographic and other traits including such information as gender, age, religion, social class, ethnicity, race, education, work, length of time in the United States, family situation, relationship status, sexual orientation, or disabilities. How does the person and/or his or her experiences compare to what you read? What does the person you interviewed recommend for the hypothetical person you are attempting to help?

In one appendix, include a list of resources that you didn't have time to look into but that you think would be important to know to have a more complete understanding of the group and a better sense of how to help the hypothetical person. In another appendix, list the questions you asked of your interviewee and a summary of the answers the person provided. In another appendix, if relevant, describe any agencies you visited related to the group you are addressing (such as a school or a social service agency). Describe, especially, the kinds of services the agency provides for the group.

Hypothetical Cases

I developed cases that would address a wide range of intersecting identity issues and that were grounded in some of the literature on the various groups. These are samples that could obviously be either revised or rewritten to fit the focus of any particular course.

1. *Native American.* Thomas is a heterosexual, able-bodied late adolescent who was raised in a residential school for American Indian children. He was told that his family sent him away when he was 3 years old. At 18, he is about to graduate from high school and doesn't know where to go or what to do. He has been forced to speak only English in the school and has forgotten his tribal language. He knows that he came from a specific Navajo reservation in the Southwest but has had no contact with anyone there. He is depressed and scared and has begun to drink more than is good for him (by his definition) to numb the pain and pass the time. Imagine that you are a counselor in an agency that works with American Indian youths and adults and that Thomas has willingly come to you for help. What can you learn about people like Thomas to better understand what he might be experiencing, and what kinds of services might make sense?

2. *Jewish.* Leah is an older Jewish woman who escaped from Nazi Germany when she was 10 years old. Her parents, siblings, and many other relatives

were murdered by the Hitler regime, and she was sent alone to the United States to live with an aunt and uncle and two cousins. Her relatives were very caring and acknowledged the horror she had been through but encouraged her not to dwell on the past and to make a new life. She did well in school, pursued a successful career as a high school teacher, married, and raised three children. Throughout most of her life in the United States, she followed her caretakers' advice and spoke very little of her early trauma related to the Holocaust. Her husband has recently died, and Leah has been thrown into a deep depression. Her children are surprised at this because they have not seen their mother so depressed before. They come to you to attempt to understand what is happening and to help her. For the first time, Leah is talking about her traumatic childhood. She speaks of anti-Semitic incidents in the United States, and of the energy it took to simply survive. She belongs to a Reform synagogue and attends services on religious holidays. She is able-bodied and in good health.

3. *Puerto Rican.* Anna and Juan are a couple in their mid-20s who are struggling economically. They were both born in Puerto Rico and moved to Boston as children. Recently, Juan was in an accident and is permanently disabled. His ability to do physical work has diminished, and he now works at a desk and earns less money than he did before the accident. On some days, he is not able to work at all due to intense pain. Anna and Juan have two children in elementary school. Anna wants to get out of the house, finish high school, and develop a career. She feels very stressed over trying to make ends meet on Juan's diminished income. Juan, however, wants Anna to work at home as she has always done and finds himself depressed and humiliated that he cannot provide adequately for his family. They have been getting by with the help of generous relatives. They are both practicing Catholics. Anna is more involved in church activities than is Juan, but since his accident he has been attending church more regularly and both have a good relationship with their priest.

4. *African American.* Bob is an African American high school student who is doing well in his academic work but who is struggling with his awareness that he is gay. He was born in the South and moved to the North with his parents and two younger siblings when he was about 5 years old. He adjusted well to his new city, enjoying the support of an extended family. Because Bob's parents are very religious and believe that homosexuality is against the teachings of the Bible, Bob is afraid to tell them what he is going through. Bob's father was recently promoted and the family moved a short distance away to an integrated but mostly white suburban setting where they feel a lot of pressure to fit in. Although Bob stayed in the same school, the male friends he was close to as a child are now very focused on dating girls, leaving him feeling awkward and left out. He is unable to pretend that he is interested in girls and has begun to withdraw from most social activities, including varsity sports. His parents both work full-time and are unaware that he retreats to his room every day after school. His younger siblings wonder why his friends don't come around anymore, but they have learned not to bother him. Bob is referred to you by one of his teachers who has noticed his withdrawal and is concerned. You are a school guidance counselor.

5. *Irish.* John's great-great grandparents on both sides immigrated to the U.S. from Ireland. All his relatives have married Irish Americans, and he has been immersed in Irish American culture in both his family and his neighborhood. He is the first in his family to attend college. He grew up in an urban working-class neighborhood and got a full scholarship to attend college based on his excellent high school performance. He is a practicing Catholic, heterosexual, and able-bodied. He works part-time to help support the family and lives at home with his parents and younger sister. His parents are struggling financially and are pressuring John to leave school to work full-time in his uncle's business. John's father's income has diminished as a result of drinking, and the tension at home is intense as John's father rants about this and that and generally frightens everyone in the family. John's mother leans on John for support. John feels very loyal to and protective of his mother and is torn between her needs and his desire to finish college. John is referred to you in the tutoring center because he can't seem to get a handle on his academic work. As you talk with him, you learn that he has no private place to study and has made no friends in school. He feels compelled to go home after classes to be there for his mother and sister.

6. *Cambodian.* Amy is a refugee from Cambodia. She is living with her aunt and uncle and her siblings, having lost her parents to illness during their turmoil-ridden last months together. She herself experienced a very traumatic escape from her country. She is currently working full-time and attending college at night. She attended high school in the United States, and her English is very good. One of her teachers has referred her to you in the college counseling center because she looks very depressed, and he encouraged her to find someone with whom to talk. Amy is heterosexual and able-bodied. She appears to be suffering from posttraumatic stress. She is Buddhist and is somewhat involved in a Buddhist community.

The Intercultural Interview

WILLIAM K. GABRENYA, JR.

On Culture Shock: Strangers in a Familiar Land

The movement of students across national boundaries for educational purposes has increased steadily since World War II, reaching well over 1 million persons per year by the 1990s. Because this mass migration has become a major component of the educational systems of the mainly American and Western host nations, the experience and adjustment of sojourners has educational, social, and economic implications for them as well as their guests. If homesickness and grief were lime and sand, they would pave a four-lane highway back to the homes of too many of these students. A broad scientific literature has developed since the 1950s as we have sought to understand the characteristics and determinants of *culture shock*, a term first proposed by the anthropologist Oberg (1954) (cf. Church, 1982; Furnham & Bochner, 1986; Klineberg & Hull, 1979). Research on participants in the American Peace Corps program (Mischel, 1965) and more recently on expatriate businesspeople (Black & Gregersen, 1991) is also useful. The flip side of helping students to adjust to our universities is developing worthwhile training programs to prepare business, government, and NGO (nongovernmental organization) personnel for overseas work (Bhawuk, 1990; Brislin & Pederson, 1976).

Church (1982) suggests that there are four types of sojourner adjustment: (a) general adjustment, including physical and mental health and overall happiness; (b) satisfaction with the sojourn; (c) attitudes toward the host country; and (d) social interaction with members of the host society. The research has identified many factors that consistently predict one or more types of adjust-ment, including the following:

Language proficiency
Age
Academic status
Culture distance
Previous cross-cultural experience
Change in social status
Personality traits and behavioral styles, including social skills
Contact with host nationals
Insufficient culture knowledge
Inappropriate expectations

Social skills is one of the best predictors of overseas adjustment (Kealey, 1989). Culture distance is the extent to which the societies differ in charac-teristics such as climate; clothing; language; educational systems; religious practices and expectations; material comfort; leisure activities; family struc-ture; dating, sexual, and marriage customs; and (most important!) food (Babiker, Cox, & Miller, 1980). Gao and Gudykunst (1990) found that general adjust-ment among overseas students was associated with the combination of high culture distance, insufficient culture knowledge, and a poor social support network. One of the most troublesome and confusing of the culture distance variables is "civil behavior": the way people behave in public settings or treat each other in day-to-day interaction, often with strangers. International stu-dents in America complain of their American peers' shallow friendliness, sexual free-for-all, alcohol addiction, and disrespect for teachers, whereas Americans in China are disgusted by their hosts' hostility toward strangers, sexual double standard, nicotine addiction, and submissiveness to teachers.

The first goal of this exercise is to help host nationals (e.g., Americans at a U.S. university) appreciate the difficulties encountered by the many inter-national students surrounding them. The focused, semistructured interview in this project is designed to lead the interviewer through the many aspects of life as a sojourning student. No amount of didactic, classroom instruction can convince a host national of the depth and difficulty of being a foreign student as can 1 hour of heart-to-heart conversation.

Foreign students are a "silent minority" on most campuses, often forming "cultural subcommittees" or communities of their own with little interac-tion with hosts. The intercultural interview sets the stage for a type of host-sojourner interaction that rarely occurs otherwise, providing a strong experi-ence that leaves a mark on both interviewer and respondent. The second goal of the interview is to facilitate such interaction for the benefit of both parties.

On Fieldwork:
Only Experience is Experiential

The third goal of the interview turns the focus from the respondent to the interviewer. Cross-cultural psychology courses often founder in communicat-ing the richness and power of culture because they are too brainy and insufficiently affective or experiential, in other words, too much like psychology and not enough like anthropology. Films and videos are nice, but the anthropologists are right: The bottom line is fieldwork. The intercultural interview, in a small, brief, safe way, is a kind of fieldwork experience for the student. The student must

— Obtain a respondent, preferable the hard way by approaching people individually
— Find a way to establish rapport and interact with the respondent
— Deal with language and communication barriers
— Perform the crucial task of interpreting the respondent's meanings and translating them to concepts familiar in his or her own culture

The interview experience forces the student to make a personal contact with another culture, through one particular member of it, in a focused manner that would be unlikely to occur otherwise, even if the student were to become a foreign student him- or herself. Many students are profoundly touched by the experience.

Time

This exercise requires a 1-hour interview, 4 hours to write a five-page report, and classroom presentation time. The student must budget enough time prior to the due date to locate a respondent and schedule an appointment for the interview.

Requirements

Sufficient international students on campus are necessary to make the project feasible. The classroom discussion portion of the project is enhanced by having a variety of different nations represented. Students can require as much as 15 minutes each to discuss their interview. Like any major project, the interview should be incorporated in the course syllabus with a clear set of deadlines. Detailed instructions should be given early in the course; a handout is provided to students with detailed guidelines and suggestions for the interview. A checklist is also provided.

Instructions

The handout supplied for this exercise is written from the perspective of American hosts, but should be useful anywhere if "the host nation" is substituted for "America" throughout. The instructions should be reviewed orally early in the term and later as needed when students actually begin to worry about the project. Students need to know (a) who they may interview, (b) where they may find the respondent, (c) general interaction guidelines, (d) hints about what to look for, (e) warnings about what to avoid, (f) ethical considerations, and (g) how to write the report. Details of each of these issues are included in the handout. It is important that respondents not be known to other students or the instructor because private details often surface in the reports. Some boundaries on access to respondents may be necessary for logistical or political reasons. Students not in the mainstream majority culture of the hosts (e.g., Latino/a and international students in the class) are required to interview someone from a different ethnic/national group. Relatives and friends should not be used. Numerous judgment calls about who are appropriate respondents should be expected. The checklist is important because, despite written and oral warnings, students will forget to use false names in the report.

Discussion Suggestions

The usefulness of the exercise can be multiplied by having students present their results to the class, generally in less than 15 minutes each. All students need not present for this strategy to be effective. The reports can be given *en masse* during one or more class periods, but a more effective method requiring some flexibility both on the part of the instructor and in the course schedule is to integrate the reports into a comprehensive lecture on sojourner adjustment. The instructor invites students to volunteer their case studies throughout a didactic lecture whenever they seem relevant to the lecture topic. For example, when the instructor is talking about problems of sexual availability, students whose respondents reported such problems can speak up. Although there is no way to predict how long such a mixed use of classroom time will require, the outcome is highly stimulating.

References and Further Reading

Babiker, I. E., Cox, J. L., & Miller, P. M. C. (1980). The measurement of culture distance and its relationship to medical consultation, symptomatology and examination performance of overseas students at Edinburgh University. *Social Psychiatry, 15,* 109-116.

Bhawuk, D. P. S. (1990). Cross-cultural orientation programs. In R. W. Brislin (Ed.), *Applied cross-cultural psychology* (pp. 325-346). Newbury Park, CA: Sage.

Black, J. S., & Gregersen, H. B. (1991). Antecedents to cross-cultural adjustment for expatriates in Pacific Rim assignments. *Human Relations, 44,* 497-515.

Brislin, R., & Pederson, P. (1976). *Cross-cultural orientation programs.* New York: Gardener.

Church, A. T. (1982). Sojourner adjustment. *Psychological Bulletin, 91,* 540-572.

Furnham, A., & Bochner, S. (1986). *Culture shock: Psychological reactions to unfamiliar environments.* London: Methuen.

Gao, G., & Gudykunst, W. B. (1990). Uncertainty, anxiety, and adaptation. *International Journal of Intercultural Relations, 14,* 301-317.

Kealey, D. J. (1989). A study of cross-cultural effectiveness: Theoretical issues, practical applications. *International Journal of Intercultural Relations, 13,* 387-428.

Klineberg, O., & Hull, W. F. (1979). *At a foreign university: An international study of adaptation and coping.* New York: Praeger.

Mischel, W. (1965). Predicting the success of Peace Corps volunteers in Nigeria. *Journal of Personality and Social Psychology, 1,* 510-517.

Oberg, K. (1954). *Culture shock.* Bobbs-Merrill Reprint Series No. A-329.

THE INTERCULTURAL INTERVIEW:
INSTRUCTIONS, GUIDELINES, AND REQUIREMENTS

I would like you to conduct a brief interview with an international student at [university] from a culture different than your own. There are three important restrictions, two of which concern who you may interview:

1. You must not use a graduate or undergraduate psychology major as a respondent.
2. You must not use employees or relatives of employees of this university.
3. You must not approach the International Student Office (ISO) for help in finding a respondent. They have too many other things to worry about.

The interview should focus on the respondent's subjective experience of being in America, psychologically important differences between the home and host societies, problems encountered by the person in adjustment, adaptation to American society, acceptance by others, and so forth. I would like you to write a short description of your findings (about five pages). I will ask some students to give oral descriptions of their findings in class. Please attach the respondent checklist to your report (at end of this handout).

Due date: See syllabus

A few suggestions and ideas for the interview

One goal of the interview is to get the respondent's *story.* Every sojourner has a story; some stories are rather standard, but some are fascinating. Many are accounts of travail and triumph that will lead you to wonder at the strength of the human spirit, but others don't come out quite so well (at least not yet). You may find that your respondent has had very little interaction with Americans even though he or she sits next to them in classes every day. The respondent may be curious about Americans and view the interview as a chance to learn something from you about America. You may find that you have to do a little self-disclosure yourself to get him or her to self-disclose. The respondent may be interested in learning about you and about American culture through you, which in a sense is his or her reward for granting the interview.

You may also find the respondent has incorrect stereotypes about psychology, such as the common "you can read my mind" or "you think everything is based on sex," and therefore may find you intimidating. Whereas these myths are also common in American folk culture, they are even stronger in some other cultures. The respondent may be embarrassed by his or her language limitations. If a respondent nods and smiles vacuously as you talk, there is a good chance that this means just what it seems to mean: He or she has gotten lost and is no longer tracking your monologue. As you may have experienced yourself, once you lose the train of thought in listening to another language it is hard to get back on track. Try speaking slowly, use common words and straightforward sentences, and avoid idiomatic English, slang, and subordinate clauses. Wait for feedback after each statement. Avoid dry humor or facetious statements at all costs!

Ethics

You must begin and end by assuring the respondent of anonymity, and *use a false name in the report*. Ask the respondent to supply a false name consistent with his or her language or nationality. If the respondent claims he or she doesn't care what people think and wants you to use his or her real name, use a false name anyway. The interview is explicitly a privileged communication, and you must never reveal the results of it in a manner that will compromise the anonymity of the respondent. As a future psychologist, you must abide by these rules of professional ethics.

An additional ethical issue that you must confront is how to deal with the respondent's potential request to see you again or continue the relationship. As you have undoubtedly learned in your course, the type of intimate interaction you have had with your respondent is more characteristic of real friendships rather than casual acquaintanceships in many cultures. Furthermore, you may find that the respondent is lonely, desperate for meaningful interaction with American hosts, or both. You may find that you need to maintain some contact with the respondent after the interview, perhaps by telephone. Different-sex interactions are additionally complicated, as you will discover. These ethical dilemmas are confronted in both psychological practice and anthropological fieldwork, albeit in somewhat different ways.

Some examples of information to glean from the interview

These lists are provided to give you some ideas about what to look for in your interview. Please do not think of them as checklists or an interview schedule. Your report need not (and probably should not) cover most of these items. Instead, hit the main points and go with the flow.

Choosing and transitioning: Why respondent (R) decided to come to America; why R chose [university];. how R felt when he/she arrived; effects of R's leaving home on his/her family

Attitudes: What R likes/dislikes about America, this area, [university]; what R sees as the important differences between home and here; attitudes/opinions about America, Americans.

Activities: What R does for recreation; special events or experiences in America; social relationships, dating, response to American sexual norms.

Somatic symptoms: Difficulty sleeping; tired, weak, fatigued; sick with colds, flu, respiratory problems; poor appetite, indigestion; stomach or intestinal disorders; diarrhea; chest pains; headache; dizziness; problems concentrating

Negative life events: Had an accidental injury; family crisis or death

Psychological problems: Bored; loneliness; depression; unhappiness; anxious or worried; problems with school or work; feelings of aimlessness, unclear goals; homesickness; frustration; heavy drinking or drug use; sexual dysfunction

Social problems: Difficulty: meeting people outside of school or work; finding sexual partners; making friends. Concerned about family, friends and conditions at home

Material problems: Difficulty: getting a job; finding a place to live; obtaining information; getting places and finding things. not having enough money

School issues: Not having enough time to study; school work too difficult

Cultural and communication problems: Object of racial discrimination; cross-ethnic identification problems (e.g., wanting to be like/not to be like Americans). Not being able to express oneself in English; having behavior misunderstood; difficulty in communication unrelated to language ability (i.e., cultural meaning of words; context issues)

THE INTERCULTURAL INTERVIEW: CHECKLIST

You must attach this checklist to the back of your report

Your name _____

Semester and year _____

Please check each item

_____ The respondent I interviewed for this report is not a psychology major (neither undergrad nor grad) at [university]

_____ The respondent I interviewed for this report is not an employee, or the child or spouse of an employee, of [university]

_____ The name I have used throughout this report for the respondent is not his or her real name.

Signature: _____

Part 2

The Distribution of Rewards

THEODORE M. SINGELIS
RICHARD W. BRISLIN

Concepts

Individualism and collectivism are the most widely called on constructs in explaining cultural differences (see Hofstede, 1980, 1991; Triandis, 1990, 1995). Individualism has been associated with many northern and western regions of Europe, America (north of the Rio Grande, especially the United States), and Australia. Cultures in Asia, Africa, South America, and the Pacific Island region have been identified with collectivism (Markus & Kitayama, 1991; Triandis, 1995). Although it is common to classify cultures according to the relative emphasis placed on individual and group goals, it is important to keep in mind individual differences within cultures as well. Overall, there are four major areas that are relevant. First, collectivists define themselves as parts or aspects of a group; individualists focus on self-concepts that are autonomous from groups. Thus, the contrast between interdependent and independent selves (Markus & Kitayama, 1991) is one of the defining attributes. Second, collectivists have personal goals that overlap with the goals of their in-groups, and if there is a discrepancy between the two sets of goals they consider it "obvious" that the group goals should have priority over their personal goals; individualists have personal goals that may or may not overlap with the goals of their in-groups, and if there is a discrepancy between the two sets of goals they consider it "obvious" that their personal goals

SOURCE: "Individualism and Collectivism as the Source of Many Specific Cultural Differences," by R. W. Brislin, 1994, in R. W. Brislin & T. Yoshida (Eds.), *Improving Intercultural Interactions: Modules for Cross-Cultural Training Programs* (pp. 71-88). Thousand Oaks, CA: Sage.

should have priority over the group goals (Schwartz, 1990). Third, among collectivists, social behavior is best predicted from norms and perceived duties and obligations (Miller, 1994); among individualists, social behavior is best predicted from attitudes and other such internal processes, as well as contracts made by the individual. Fourth, among collectivists, relationships are of the greatest importance, and even if the costs of these relationships exceed the benefits individuals tend to stay with the relationship; among individualists when the costs exceed the benefits the relationship is often dropped (Kim, Triandis, Kagitcibasi, & Yoon, 1994). Whereas these differences are evidenced in a variety of behaviors, reward allocation is a particularly clear and important process that is influenced by individualism and collectivism. The exercise in this chapter shows how the two cultural orientations diverge in their assessment of what is a fair way to divide rewards.

In individualist cultures, people tend to see group efforts as an aggregation of individual inputs. Therefore, a reward to the group tends to be divided according to the work that each member has contributed—equity. On the other hand, in collectivist cultures the group is viewed as a basic unit and although individual efforts may differ on a given project, the rewards to the group tend to be allocated equally according to membership rather than contribution—equality (see Leung & Bond, 1984).

The exercise also brings to light how individualism and collectivism can affect the ways that people deal with the issue of needs in allocating rewards. Specifically, collectivists tend to take into account the needs of the individual when allocating rewards. The group will allocate additional resources to one who has a clear need. However, in individualist cultures the decision to help a group member in need tends to be left to individual discretion. Thus, the person in the scenario below whose father died would more likely receive a larger share of the reward in a collectivist culture. In an individualist culture, this situation might well result in someone taking up a collection for the person in need, allowing group members to decide on their own if each wished to contribute.

Time

This exercise requires 20 to 60 minutes, depending on discussion time and number of participants.

Requirements

Other than the handout included here, there are no special requirements for this exercise, although a chalkboard is useful for displaying the final results. The activity works quite well in both homogeneous and heterogeneous groups. In homogeneous groups, it works best when the students have some understanding of individualism and collectivism before starting the exercise. In heterogeneous groups, the exercise can be used as an introduction to the concepts (see Variations).

Instructions

After presenting the basics of the individualism-collectivism dimension and some of the behaviors that result, the instructor might introduce the exercise by saying something like: "Another distinction between individualist and collectivist cultures occurs when there are rewards to be distributed. If different people in a group contribute in varying degrees to the accomplishment of a task, how are the rewards for task accomplishment to be distributed?" Students are then divided into groups of five or six and asked to read the scenario. Each group must then decide how to distribute the bonus money. It is useful to emphasize that students should note why they are allocating money.

While the groups are working on the task, the instructor can draw a grid on the board in which the groups can write their allocations. This grid should have the same rows as the handout (one for each individual in the scenario) and enough columns for each group to indicate its individualist and collectivist distributions. It is best to divide the grid vertically in half with collectivist allocations on one side and individualist allocations on the other. This way the two types of distribution can be readily identified. When groups have finished (usually about 10 minutes), the instructor asks each group to write its distributions on the board. The trends are then compared. In our experience, two clear patterns have always emerged as expected. The instructor should identify the different distribution patterns as "equality" and "equity."

Variations

This exercise can be used to introduce or emphasize the individualism and collectivism dimension when both types of culture are well represented in your group. In this case, participants are divided into homogeneous groups according to their cultural background. Each group, then, completes the distribution only once, as they would in their own culture. (You may alter the handout to remove one of the response lists and the instructions about assuming to work in an individualist or collectivist society.) The exercise proceeds as above with final comparisons of the distributions representing the different group preferences.

Discussion Suggestions

One starting point for discussion is the reasoning students used for the different distributions. Asking each group to provide their rationale emphasizes the characteristics of the individualism and collectivism dimension. Consideration of the special cases (Persons E and F) can lead to discussions of high and low context and/or the hierarchical nature of collective cultures.

An excellent question to ask students is, "Which distribution system is *fair*?" The question of fairness is a central feature of many intercultural conflicts and this exercise demonstrates that fairness is constructed from cultural guidelines. What is fair clearly depends on culture. The fact that collective cultures tend to have longer-term relationships with more loyalty to their group is a key factor in making the equal distribution work well. The people who worked hardest on this project may not contribute as much on the next, but will still be rewarded equally then. In individualist cultures, there is a good possibility that the member who contributes the most will not still be a part of the group when the next project comes around.

Finally, asking students how they would *feel* if they were rewarded under a system not typical of their culture brings up the emotional aspects of intercultural interactions. How would they deal with such a situation?

References and Further Reading

Brislin, R. W. (1994). Individualism and collectivism as the source of many specific cultural differences. In R. W. Brislin & T. Yoshida (Eds.), *Improving intercultural interactions: Modules for cross-cultural training programs* (pp. 71-88). Thousand Oaks, CA: Sage.

Hofstede, G. (1980). *Culture's consequences.* Beverly Hills, CA: Sage.

Hofstede, G. (1991). *Cultures and organizations: Software of the mind.* London: McGraw-Hill.

Kim, U., Triandis, H. C., Kagitcibasi, C., & Yoon, G. (Eds.). (1994). *Individualism and collectivism: Theoretical and methodological issues.* Thousand Oaks, CA: Sage.

Leung, K., & Bond, M. (1984). The impact of cultural collectivism on reward allocation. *Journal of Personality and Social Psychology, 47,* 793-804.

Leung, K., & Iwawaki, S. (1988). Cultural collectivism and distributive behavior. *Journal of Cross-Cultural Psychology, 19,* 35-49.

Markus, H. R., & Kitayama, S. (1991). Culture and the self: Implications for cognition, emotion, and motivation. *Psychological Review, 98,* 224-253.

Miller, J. G. (1994). Cultural diversity in the morality of caring: Individual oriented versus duty-based interpersonal moral codes. *Cross-Cultural Research, 28,* 3-39.

Schwartz, S. H. (1990). Individualism-collectivism: Critique and proposed refinements. *Journal of Cross-Cultural Psychology, 21,* 139-157.

Triandis, H. C. (1990). Cross-cultural studies of individualism and collectivism. In J. Berman (Ed.), *Nebraska Symposium on Motivation 1989* (pp. 41-133). Lincoln: University of Nebraska Press.

Triandis, H. C. (1995). *Individualism and collectivism.* Boulder, CO: Westview.

Triandis, H. C., Brislin, R., & Hui, H. C. (1988). Cross-cultural training across the individualism-collectivism divide. *International Journal of Intercultural Relations, 12,* 269-289.

THE DISTRIBUTION OF REWARDS

Assume that you are employed in a company (for profit) that contracts to do construction work (e.g., roads, water treatment facilities) in rural areas of the community where you live. The company recently received a contract for $800,000 dollars (U.S.) to build a road. Given a number of fortunate circumstances, such as good weather, the project was completed for $700,000. It is now the end of the fiscal year and the board of directors has decided that the extra $100,000 can be distributed the way people (who were involved in the road construction project) decide. The following people are involved. All have been in the company for at least 5 years and get along well with each other.

Person A was the hardest worker and was clearly responsible for supervising a great deal of the actual day-to-day work on the project. At least 40% of the day-to-day work on the project was done by him. Persons B, C, and D were solid but not spectacular contributors. They were competent workers but not outstanding. Each contributed about 15% of the actual day-to-day work on the project. Person E is a very high status and wealthy person in the organization and in the community. Although he did not engage in any of the day-to-day work on the road construction project and did not write the proposal for funding, it is known within the organization that he called on his connections and used his influence so that the original $800,000 contract would go to the company.

Person F is a contributor much like B, C, and D. His contribution was about 15% of the work needed for the project's completion. His father died recently, however, and Person F has considerable expenses associated with the funeral, nursing care for his mother, and the education of his much younger brothers (his father left no estate).

Note that the contributions of A, B, C, D, and F total 100% of the project's workload.

You are not associated with the project but are asked to help in the decision making concerning the distribution of the $100,000. How would you distribute the money?

If you need to make other assumptions or to presuppose other facts so that the negotiations can proceed, please write these down here.

Assume that you are working in an individualist society. What is the final distribution of money?

	Amount	*A few words of explanation (Why?)*
Person A		
Person B		
Person C		
Person D		
Person E		
Person F		
Another person		
Total =	$100,000	

Now assume that you are working in an collectivist society. What is the final distribution of money?

	Amount	*A few words of explanation (Why?)*
Person A		
Person B		
Person C		
Person D		
Person E		
Person F		
Another person		
Total =	$100,000	

Who Should Be Hired?

PAMELA M. NORWOOD
DEBORAH CARR SALDAÑA

Concepts

According to Sue and Sue (1990), one of the significant characteristics of culturally sensitive professionals is that they have actively examined their personal assumptions about human behavior, ethnocentric attitudes, personal values, and limitations. Professionals who are aware of their own beliefs, feelings, and attitudes are thought to be better able to begin considering how these are likely to affect their interactions with both clients and colleagues in culturally pluralistic settings. The questioning of the folkways, patterns of communication, worldviews, and ideas involves several stages of personal growth. Approached in a careful and developmental manner, new relationships across cultural boundaries can be explored so as to transcend "natural" and "traditional" ethnocentrism (Bennett, 1993).

Bennett's (1993) developmental model of cultural sensitivity "posits a continuum of increasing sophistication in dealing with cultural difference, moving from ethnocentrism through stages of greater recognition and acceptance of difference" (p. 22). Termed *ethnorelativism*, the most sophisticated endpoint of the continuum is an acceptance of and adaptation to cultural differences. On the least sophisticated end of the continuum are the ethnocentric stages: (a) a denial of differences, (b) a defensive posture taken to counter the impact of cultural differences perceived as threatening, and (c) the preservation of the centrality of one's own worldview by minimizing cultural difference.

The process of developing intercultural sensitivity may be initiated by having professionals explore their perceptions of persons who differ from them in terms of race, ethnicity, culture, political ideology, or sexual preference. The discussion of person perception must begin with a discussion and explanation of ethnocentrism, a loyalty to the values, beliefs, and members of one's own group. In describing the defensive stage of ethnocentricism, Bennett (1993) explains that behaviors may involve the denigration of indicators of difference, a common strategy used to counter the threat of difference. Persons at this stage of ethnocentrism may hold negative views of "out-groups" or groups that are different from one's own. The out-groups are constantly evaluated in terms of one's own values, ways of knowing, and frame of reference. These negative views are then manifested in prejudices and stereotypes (Feagin, 1989; Williams, 1964).

Prejudice is defined as "an avertive or hostile attitude toward a person who belongs to a group simply because he belongs to that group and is therefore presumed to have the objectional qualities ascribed to the group" (Allport, 1958, p. 8). Individuals who make unsupported and biased judgments about others based on faulty and inflexible generalizations, even when exposed to new information or knowledge, are considered prejudiced. Such generalizations or overcategorizations lead to the development of stereotypical beliefs, which then serve to rationalize conduct or justifications for the prejudice (Allport, 1958).

Stereotyping, on the other hand, has been defined as "the prejudicial attitude of a person or group that superimposes on a total race, sex, or religion, a generalization about behavioral characteristics" (Lum, 1992, p. 158). Both prejudiced and nonprejudiced individuals often base their perceptions of others on stereotypical beliefs rather than on individual behaviors or actions. Axelson (1985) identifies the following as being among the major characteristics of stereotypes:

1. Stereotypes are pervasive; most people have their own "pet" personality theories about the characteristics of others.
2. Stereotypes are most often negative when applied to characteristics of individuals and groups different from oneself or one's own group.
3. Stereotypes are habitual and routinized, unless they are challenged.
4. Stereotypes impair the ability to assess others accurately, leading to misinterpretations.

To function more effectively in cross-cultural situations, people must be prepared to identify their own mental images of other groups that may possibly be unfair or untrue. The self-awareness exercise in this chapter is designed to facilitate the exploration of personal attitudes, beliefs, and perceptions. In addition, it is designed to foster critical thinking about bias and the role that prejudices and stereotypes play in the lives of individuals and groups. Participants engaging in self-reflection learn to analyze systematically possible points of cultural conflict that may affect their ability to handle situations in which aspects of cultural diversity may play a part.

Time

The estimated time needed for the exercise, debriefing, and discussion of the relevant concepts is 2 hours.

Requirements

There are no specific equipment, room, or participant requirements, other than the handout at the end of this chapter. The exercise has been used with both heterogeneous and homogeneous groupings as well as with individuals who have had some prior exposure to topics related to cultural diversity and those who have had none.

Instructions

The class should be randomly assigned to groups of five or six persons. Ask the members of each group to go over the given biographical information and make their individual selections first. Each group is then given approximately 45 minutes to select the seven replacements who will be hired on a 1-year contract. In addition, each group is given the same ground rules to abide by during their discussion: (a) Every group member's contribution and point of view is to be respected; (b) candor, courtesy, and consideration are to be modeled at all times; and (c) everyone in the group must participate.

As the leader circulates among the groups, he or she must be sure to encourage participants not to give in just because others disagree with them. The leader must also encourage all of the participants to persist with the discussion even if they begin feeling uncomfortable with the views and statements espoused by their fellow group members. Minority members of the groups (if present) may especially be in need of such encouragement. Any and all aggression and group dominance by individual members should be tactfully and gently dealt with to keep the group on task.

As the exercise instructions indicate, there must be consensus in the selections. If one person in the group does not wish to hire a candidate, then the candidate must be rejected. They must agree, however, on seven candidates by the end of the time period given. Following the small group discussion, the entire class is brought back together for debriefing with the participants remaining in their groups.

The exercise is inductively structured and works well as the first activity in a course or professional development program on cultural diversity. The perceptions that underlie and dictate the participant's decision making are brought to a level of consciousness in a very natural and nonthreatening manner. The discussion can be further extended to include an examination of the mental images that are actually generated based on the descriptions provided in the handout, as well as the possible sources of their origin.

Variations

This exercise can easily be adapted to suit professions other than education. The descriptions have been successfully altered for social workers by using a social service agency context and changing the nature of the work experiences. This can be done for any of the professions.

Discussion Suggestions

After each group has selected the individuals whom it feels should be hired, each candidate is then discussed by the entire class. The name of each candidate is placed on the board and his or her qualifications discussed by the class. The class must decide whether or not a candidate is hired. This must also be done by consensus. If one group did not accept a candidate, then the candidate must be rejected by the entire class. During this discussion, each group tells why it felt a candidate should or should not be hired. Usually, there are only two or three candidates on which the entire class can agree on based on their group's work. Students tell why they as individuals preferred or rejected a candidate; however, the results tallied from each group on every candidate determines who the class feels should be hired. It is interesting to note that during the discussion, participants begin to see how their stereotypical beliefs or images can be triggered by certain specific language.

Students should be queried as to whether they considered that the appointment was only for 1 year. They should be encouraged to explain why they rejected an individual. Questions about how a person's sexual preferences or religion affects their ability to be successful in his or her professional life will help students explore issues dealing with personal life choices versus professionalism (e.g., misconceptions among heterosexuals that all homosexuals wish to convert other individuals to their lifestyle). Other questions to be initiated are those related to persuasive language such as "reported," "community activist organizations," "bitter," "moral things," and "religionist." Participants will begin to examine how persuasive language can be used to incite erroneous views and perceptions. It is imperative that the discussion leader assist the students in evaluating the applicants only on their merits or lack thereof for the position.

Finally, ask students to reflect on their initial choices after group discussion and class discussion to determine if they would now consider some candidates whom they had previously rejected.

References and Further Reading

Allport, G. (1958). *The nature of prejudice.* New York: Doubleday, Anchor Books.

Appleton, N. (1983). *Cultural pluralism in education.* New York: Longman.

Axelson, J. (1985). *Counseling and development in a multicultural society.* Monterey, CA: Brooks/Cole.

Bennett, M. J. (1993). Towards ethnorelativism: A developmental model of intercultural sensitivity. In R. M. Paige (Ed.), *Education for the intercultural experience* (pp. 21-71). Yarmouth, ME: Intercultural.

Feagin, J. (1989). *Racial and ethnic relations.* Englewood Cliffs, NJ: Prentice Hall.

Lum, D. (1992). *Social work practice and people of color: A process-stage approach.* Monterey, CA: Brooks/Cole.

Paige, R. M. (Ed.). (1993). *Education for the intercultural experience.* Yarmouth, ME: Intercultural.

Rothenberg, P. (Ed.). (1992). *Race, class, and gender.* New York: St. Martin's.

Shorter, C. A. (1980). *Who should be hired?* Chicago: University of Illinois at Chicago, College of Education.

Simpson, G., & Yinger, J. (1985). *Racial and cultural minorities: An analysis of prejudice and discrimination.* New York: Plenum.

Sue, D. W., & Sue, D. (1990). *Counseling the culturally different: Theory and practice.* New York: John Wiley.

Williams, R. (1964). *Strangers next door.* Englewood Cliffs, NJ: Prentice Hall.

WHO SHOULD BE HIRED?
EXERCISE

You are a member of a community advisory committee. Seven of the teachers on the school faculty resigned shortly before school opened. The principal has asked the committee to choose seven replacements from fifteen applications on file. Time will not allow you to interview the applicants. Your only information is the completed applications, references, and principal's notes based on the interviews he has conducted.

Below is a summary of the information given you about each of the applicants. Use this information to choose the seven teachers to be hired on a 1-year contract. The group decision must be both consensual and unanimous. The principal will present your recommendations to the district superintendent for consideration.

Case Descriptions

1. *Martha Atler*—27, white, no religious affiliation, M.S. degree, has 4 years of successful teaching experience (2 years in a middle-class, predominantly white community and 2 years in a racially mixed community). She is reported to have ties to a military militia group.

2. *Robert Simpson*—51, white, Protestant, a professed segregationist with a B.A. degree and 27 years of teaching experience. Does not want to teach minority children. Married and father of two adult sons.

3. *Nannette Freeman*—29, black, Muslim. Nannette has an M.S. degree and 6 years of fairly good experience. She is in good health and is an active member of several community activist organizations.

4. *Maxine Liberman*—21, white, Jewish, B.A. from Vassar. Maxine has traveled extensively and is well versed in many areas. She has no prior teaching experience.

5. *James Crow*—35, Native American, tribal religion. James has a B.A. degree and has worked for 11 years. He taught on several Indian reservations and for the Peace Corps. He is bitter about the conditions of his people. Single, no children.

6. *Mary Weaver*—38, white, Pentecostal minister. Mary has a B.A. degree and has 15 years of experience. She has taught in church schools and in public schools. She feels strongly that a child's education should include a focus on moral things as well as academic.

7. *Marie Vitalie*—32, Italian, Catholic. Marie has an M.S. degree and 5 years of teaching experience. She is reported to have lesbian tendencies.

8. *Bernice Johnson*—22, black, Catholic. Bernice has a B.A. degree and 1 year of teaching experience in the middle-class community in which she was reared. She is a sports enthusiast.

9. *Julio Rodriguez*—28, recently arrived from Mexico. Received a chemical engineering degree from University of Guadalajara. Originally certified through the alternative certification program. Speaks limited English but feels able to communicate effectively with children.

10. *Herbert Brown*—49, black, Baptist, M.S. degree. Herbert was an active member of the Black Panther organization of the 1960s and has taught for 4 years. His experience included Afrocentric freedom schools in the United States and Africa.

11. *Sister Robertann*—40, white, a nun. Sister Robertann is a strict disciplinarian who has taught in church schools for 19 years. She has a provisional certificate and permission from her order to teach in a public school system. She has been a religionist since she was 19 years old.

12. *Nguyen Nguyen*—28, Vietnamese, Buddhist, B.A. degree with no teaching experience. Nguyen assisted in the literacy programs conducted in the factory where he has been a part-time employee since the age of 16.

13. *Mary Jones*—25, black, Methodist. Mary has a B.S. degree and 1 year of successful teaching experience. Single with one child. She was involved in a drug raid during her freshman year in college.

14. *Maria Garcia*—39, Mexican American, Catholic. Maria is a former welfare recipient who received a B.A. degree by attending night school. She has worked for 6 years in a day care center. She is married and has 10 children, ranging in age from 9 to 21 years old.

15. *Brian Nelson*—25, white, no religious affiliation. Brian has a B.A. degree and has been asked to leave two schools in the 2 years that he has worked. He considers himself a liberal and feels that this contributed to his problems with his former principals.

SOURCE: Developed by Constance A. Shorter (1980). *Who should be hired?* Chicago: University of Illinois at Chicago, College of Education. Adapted by Pamela M. Norwood and Deborah Carr Saldaña.

Applying Berry and Kim's Acculturative Framework to Documentaries on Culture Contact

KYLE D. SMITH

This chapter describes an exercise combining documentaries on culture contact—often rich in examples of responses to outside cultures, but poor in structure—with a model of acculturation best learned by example.

Intercultural courses can profit greatly from audiovisual material. Image-rich presentations of culturally revealing behaviors, for example, in documentaries on culture contact, enhance students' interest in the material. Yet such documentaries often proceed at a rapid pace and with little obvious structure. They offer potentially important examples of how people respond to influence from an outside culture, but without some idea of what to look for, students may fail to notice these examples or fail to appreciate their significance. Prior exposure to theory concerning cultures in contact should help.

Berry and his colleagues have addressed the changes an individual in one culture experiences as that culture interacts with another—a process of *psychological acculturation*—in a well-developed model (Berry, 1990; Berry & Kim, 1988). According to the model, one culture (the *donor*) typically exerts more influence over the other. Individuals in the latter, *receptor* culture develop preferences for responding in one of four predictable ways. These four

AUTHOR'S NOTE: Portions of the material in this chapter were presented at the Ninth Summer Workshop for the Development of Intercultural Coursework at Colleges and Universities, July 12-21, 1995, East-West Center, Honolulu.

acculturation attitudes obtain as a function of two decisions: (a) whether to remain culturally what one has been, and (b) whether to pursue relationships with members of the donor culture.

In *assimilation,* the acculturating person disengages from his or her original culture and pursues daily interaction with members of the donor culture. In *integration,* the person maintains relationships within the original culture and also pursues interaction with the donor culture. *Separation* affirms one's original cultural identity and rejects the donor culture. *Marginalization* involves a rejection of (or alienation from) both cultures.

Berry's theory makes sense of a variety of phenomena covered in courses on culture, ethnicity, and diversity.[1] It also seems relatively straightforward. Yet I have found that students often struggle with the theory and seem hard-pressed to suggest from their own experience even one example of a behavior relevant to an acculturation attitude.

Combining this theory with documentaries in the following exercise seems to reinforce both. The exercise provides clear and concrete examples of the acculturation attitudes in practice; structures and improves retention for specific information from films; and prepares students to generate examples of the acculturation attitudes expressed in their own experience.

Time

The time required for this exercise will depend on the length of the film you choose and the amount of discussion you prefer. I recommend using two 80-minute classes or three 50-minute classes. This allows time for an introductory lecture (20 minutes) and a documentary (50-60 minutes), for students to sort through and classify examples of behaviors from the film (30-40 minutes), and for extensive discussion.

Requirements

Students do not need prior familiarity with the concepts. You will need access to a film addressing multiple cultures and contacts between them. The documentaries listed below work well. Cards prepared from Handout 1 or Handout 2 are needed for use with the films listed below.

A Clash of Cultures (1986). This 50-minute film covers Western, Islamic, and traditional influences in a variety of African cultures. It is Part 8 in the series "The Africans," from WETA's Annenberg/CPB Collection (ISBN 0-89776-573-7), distributed by Intellimation, P.O. Box 1922, Santa Barbara, CA 93116-1922, telephone (805) 968-2291.

Return to Paradise (1987). This 60-minute film covers cultural change and cultural resilience in Melanesia, Polynesia, and (to a lesser extent) Micronesia. It is part of the New Pacific Series produced by the BBC and distributed by Films Incorporated, 5547 N. Ravenswood, Chicago, IL 60640-1199, telephone (773) 878-2600.

For suggestions on adapting the exercise to other films (including feature films), please refer to the section Variations.

Instructions

First, prepare decks of cards listing the four acculturation attitudes and relevant behaviors from the film that you have selected. Handouts 1 and 2 list the attitudes and the behaviors that I have observed in multiple viewings of *A Clash of Cultures* and *Return to Paradise,* respectively. Each entry in Handout 1 or Handout 2 should appear on one card (or label for a card) per deck.[2] Make one complete set of labels for every four students in your class, and transfer them to index cards.

Table 11.1 classifies 16 behaviors from the films according to the acculturation attitude that seems most relevant to each. The table appears here to give you a feel for the exercise, and not as a handout; students will probably learn more by classifying each behavior themselves, and they may make a good case for putting a particular behavior in an alternate category.

Second, lecture briefly to introduce the concepts of psychological acculturation and the acculturation attitudes. Figure 11.3 from Berry (1990), which presents the attitudes in an outcome matrix, makes a good visual aid.

Because students may be skeptical about inferring a person's attitudes from brief encounters on film, discuss briefly the relationship between attitudes and behavior. Attitudes cannot be observed directly, but are often inferred from behavior (e.g., prejudice from discriminatory treatment). Also, behaving in a way contrary to one's preexisting attitudes (especially under conditions of apparent free choice) creates pressure to bring one's attitudes in line with the behavior. You will ask students to look for behaviors that (a) might express a particular acculturation attitude, or (b) would contribute to such an attitude if repeated often enough. Chapters in introductory social psychology texts covering *cognitive dissonance* and the link between attitudes and behavior will supply ample information for you to summarize here if need be (e.g., Aronson, Wilson, & Akert, 1994; Worchel, Cooper, & Goethals, 1991).

Third, screen your film. Ask students to watch for behaviors that suggest each of the acculturation attitudes. Emphasize that this is more important than making a complete record of the film in their notes.

Fourth, bring your decks of cards (and a list of the behaviors for your own reference) to the next class meeting. Divide your class into groups of three to five (groups of four work best). Give each group a deck of cards. Try the following instructions.

I'd like each team to compare examples of behaviors from the film with the concepts I introduced at the beginning of our last class. Each team has a deck of cards: four cards defining the acculturation attitudes, and the rest listing one behavior apiece. Each behavior can be classified as a particular way of responding to pressure from an outside culture. That is, each behavior expresses or contributes to assimilation, integration, separation, or marginalization.

TABLE 11.1 Sample Behaviors Illustrating Acculturation Attitudes in Two Documentaries

	Documentary	
Acculturation attitude	*Return to Paradise*	*A Clash of Cultures*
Assimilation	A 15% French population forces Tahitians to learn French language and history; Tahitian courses are forbidden.	Cities in Africa use primarily Western building materials and architectural styles.
	TV encourages Pacific people to imitate the lifestyles depicted and to buy slickly advertised consumer goods.	Many African cultures have adopted Western standards of feminine beauty, and the white wedding gown as a symbol of "purity."
Integration	"Japanese spirit, Western technology" (an official motto).	A university in Nigeria offers a course in traditional methods of divination in its science curriculum.
	Papua New Guinea's leading rock band combines traditional instruments with rock's to create a distinctly P.N.G. style.	A newspaper in Swahili publishes news in the form of traditional poetry.
Separation	Tahitians gather on the island of Mooréa to salvage remnants of their culture (e.g., songs and weaving).	A 500-year-old university in Cairo rejects Western curricula, and non-Muslim predecessors in Egypt, as "ignorant."
	New Maori meeting houses reject European culture, produce authentic art, and teach Maori youths "who they are."	Zaire encourages "authenticity" in hairstyles and dress by outlawing jeans and neckties.
Marginalization	Frustrated by a lack of wage employment in Samoa, 100,000 emigrate for New Zealand's most menial jobs.	African women once yielded to missionaries' insistence that they cover their breasts; later they are mystified at bare-breasted European tourists at the beach.
	50% of New Zealand's prison population are indigenous Maori people.	Africans no longer know whether giving something as a sign of appreciation to a leader is good or corrupt behavior.

Please sort the behaviors, card by card, into these four categories. Make a separate stack for each of the four acculturation attitudes. For example, cards in your stack for assimilation will list behaviors that suggest turning one's back on one's original culture, adopting the outside culture's customs or ideas instead. Decide as a group how to classify each behavior. If you can't agree on a particular card, you may place it in a "discard" pile, but try to do this with no more than one or two cards. When you've finished, we'll compare notes on how the teams classified each of these behaviors.

If time is short, have each group assign one member to each of the four attitudes. These "attitude specialists" can scan the spread-out cards for examples, collect them, and then list their choices for other members of the group to consider possible reassignments. This reduces intragroup discussion and saves time for class discussion.

Fifth, ask one group to use the board to list the four categories and the behaviors it sorted into each. (A few words from each card will suffice.) Then ask each of the other groups whether they classified any of the behaviors differently. Writing letters for the alternate categories next to the behaviors in question helps to keep track of the disagreements. When groups disagree, ask them to consider the decisions implicit in the behavior in question. Is the person behaving in a way that will maintain his or her role in the original culture, or weaken that role? Is he or she adopting or rejecting the donor culture's practices? These questions will help to clarify differences between the attitudes.

This discussion works well in seminars (8-10 students) and also in medium-sized classes (25-40). Larger classes could attend the lecture and film in a regular meeting, and try the exercise and discussion in quiz sections.

Variations

You may want to adapt the exercise to a documentary addressing cultures of particular relevance to your course, or to a feature film based on cultural clashes (e.g., *Dances With Wolves, Moscow on the Hudson, Mr. Baseball, My Beautiful Laundrette*). You will want to preview the film to be sure that it contains enough examples of acculturation and to prepare your list.

Discussion Suggestions

1. Ask students to draw examples of behaviors relevant to each of the acculturation attitudes from cultures represented on your campus or in the surrounding community. These personally meaningful examples usually spark some debate and encourage students to think about acculturation after leaving the class. You may also find that these examples enrich your subsequent presentations on acculturation to audiences from the same community.

2. Ask your class to speculate on which of the four attitudes leaves the acculturating person most vulnerable to stress. This creates a natural opening for expanding the discussion to material from Berry and Kim (1988), which links marginalization to increased stress and to psychological disorders in migrants, refugees, and sojourners.

Notes

1. The model (only part of which appears here) also covers phases in developing relations between the two cultures, and differences in how various acculturating groups (e.g., refugees, migrants, sojourners) experience their contact with the donor culture.

2. If you prefer, send the author a Macintosh-formatted diskette with a self-addressed stamped envelope for copies of Hypercard files listing these behaviors. Kyle Smith, Social/Behavorial Sciences, University of Guam, Mangilao, GU 96923, USA.

References and Further Reading

Aronson, E., Wilson, T. D., & Akert, R. M. (1994). *Social psychology: The heart and the mind.* New York: HarperCollins. [Includes an in-depth discussion of dissonance-induced attitude change]

Berry, J. W. (1990). Psychology of acculturation: Understanding individuals moving between cultures. In R. W. Brislin (Ed.), *Applied cross-cultural psychology* (pp. 232-253). Newbury Park, CA: Sage.

Berry, J. W., & Kim, U. (1988). Acculturation and mental health. In P. Dasen, J. W. Berry, & N. Sartorius (Eds.), *Health and cross-cultural psychology* (pp. 207-236). London: Sage.

Padilla, A. (1994). Bicultural development: A theoretical and empirical examination. In R. G. Malgady & O. Rodriguez (Eds.), *Theoretical and conceptual issues in Hispanic mental health* (pp. 20-51). Malabar, FL: Krieger. [Discusses the advantages of integration for people equally at home in two cultures]

Worchel, S., Cooper, J., & Goethals, G. R. (1991). *Understanding social psychology* (5th ed.). Pacific Grove, CA: Brooks/Cole. [Includes a chapter on consistency between attitudes and behaviors]

HANDOUT 1:
LABELS FOR AN ACCULTURATION EXERCISE BASED ON *A CLASH OF CULTURES*

ASSIMILATION: Adopting the attitudes and behavior of the larger society; abandoning one's own cultural heritage in the process	INTEGRATION: Maintaining one's own cultural heritage while participating actively in the larger society	SEPARATION: Maintaining and promoting one's cultural heritage while rejecting the culture of the larger society
MARGINALIZATION: Losing ties with one's own culture and failing to establish ties with the culture of the larger society	Including a course in traditional methods of divination in the science curriculum at a university in Nigeria	Ethiopian Jews ostracized by the Israelis
Traditional Africans are not easily alarmed by moralizing preachers	Mixing hypnosis and magic with wrestling	Preference for Muslim healers in Zaire, even on the part of non-Muslims
Bullfighting with unarmed matadors	Use of Western building materials and architectural styles	Accepting Western standards of feminine beauty
Yielding to Western missionaries' insistence that women cover their breasts	Mystification at bare-breasted European women on African beaches	A return to some building techniques developed by the ancient Egyptians
A 500-year-old university in Cairo rejects Western curricula, and non-Muslim predecessors in Egypt, as "ignorant"	Combining a large number of Western influences with the Islamic societies of Northern Africa	Looking for an alternative to the Western system of law as a response to increasing crime rates

Africans no longer know whether giving something as a sign of appreciation to an official or leader is good behavior or corrupt behavior	Practicing exorcism as a means of curing mental illnesses	Frenzied individual prayers in the African style as a component of large-scale Christian services
An increase in use of traditional healing as economies decline	Adopting the white wedding gown as a symbol of purity	Zaire encouraging "authenticity" in hairstyles and dress; outlawing jeans and neckties
Using English, French, and Arabic as pan-African media of communication	A newspaper in Swahili (with poetry)	

HANDOUT 2:
LABELS FOR AN ACCULTURATION
EXERCISE BASED ON *RETURN TO PARADISE*

ASSIMILATION: Adopting the attitudes and behavior of the larger society; abandoning one's own cultural heritage in the process	INTEGRATION: Maintaining one's own cultural heritage while participating actively in the larger society	SEPARATION: Maintaining and promoting one's cultural heritage while rejecting the culture of the larger society
MARGINALIZATION: Losing ties with one's own culture and failing to establish ties with the culture of the larger society	Foreign videos (including horror and sexploitation films) are available everywhere in the Pacific	An ancient martial art is now taught in sensationalistic style to 4-year-olds training to earn money in films
TV encourages Pacific people to imitate the lifestyles depicted and buy slickly advertised consumer goods	The People's Republic of China declares war on "cultural pollution" and promotes traditional values	The Japanese make use of foreign products, but remain little changed by them
Tokyo Disneyland opened with Shinto ceremony, run by Japanese, profits stay in Japan	An official motto: "Japanese spirit, Western technology"	Papua New Guinea's leading rock band combines traditional instruments with rock's to create a distinctly P.N.G. style
Papua New Guinean actors combine many New Guinea styles to create a national style of "folk opera"	Plays teach P.N.G. villagers about cultural change, for example, how to get money out of scheming politicians	P.N.G. ministers use foreign aid to live like kings, earning the wrath of their own people and, eventually, of the World Bank

France funds the island Pacific's "highest standard of living" to reduce Tahitian opposition to dangerous nuclear tests	A 15% French population forces Tahitians to learn French language and history; Tahitian courses are forbidden	To earn tourist dollars, Tahitians perform dances in an inauthentic style that emphasizes sex over poetry
Tahitians re-enact an ancient Polynesian coronation, relying on foreigners' written histories for authentic detail	Tahitians gather on the island of Mooréa to salvage remnants of their culture, for example, songs and weaving	Trying to get a better wage-paying job with traditional Samoan status-conferring tattoos
At Samoan funerals, traditional exchanges of gifts (e.g., mats) continue, and now include bus fare given because "We are Christians"	A funeral for a chief in Samoa includes traditional gifts for the Christian church, just as would have been offered to the Polynesian gods	The U.S. deluges American Samoa with dollars, but fosters a very high crime rate (4 times Western Samoa's per capita police force)
Samoans play English cricket with an American bat and with indigenous elements like humorous dances	90% of American Samoan children speak only Samoan before they begin school in English	"Americanization in Samoa is a veneer. They're still truculently Samoan, almost arrogantly so"
Frustrated by the lack of wage employment in Samoa, 100,000 emigrate for New Zealand's most menial jobs	New Zealand managers require Samoans and Cook Islanders to converse with one another in English, so no one is at a disadvantage	Remittances of money from New Zealand's immigrant Samoans become a mainstay of their relatives' lifestyles in Samoa
Samoans and Cook Islanders compete with indigenous Maoris for wage employment in New Zealand; 40% of unemployed are Maori	50% of New Zealand's prison population are indigenous Maori people	Maori cycle gangs force Maoris to pay rents to European slumlords. These gangs are seen as a "new identity" for Maoris

Factory-produced Maori "folk art" is stained black for tourists who expect "dark things from dark people"	New Maori meeting houses reject European culture, produce authentic art, teach Maori youths "who they are," and give them "a place to stand"	"Maoris are an impotent minority in the land of their birth. Many are unsure of who they are"
Many Maori do not even know what tribe they come from	Rights to land were important in traditional Maori culture, but they have lost ownership of all but 4% of New Zealand's land	"Hawai'ian Renaissance" combines once-banned ancient hula with recent costumes, modern performance halls, and a faster pace
In Hawai'i, the hula is no longer a way of worshiping natural deities, but a form of public competition	Hula dancers exemplify a new confidence in Hawai'ian identity, based not on language or Hawai'ian blood, but on customs and art	

Attribution Across Cultures

One's Effort Is Another's Ability!

JO ANNE SHWAYDER
DHARM P. S. BHAWUK

Concepts

*M*aking attributions about the cause of people's behavior is not always easy within one's own culture, and the process is further complicated in intercultural interactions by the existence of different cultural standards, norms, and references. Let us say a person is hospitalized for surgery. When this person receives flowers and a "get well soon" card from a friend, what attribution should he or she make? Should the patient be thankful to the friend for the consideration shown and consider the person a close friend, or should the patient think of the person as not a close friend and someone who cannot find the time to visit the patient at the hospital? In some cultures, it is appropriate to send flowers to friends who are in the hospital, whereas in other cultures it is more appropriate to visit them personally. Depending on one's cultural background, one may make either of the two attributions. If the flower sender and receiver both make the first attribution (or the second), then they are making isomorphic attributions (Triandis, 1975). But if they make different attributions, then they will have to deal with intercultural misunderstanding.

Making correct attributions is very important in intercultural interactions, especially in the classroom because misunderstanding can hamper students' learning. For example, if a student looks down while a teacher is admonishing the student, what attribution should the teacher make? If the student is Hawai'ian and the teacher attributes this behavior to not paying attention to the teacher, the teacher is not making the same attribution as the student, but if the teacher attributes the behavior to showing respect, the teacher is making the same attribution as the student, that is, an isomorphic attribution.

Making isomorphic attributions in a diverse school population is critical to student-teacher relationships as well as academic effectiveness. Hence, it is important for teachers to know about cultural variation in making attributions about many everyday behaviors, especially because teachers give positive or negative reinforcement to students based on the attributions they make.

Cultural differences in attributions of school events has been well documented. Asian students tend to make attributions of low effort to their school failures, whereas American students tend to make attributions of low ability to their failures in school (Holloway, 1988; Omura, Kambara, & Taketsuna, 1990; Watkins & Regmi, 1994). The root of the differences is not exactly clear yet, although there is some evidence that students may make different attributions to the same event. This is shown in the cultural differences (Bae & Crittenden, 1989; Nurmi, 1991) in the Attributional Style Questionnaire (Peterson et al., 1982), which asks respondents to chose an attribution for a certain event out of context.

On the other hand, other more contextually based studies have shown that a teacher's behavior has a strong impact on students' attributions (Butler, 1994; Graham, 1991). Showing pity, giving praise for an easy task, and giving much unsolicited help cues students to making attributions of low ability following failure. Showing anger, showing blame, and not giving unsolicited help cues students to make attributions of low effort following failure (Graham, 1991).

The purpose of the exercise in this chapter is to sensitize teachers to the following three dimensions of attribution proposed by Weiner (1985).

> *Locus of causality* refers to where the cause of the outcome originated. This dimension is perceived by actors as either internal (e.g., ability) or external (e.g., luck) to themselves.
> *Stability* refers to whether the cause of the outcome is thought to be stable over time (e.g., ability) or temporary (e.g., effort).
> *Controllability* refers to whether the cause is perceived as controllable by the actor (e.g., effort) or uncontrollable (e.g., ability).

An example will illustrate the value of understanding cross-cultural differences in attribution making. Whereas a teacher might make one attribution of a student's achievement in school, that student may make another. For instance, a teacher might think that one female student is just not very good at math and so should not waste effort on it. After all, the student is very good at reading, writing, and expressing herself. The student can pick up on the cues the teacher gives and may herself start attributing her failure in math to low mathematical aptitude. In fact, the student might have the ambition to become an astronaut. Before her encounters with this teacher, she may have been encouraged by her parents to try harder to succeed in math and to reach her goal. Now she is receiving mixed messages from her teachers and her parents.

Additionally, the teacher probably does not know that the attributions he is making about his student's failure are also received by that student. Graham (1991) has shown that students can pick up on certain subtle cues from teachers that show their attributions of student's successes and failures.

Teachers should be aware that there are many differing attributional styles and that they may have an influence on the attributional styles of their students. Some styles have been called pessimistic and can lead to learned helplessness. These are internal, uncontrollable, and stable attributions of failure, for instance, low scholastic ability. Some have been called optimistic. They are controllable attributions of failure, for instance, low effort. Attributions children make can help lead them to further failures and perhaps chronic failure, learned helplessness, or turn the tide and lean them toward success.

Time

This exercise requires about 50 minutes.

Requirements

The included questionnaire is the only requirement.

Instructions

The questionnaire should be given to the participants before an explanation of attribution theory is given. The participants should be able to fill out the questionnaire in about 10 minutes. Then the participants can total their answers and find their place on three scales (one for each dimension—controllability, locus of causality, and stability) based on the chart below:

Controllability	Locus of causality	Stability
Question 1　A = 1, B = 2	Question 2　A = 1, B = 2	Question 6　A = 2, B = 1
Question 5　A = 2, B = 1	Question 3　A = 1, B = 2	Question 9　A = 2, B = 1
Question 8　A = 2, B = 1	Question 4　A = 2, B = 1	Question 12 A = 1, B = 2
Question 10 A = 1, B = 2	Question 7　A = 2, B = 1	Question 13 A = 2, B = 1
Question 14 A = 1, B = 2	Question 11 A = 2, B = 1	Question 15 A = 2, B = 1

Now that students have three scores on the three subscales, the facilitator can explain the three subscales and/or the three dimensions associated with them. These provide quick familiar examples, and then participants learn where they tend to stand on each dimension. Students can first compare subscale totals, then they can compare answers on specific questions.

Finally, if most of the students answer similarly, the facilitator should lead the group to the discussion of other attribution styles by choosing different answers to the items in the questionnaire.

Variations

The questionnaire itself can be varied according to the needs of the class. If the participants are parents, "student" in the questionnaire can be substituted for "child," or "your child." Similarly, "student" can be replaced by "college student."

The next variation comes in the way of presentation. If you wish to use the exercise to introduce the students to the three dimensions of attribution and then want them to have a little more hands-on experience understanding the dimensions, you can use this variation.

First, give the questionnaire to the students. Then let them put it aside (or you could give them just the scores—i.e., Question 1 A = 1, B = 2, Question 2 A = 1, B = 2, etc.). Then the first three dimensions of attribution can be explained. Next the facilitator can ask the students to find in groups which questions belong in the three subscales.

Discussion Suggestions

Once the participants understand the three dimensions, they can discuss the implications of the different attributions that people make of their own actions and of others' actions.

References and Further Reading

Bae, H., & Crittenden, K. S. (1988). From attributions to dispositional inferences: Patterns of Korean students. *Journal of Social Psychology, 129*, 481-489.

Barker, G. P., & Graham, S. (1987). Developmental study of praise and blame as attributional cues. *Journal of Educational Psychology, 79*, 62-66.

Butler, R. (1994). Teacher communications and student interpretations: Effects of teacher responses to failing students on attributional inferences in two age groups. *British Journal of Educational Psychology, 64*, 277-294.

Ferris, G. R., Bhawuk, D. P. S., Fedor, D. B., & Judge, T. A. (1995). Organizational politics and citizenship: Attributions of intentionality and construct definition. In M. J. Martenko (Ed.), *Advances in attribution theory: An organizational perspective* (pp. 231-252). Delray Beach, FL: St. Lucie.

Graham, S. (1991). A review of attribution theory in achievement contexts. *Educational Psychology Review, 3*, 5-39.

Holloway, S. D. (1988). Concepts of ability and effort in Japan and the United States. *Review of Educational Research, 58*, 327-345.

Nurmi, J. (1991). Cross-cultural differences in self-serving bias: Responses to the Attributional Style Questionnaire by American and Finnish students. *Journal of Social Psychology, 132*, 77-86.

Omura, A., Kambara, M., & Taketsuna, S. (1990). A causal attribution model of academic achievement in senior high school. *Japanese Psychological Research, 32*, 137-147.

Peterson, C., Semmel, A., Baeyer, C., Abramson, L. Y., Metalsky, G. I., & Seligman, M. E. P. (1982). The Attributional Style Questionnaire. *Cognitive Therapy and Research, 6*, 287-300.

Seligman, M. E. P., Peterson, C., Kaslow, N. J., Tanenbaum, R. L., Alloy, L. B., & Abramson, L. Y. (1984). Attributional style and depressive symptoms among children. *Journal of Abnormal Psychology, 93*, 235-238.

Triandis, H. C. (1975). Culture training, cognitive complexity, and interpersonal attitudes. In R. Brislin, S. Bochner, & W. Lonner (Eds.), *Cross-cultural perspectives on learning* (pp. 39-78). Beverly Hills, CA: Sage.

Watkins, D., & Regmi, M. (1994). Attributing academic success and failure in Nepal. *Journal of Social Psychology, 134,* 241-242.

Weiner, B. (1985). An attributional theory of achievement motivation and emotion. *Psychological Review, 92,* 548-573.

STUDENTS' ATTRIBUTIONAL STYLE QUESTIONNAIRE

Following are some events that may happen to your students and some reasons why they might have happened. Imagine that it is happening to one of your students and circle which of the two given reasons best describes why that event would happen.

1. A student gets an "A" on a test.
   a. The student is smart.
   b. The student tries hard on tests.

2. A student plays a game with some friends and wins.
   a. The people that the student played with did not play the game well.
   b. The student plays that game well.

3. A good friend of a student tells the student that he hates him.
   a. The friend was in a bad mood that day.
   b. The student was not nice to his friend that day.

4. A student tells a joke and no one laughs.
   a. The student does not tell jokes well.
   b. The joke is so well known that it is no longer funny.

5. A teacher gives a lesson and a student does not understand it.
   a. The student did not pay attention to anything that day.
   b. The student could not understand anything that day.

6. A student fails a test.
   a. That student's teacher makes hard tests.
   b. The past few weeks that student's teacher has made hard tests.

7. A student's parents praise something that the student made.
   a. The student is good at making some things.
   b. That student's parents like some things that the student makes.

8. A student plays a game and wins money.
   a. The student is a lucky person.
   b. The student plays games well.

9. A student almost drowns when swimming in a river.
   a. That student is not a very cautious person.
   b. The student is not always cautious.

10. A student does a group project and it turns out badly.

a. The student did not work well with the group.

b. The student did not *try* to work well with the group.

11. A student gets a bad grade in school.

a. The student is stupid.

b. Teachers are unfair graders.

12. A bus arrives so late that a student misses a movie.

a. The past few days there have been problems with the bus being on time.

b. The buses are almost never on time.

13. A team that a student is on loses a game.

a. The team members do not play well together.

b. That day the team members did not play well together.

14. A student finishes her homework quickly.

a. Lately, her schoolwork has been easy.

b. Lately, that student has been doing schoolwork quickly.

15. A teacher asks a student a question and the student gives the wrong answer.

a. The student gets nervous when having to answer questions.

b. That day the student got nervous when having to answer questions.

SOURCE: Adapted from Seligman et al., 1984.

Conversational Constraints as a Tool for Understanding Communication Styles

Concepts

In our modern, socially diversified and specialized urban societies, intensive communication with speakers of differing backgrounds and assumptions is the rule rather than the exception. Conversing and communicating competently across cultures is becoming a major concern for many people. The growth in foreign travel for business, study, and pleasure; the migration of people seeking work in other countries; and the expansion of international trade have all naturally led to an increase in contacts across national and ethnic borders, together with severe communication problems and conflict situations. These problems and conflicts are partially due to divergent, culture-specific styles of communication. In the past 20 years, there has been a plethora of studies addressing interpersonal conflict styles (e.g., Folger & Poole, 1984; Putnam & Wilson, 1982; Rahim, 1983). Although these studies have addressed many issues pertaining to conflict styles, there has been little theoretical explanation as to why members of different cultures or across a set of cultures engage in certain conflict management styles in preference to others. The exercise in this chapter is an attempt to understand the critical role of the *cultural context* in a conflict situation. Why do people say what they say? or Why do speakers choose one conflict strategy over another?

Kim (1994, 1995; Kim, Sharkey, & Singelis, 1994) has recently suggested that certain interactive constraints appear to account for cross-cultural conversational styles. These interactive constraints are as follows:

1. Concern for clarity
2. Concern for avoiding hurting the hearer's feelings
3. Concern for avoiding negative evaluation by the hearer
4. Concern for minimizing imposition
5. Concern for effectiveness

Clarity, as applied to conversational behavior, is defined as the likelihood of an utterance making one's intention clear and explicit. *Concern for the hearer's feelings* refers to the speaker's perceived obligation to support a hearer's desire for approval seeking, or the hearer's positive self-image. *Avoiding negative evaluation* refers to the desire to avoid negative evaluation by the hearer. *Minimizing imposition* refers to the degree to which an utterance avoids imposing on the hearer or interfering with the hearer's freedom of action. *Effectiveness* refers to an individual's concern for achieving the end results desired from an interaction. To summarize, the current exercise is based on the assumption that these five constraints may function as general motivating forces in the selection of conflict strategies and tactics and may thus serve as important determinants of "cultural ways of speaking" (cf. Katriel, 1986).

Kim's previous research, focusing on styles of making requests, paints a picture that is generally consistent with the existing cultural stereotypes about request styles in Korea and the United States. Specifically, her results suggest that Americans and Koreans differ in their overall approach toward achieving their goals: Americans focus on task constraints (conveying the message clearly and efficiently), whereas Koreans focus on social-relational constraints (avoiding damage to the relationship or loss of face by the hearer) (see Kim, 1994; Kim, Hunter, Miyahara, Horvath, Bresnahan, & Yoon, 1996).

The basic idea is that the dimension of collectivism-individualism will systematically affect the salience of each conversational concern in conflict situations. In dealing with the construct of individualism-collectivism, Triandis (1989) posits that the emphasis is usually more on people than on the task in collectivist cultures and that the reverse happens in individualist cultures. In other words, individualism is defined as the tendency to be more concerned about one's behavior for one's own needs, interests, and goals, whereas collectivism refers to the tendency to be more concerned about the consequences of one's behavior for in-group members and to be more willing to sacrifice personal interests for the attainment of harmony and collective interests.

Recent cross-cultural research on the self has suggested that self-concept is an important mediator of cultural behavior patterns (Singelis, 1994; Singelis & Brown, 1995; Ting-Toomey, 1988; Triandis, 1988). For instance, Markus and Kitayama (1991) delineated two types of self-construal (independent and interdependent). These two images of self were originally conceptualized as reflecting the emphasis on connectedness and relations often found in "non-Western" cultures (interdependent) and the separatedness and uniqueness of the individual (independent) stressed in "the West." In the *independent* construal, most representations of the self (i.e., the ways in which an individual thinks of himself or herself) have as their referent an individual ability, characteristic, attribute, or goal ("I am friendly" or "I am ambitious"). Thus, the goals of persons in such cultures are to "stand out" and to express their own unique internal characteristics or traits.

By contrast, in the *interdependent* construal the self is connected to others; the principal components of the self are one's relationships to others. So one's behavior in a given situation may be a function more of the needs, wishes, and preferences of others than of one's own needs, wishes, or preferences. As a result of this interdependent construal of the self, one may attempt to meet the needs of others and to promote the other's goals.

These ideas, as applied to conflict management styles, would mean that individuals with interdependent self-construals have, as an overall goal, the desire to avoid loss of face and to be accepted by in-group members. These values tend to foster passive, indirect styles in the management of conflict (due to high concern for relational concerns, such as avoiding hurting the other's feelings, minimizing imposition, and avoiding negative evaluation). The independent self-image places a higher priority on maintaining independence and asserting individual needs and goals. It is the individual's responsibility to "say what's on her or his mind" if he or she expects to be attended to or understood (Markus & Kitayama, 1991). Thus, individuals with independent self-construals tend to satisfy their concerns and to stress a direct style of communication (due to high concern for clarity and effectiveness). Thus, styles of managing conflict may differ across individuals of different cultural orientations, presumably due to differing importance attached to different conversational constraints.

The frequent misunderstanding among speakers of different cultures stems from the fact that "our" ways of communicating seem self-evidently natural and appropriate to us. We don't think of changing tactics because ways of achieving conversational goals seem self-evidently appropriate. People instinctively feel that their ways of expressing things and of being polite or rude are "natural" and "logical." Given that these assumptions are hard to change, the danger of misinterpretation is greatest among speakers who actually speak different native tongues, or come from different cultural backgrounds. Cultural difference, in the form of shared cognitive orientations, necessarily implies different assumptions about natural and obvious ways to achieve communication goals. The differences in conversational styles can lead to difficulties in cross-cultural interactions.

This exercise can systematically explain how the interactive constraints guide the preference of communication strategies across cultures. It can also help participants understand culturally diverse others and more effectively work with them.

Time

About 40-50 minutes are required, depending on the depth of discussion and number of participants.

Requirements

A heterogeneous group of participants (in terms of gender and ethnic background) is preferred. The Sample Conflict Situations handout included at the end of this chapter should be distributed to the participants.

Instructions

After presenting the basics of the conversational constraints and cultural values, the instructor might introduce the exercise by saying: "Conversational style is not what people say but the way they say it. One way to understand others' conversational styles is to know the different concerns people have in conversations." After being presented with a conflict situation, participants are asked to rate the perceived importance of each constraint in that situation. Participants are then divided into heterogeneous groups of five or six, and each person, in the group, then shares his or her ratings with others. It is useful to emphasize that participants should note why they are rating each conversational constraints the way they do. Then they collectively compose two different sets of verbal responses: (a) one from the perspective of someone with highest concern for task orientations (clarity and effectiveness), and (b) the other from the perspective of someone with highest relational concerns (negative evaluation, minimizing imposition, and avoiding hurting feelings). Again, based on each of the responses (presumably one with very direct message, and the other very indirect message), each person writes down his or her attributions about the person who would say each of the responses. Each person then compares his or her attributions with others in the group.

Variations

This exercise can be used to introduce or emphasize the contrast in conversational styles when there are two contrasting (homogeneous within a group) groups of participants (in terms of culture). In this case, participants are divided into homogeneous groups according to their cultural background. Each group then completes the ratings as a group and writes down one or two typical responses based on their constraint ratings. The instructor then collects those responses and writes them down on the blackboard and asks for attributions from each of the groups.

This exercise can also be used to demonstrate gender differences in conversational styles. In this case, participants are divided into female and male groups. The exercise proceeds as above with final comparisons of constraint ratings of two groups and their attributions.

Discussion Suggestions

One starting point for discussion is the contrasting ratings of conversational constraints. Ask each person to provide his or her rationale for emphasizing clarity versus face-concern dimensions. Considerations of clarity concern can lead to discussions of value for task orientation and efficiency. A question to ask participants is, "Which style is better?" The claim that "my own style is better" becomes a central feature of many intercultural conflicts.

Finally, asking participants how they would feel if they were responded in a certain way not typical of their culture brings up the emotional aspects of intercultural communications. "Before doing this exercise, how would you deal with such a situation? What would be your typical attributions? After knowing different conversational styles, how would you deal with such a situation now?"

This exercise brings to light our ethnocentric tendency to think that it is the other person who needs fixing. Understanding each other's styles, and motives behind them, is a first move in overcoming intercultural misunderstanding. This answer is not to apply the standards of one group to judge the conversational styles of the other. Determining the influence of interactive constraints on conversational behavior is an important and necessary endeavor, particularly because, in the "global village," intensive communication with speakers of differing backgrounds is becoming the rule rather than the exception.

References and Further Reading

Folger, P., & Poole, M. S. (1984). *Working through conflict: A communication perspective*. Glenview, IL: Scott, Foresman.

Katriel, T. (1986). *Talking straight: Dugri speech in Israeli Sabra culture*. Cambridge, UK: Cambridge University Press.

Kim, M. S. (1994). Cross-cultural comparisons of the perceived importance of conversational constraints. *Human Communication Research, 21*, 128-151.

Kim, M. S. (1995). Toward a theory of conversational constraints: Focusing on individual-level dimensions of culture. In R. L. Wiseman (Ed.), *Intercultural communication theory* (pp. 148-169). Thousand Oaks, CA: Sage.

Kim, M. S., Hunter, J. E., Miyahara, A., Horvath, A.-M., Bresnahan, M., & Yoon, H. (1996). Individual- vs. culture-level dimensions of individualism and collectivism: Effects on preferred conversational styles. *Communication Monographs, 63*, 29-49.

Kim, M. S., Sharkey, W. F., & Singelis, T. M. (1994). The relationship between individuals' self-construals and perceived importance of interactive constraints. *International Journal of Intercultural Relations, 18*, 117-140.

Markus, H. R., & Kitayama, S. (1991). Culture and the self: Implications for cognition, emotion, and motivation. *Psychological Review, 98*, 224-253.

Putnam, L. L., & Wilson, C. E. (1982). Communication strategies in organizational conflicts: Reliability and validity of a measurement. In M. Burgoon (Ed.), *Communication yearbook 6* (pp. 629-652). Beverly Hills, CA: Sage.

Rahim, M. A. (1983). A measure of styles of handling interpersonal conflict. *Academy of Management Journal, 26,* 368-376.

Singelis, T. M. (1994). The measurement of independent and interdependent self-construals. *Personality and Social Psychology Bulletin, 20,* 580-591.

Singelis, T. M., & Brown, W. J. (1995). Culture, self, and collectivist communication: Linking culture to individual behavior. *Human Communication Research, 21,* 354-389.

Ting-Toomey, S. (1988). Intercultural conflict styles: A face-negotiation theory. In Y. Y. Kim & W. B. Gudykunst (Eds.), *Theories in intercultural communication* (pp. 213-235). Newbury Park, CA: Sage.

Triandis, H. C. (1988). Collectivism vs. individualism: A reconceptualization of a basic concept in cross-cultural social psychology. In G. Verma & C. Bagley (Eds.), *Cross-cultural studies of personality, attitudes, and cognition* (pp. 60-95). London: Macmillan.

Triandis, H. C. (1989). The self and social behavior in differing cultural contexts. *Psychological Review, 96,* 506-520.

SAMPLE CONFLICT SITUATIONS

Situation 1 (Roommate)

Imagine you moved into an off-campus house with three other friends, each of whom you have known for 2 years. You and your roommates each has a private bedroom, and you all share a living room and kitchen. Because your personal computer is in your bedroom, you do a good deal of studying there.

Sometimes you or your roommates have people over for parties on weekends, but you have an informal agreement to limit entertaining during the week so people can study. However, over the past 2 months Chris, one of your roommates, frequently has had friends over and played music loudly during the week. Talking to your other roommates, you found that Chris also has had noisy weeknight parties when they were at home. Chris certainly has been noisier than your other roommates on weeknights.

Suppose it is a Tuesday evening, and you are in your bedroom writing a term paper that is due tomorrow. A few minutes ago, Chris came home with several friends and turned on the stereo loudly. You don't want to leave, because you are writing your paper on your computer. You decide to talk to Chris about the situation.

Perceived Importance of Conversational Concerns

This exercise focuses on the objectives of conversational situations and your attitude toward various ways you could go about achieving them. Please read the above situation and answer the following questions.

1. In this situation, I feel it is very important to make my point as clear and direct as possible.

   strongly agree   1   2   3   4   5   6   7   strongly disagree

2. In this situation, it is very important to get the other person to do what I want.

   strongly agree   1   2   3   4   5   6   7   strongly disagree

3. In this situation, I feel it is very important to avoid hurting the other's feelings.

   strongly agree   1   2   3   4   5   6   7   strongly disagree

4. In this situation, it is very important to avoid imposing on the other person.

   strongly agree   1   2   3   4   5   6   7   strongly disagree

5. In this situation, it is very important to avoid looking negative in the eyes of the other person.

   strongly agree   1   2   3   4   5   6   7   strongly disagree

Situation 2 (Office Manager)

Imagine that after graduation you were hired as an assistant manager. The manager often leaves you in charge of the office where you work. Imagine that a friend of yours, Pat, also is an employee at this office. Pat's work is satisfactory in most respects, but Pat constantly has been 5 to 10 minutes late returning from lunch when you are left in charge. Moreover, Pat rarely is late when the manager is present. The other employees nearly always return from lunch on time, regardless of whether you or the manager are in charge. In sum, the other employees manage to be punctual, yet Pat repeatedly is tardy when the manager is gone and you are in charge.

Today Pat returned from lunch 30 minutes late. You feel obligated to talk with Pat, because the manager recently mentioned the importance of employees being on time.

Perceived Importance of Conversational Concerns

This exercise focuses on the objectives of conversational situations and your attitude toward various ways you could go about achieving them. Please read the above situation and answer the following questions.

1. In this situation, I feel it is very important to make my point as clear and direct as possible.

    strongly agree   1   2   3   4   5   6   7   strongly disagree

2. In this situation, it is very important to get the other person to do what I want.

    strongly agree   1   2   3   4   5   6   7   strongly disagree

3. In this situation, I feel it is very important to avoid hurting the other's feelings.

    strongly agree   1   2   3   4   5   6   7   strongly disagree

4. In this situation, it is very important to avoid imposing on the other person.

    strongly agree   1   2   3   4   5   6   7   strongly disagree

5. In this situation, it is very important to avoid looking negative in the eyes of the other person.

    strongly agree   1   2   3   4   5   6   7   strongly disagree

Situation 3 (Group Project)

Imagine that you have been assigned to a group project in one of your classes. The class is in your major and it is important that you get a good grade in this class. The final grade will depend to a great extent on how well the group project turns out. You were designated by the course instructor to be the leader of the group.

One group member, Dale, has been causing some problems. From the start of the group project, Dale has seldom made it to group meetings on time and entirely skipped one meeting without ever calling anyone. Talking to people who have been in courses with Dale in prior terms, you found that Dale sometimes skipped class meetings in the past. Among the members of your group, Dale is the only person who is creating this problem.

Suppose the group project is due in 2 weeks. Dale again skipped today's meeting in which the group planned to put together the final draft of its report next week. As group leader, you decide to talk to Dale about the situation.

Perceived Importance of Conversational Concerns

This exercise focuses on the objectives of conversational situations and your attitude toward various ways you could go about achieving them. Please read the above situation and answer the following questions.

1. In this situation, I feel it is very important to make my point as clear and direct as possible.

   strongly agree   1   2   3   4   5   6   7   strongly disagree

2. In this situation, it is very important to get the other person to do what I want.

   strongly agree   1   2   3   4   5   6   7   strongly disagree

3. In this situation, I feel it is very important to avoid hurting the other's feelings.

   strongly agree   1   2   3   4   5   6   7   strongly disagree

4. In this situation, it is very important to avoid imposing on the other person.

   strongly agree   1   2   3   4   5   6   7   strongly disagree

5. In this situation, it is very important to avoid looking negative in the eyes of the other person.

   strongly agree   1   2   3   4   5   6   7   strongly disagree

Negotiating Across Cultural Boundaries

Implications of Individualism-Collectivism and Cases for Application

JEFFREY C. ADY

Concepts

This exercise is designed to raise learners' general awareness of how cultural differences, described through the lens of individualism-collectivism, can affect negotiation across cultures.

Negotiations are often conflictual, especially when parties to the negotiation do not enjoy great flexibility in positions they represent. Negotiations across cultural boundaries can be much more conflictual because there are frequent clashes between parties regarding culturally defined roles for negotiation. In many cases, negotiations are less satisfying—and, at worst, unsuccessful—because of differences in task interaction patterns and negotiation preferences.

The importance of culture to negotiation is that cultural differences—and conflict resulting from difficulties with those differences—may cause inter-negotiator conflict about how to negotiate. Negotiators may therefore experience conflict within the negotiation process that may prevent resolution of the issues that bring them together as negotiators! The result may be that the negotiation may never move substantively forward because of excessive time and energy spent on meta-negotiation—the interaction is monopolized by is-sues of how to negotiate.

One of the most widely accepted and researched focus of cultural differ-ences between people groups is the construct of individualism-collectivism. Articulated initially by Hofstede (1980) and widely cited since, individual-ism-collectivism has proved useful in explaining many differences in social behavior between cultures. The utility of the construct for the purposes of this exercise is that many people groups are strongly individualist and other people groups are strongly collectivist.

Although people differ from one another within their own culture, people groups and their cultures tend to exhibit characteristics toward self- and other orientation, which are described by the constructs of individualism and col-lectivism. Individualism-collectivism "has a direct effect on communication because it affects the norms and rules that guide behavior" (Gudykunst et al., 1996, p. 511). Found in most northern and western regions of Europe and in North America (Triandis, Brislin, & Hui, 1991), individualism can be summa-rized as individuals putting their goals ahead of the goals of any group of people with which they may be associated. Individualists are idiocentric in that they pay more attention to their own needs and values than they do to those of a larger group. Collectivism, on the other hand, can be characterized as individual people holding their goals as secondary to those of a group of people to which they belong. Such people are allocentric in that they use group needs and values as the primary reference point for action. Collectivism can be found in Asia, South America, and the Pacific (Triandis et al., 1991).

Individualism-collectivism operates at the cultural level, and it has been argued that individuals' behaviors cannot be explained alone by dimensions of cultural variability such as individualism-collectivism (Kashima, 1989). One individual-level contributor to behavior, seen as a link between culture-level individualism-collectivism and individual behavior, is self-construal (Kashima, 1989; Markus & Kitayama, 1991, 1994). Whereas cultures are pre-dominantly individualist or collectivist, individuals within cultures have both an "independent" and an "interdependent" view of themselves (Singelis & Brown, 1995), though the prevailing self-construal usually reflects the dominant culture-level individualism or collectivism. A dominant independent self-construal, reflecting cultural individualism, leads one to be unique, strive for one's own goals, express one's self, and communicate directly (Markus & Kitayama, 1991). A dominant interdependent self-construal, on the other hand, reflects cultural collectivism's imperatives in that the individual must mesh with his or her in-group, act appropriately, promote in-group goals, commu-nicate indirectly, and understand what others are thinking.

Brislin (1993) notes that the differences between individualist and collec-tive cultures have important implications for everyday behaviors, and this leads to the importance of the construct for task interaction in general and negotiation in particular. Triandis's (1994) work on individualism-collectivism serves as a template for understanding how loci of cultural differences such as individualism-collectivism can give rise to difficulties in task interaction and negotiation. Triandis identified many facets or characteristics of indi-vidualism and collectivism, a number of which have been adapted to form the table in the handout at the end of this chapter, which comprises the foun-dation for this exercise. It is important to understand, though, that not all individuals within cultures behave in the same ways. Rather than thinking of "all Indonesians" behaving according a certain stereotype, it is better to conceive of a range of behaviors, at various points within which most Indonesians would cluster. Not all individuals within a culture behave identically, but there are general forces that operate in a collectivist culture that attach positive value to, and prescribe, behaviors that are allocentric and interdependent, though it is possible for a person to behave independently. Idiocentrism and independent behaviors and self-construals are favored in individualist cultures, but allocentrism and interdependence are certainly possible.

Individualism-collectivism cannot explain everything that occurs as people from different cultures interact, but it is a powerful construct that captures the essence of many meaningful differences between cultures and people groups, particularly when task interaction and negotiation are in focus.

Time

The exercise requires from 1 to 2 hours, depending on the time devoted to examining the specific elements of the table and how much attention is given to the two cases.

Requirements

Each participant should be given a packet that includes the table, the two attached cases or cases provided by the teacher/trainer, and several blank sheets of paper for case notes.

Instructions

a. The facilitator should introduce the problem of task interaction and negotiation following packet distribution.

b. Discuss individualism-collectivism and independent-interdependent self-construals as useful vehicles for explaining difficulties in intercultural task interaction. The teacher/trainer should have sufficient grasp of the individualism-collectivism construct to explain it in terms understandable to participants.

c. Introduce the table to participants. Explain the purpose of each of the four columns of information.

The first column, Attribute, lists the general attributes of cultures that are focused on in this exercise.

The second column, Collectivists, describes how people in collective cultures tend to experience that general attribute.

The third column, Individualists, describes how people in individualist cultures tend to experience that general attribute.

The fourth column, Implications for Negotiation, describes how that attribute may manifest itself behaviorally in negotiation, particularly in describing how collectivists (*Cs*) and/or individualists (*Is*) may behave.

d. Depending on teacher/trainer and participant interest and time available, move through as many attributes as the teacher/trainer judges is best. For each attribute, the focus should be on the fourth column; the discussion of what it means to negotiators behaviorally.

e. If questions or comments have not been offered from participants by the time the teacher/trainer is finished with the discussion of the table, the teacher/trainer should ask for them before moving on to the cases.

f. I recommend a short break at this juncture.

g. The teacher/trainer should provide participants with an opportunity for applying the information from the table. The two cases provided with this exercise were designed to have participants identify attributes, manifestations, and behavioral characteristics from the table that would arguably be the reasons for the scenarios depicted in the cases. For both cases, have participants read the case and follow the directions given at the bottom of each case.

h. Once participants have read each case and identified for themselves which table elements may have been responsible for the events in each case, start with Case 1 and ask several participants to identify the likely contributors to the events described in that case. The facilitator's role at this stage is to evoke opinions from participants and attempt to move the group toward a consensus around the table elements that indeed act to explain case events most realistically. It is possible that up to five, six, or even eight elements may be strong contributors to the explanation of case events. I have deliberately not identified here which elements I tap for each of the two cases, because the facilitator ought to be fairly convinced of his or her judgment on that issue before addressing either case with the group. Do the same for Case 2.

i. The teacher/trainer should ask for comments or questions following the case discussions.

j. The teacher/trainer should conclude the session by reemphasizing the importance of practical differences across cultures in task interaction behavior and the importance of knowing how those differences may affect task interaction and negotiation across cultures.

Variations

I have found that assigning one case to one half of the group, and the other case to the remainder of the group, saves some time and builds interest as one cohort listens to the work of another cohort. The disadvantage of this, of course, is that each cohort does not derive the full benefit of having worked with both cases.

Discussion Suggestions

There are several profitable questions that can be asked of the group following the activity. One, particularly useful when the learner/trainee group is culturally diverse, is to ask for examples from learners' cultural backgrounds of the behavioral expressions of attributes identified in the table. Another is useful for learners/trainees who have had intercultural task interaction experience: Ask for stories illustrating the basic principles elucidated by the exercise.

References and Further Reading

Brislin, R. (1993). *Understanding culture's influence on behavior.* Fort Worth, TX: Harcourt Brace College.

Gudykunst, W., Matsumoto, Y., Ting-Toomey, S., Nishida, T., Kim, K., & Heyman, S. (1996). The influence of cultural individualism-collectivism, self-construals, and individual values on communication styles across culture. *Human Communication Research, 22,* 510-543.

Hofstede, G. (1980). *Culture's consequences.* Beverly Hills, CA: Sage.

Kashima, Y. (1989). Conceptions of persons: Implications in individualism/collectivism research. In C. Kagitcibasi (Ed.), *Growth and progress in cross-cultural psychology* (pp. 104-112). Amsterdam: Swets & Zeitlinger.

Markus, H., & Kitayama, S. (1991). Culture and the self: Implications for cognition, emotion, and motivation. *Psychological Review, 98,* 224-253.

Markus, H., & Kitayama, S. (1994). A collective fear of the collective: Implications for selves and theories of selves. *Personality and Social Psychology Bulletin, 20,* 568-579.

Singelis, T. M., & Brown, W. J. (1995). Culture, self, and collectivist communication: Linking culture to individual behavior. *Human Communication Research, 21,* 354-389.

Triandis, H. (1994). *Culture and social behavior.* New York: McGraw-Hill.

Triandis, H., Brislin, R., & Hui, C. (1991). Cross-cultural training across the individualism-collectivism divide. In L. Samovar & R. Porter (Eds.), *Intercultural communication: A reader* (pp. 370-382). Belmont, CA: Wadsworth.

NEGOTIATING ACROSS
CULTURAL BOUNDARIES EXERCISE

The table describes, from the left, general attributes, how various attributes of social behavior are experienced by collectivists and by individualists, and the behavioral implications of each attribute for negotiation.

Attribute	Collectivists	Individualists	Implications for Negotiation
Self	The ideal is modest and cooperative.	The ideal is distinct from others, better than others, competitive, exhibitionist.	Cs^a may perceive *Is* to be brash, pushy, or uncooperative. *Is* may perceive *Cs* to be unresponsive and/or indecisive.
Focus on:	Groups as the basic unit of social perception	Individuals as the basic unit of social perception.	*Cs* make more references to nonpresent in-group parties to the negotiation.
	The needs of one's in-group (obligations).	Individual needs, rights, capacity (contracts).	*Is* emphasize contractual relationships. *Cs* emphasize reciprocity, sensitivity.
Group relationships	Few, but relationship to them is close, with much concern for their integrity.	Many; relationships are casual; little emotional involvement.	*Is* display easy attachment to negotiation counterparts; *Cs* may be offended at later expressions of easy *un*attachment (e.g., threats of breaking off talks).
	Difficult entry into groups and friendships, but relationships are intimate after establishment.	People appear sociable, but relationships are superficial and depend on social exchanges and contracts.	*Cs* are likely to be dismayed at *Is'* apparent lack of regard for protocol and trust-building needs. *Is* are likely to be frustrated at *Cs'* apparent lack of responsiveness to friendship messages.
	In-group harmony is required.	Debate, confrontation are acceptable within in-group.	*Cs* may want to present a unified face to counterparts and perceive *Is'* in-group disagreements as weakness.
Goals	Role-relevant goals are greatly valued.	Clearly articulated goals are greatly valued.	Disagreements over which goals are important are very likely.

Attribute	Collectivists	Individualists	Implications for Negotiation
	Goals are long term.	Goals are short term.	*Cs* may press for long-term goals, whereas *Is* may press for short-term solutions.
Values	Concern for "virtuous action" (situation-appropriate action).	Concern for "the truth" instead of established rules.	*Is* are likely to be offended at *Cs*' apparent lack of principles; *Cs* are likely to perceive *Is* as inflexible.
	Persistence	Visible, immediate rewards for action.	Conflicts in long-term versus short-term goals and rewards are likely.
Attributions	Success is attributed to help from others.	Success is attributed to ability.	*Is* may perceive *Cs* as too modest; *Cs* may perceive *Is* as boastful and ungrateful.
	Failure is attributed to lack of effort.	Failure is attributed to external factors (i.e., difficulty, bad luck).	*Is* may perceive *Cs* as unempathetic; *Cs* may perceive *Is* as evading responsibility for failure.
Social behavior	Frequent use of "we."	Frequent use of "I."	*Is* may perceive *Cs* as nondisclosive ("he or she never speaks as an individual").
	Communication consists of context.	Communication consists of content.	*Is* may appear to be more task oriented; *Cs* may not appear to "get to the point."
	Reciprocity is obligatory and long term.	Reciprocity is voluntary and short term.	*Is* and *Cs* may initially appear unresponsive, but for differing reasons.
	Mutual face-saving, regulated by in-group norms.	Personal face-saving, regulated by personal needs, as well as cost-benefit computations.	*Is* may be more comfortable with overt disagreements with counterparts and may decide to express disagreement more quickly.

SOURCE: Adapted from H. Triandis (1994). *Culture and social behavior,*, pp. 168-172. New York: McGraw-Hill.
a. *Cs* = collectivists; *Is* = individualists.

Case 1: Getting Down to Business?

Korean midlevel managers of the manufacturing firm Young, Park, and Lee met Dan Smith and Tom Norman, representatives of a U.S. firm, just a few hours after Smith and Norman landed at Seoul International. Mr. Young and his two colleagues work for a company in Seoul that manufactures mounting plates for personal computer motherboards; their firm has been looking for an extreme-high-quality metal stamper for a new mounting plate they will produce beginning in 1998. Smith and Norman are in Seoul to negotiate a sales contract for 20 metal stampers with the Korean company—a deal worth millions of dollars. But talks were difficult from the very beginning as the five men sat down together in a restaurant in the lobby of Smith and Norman's hotel.

Young, Park, and Lee were surprised when Smith, only 15 minutes into their first meeting, said, "Well, it's been nice getting to know you, but we need to get down to business. I think $US 3.8 million is a fair price for the 20 stampers, considering the fact that we're offering you a 15% discount to cover relevant tariffs and reimbursement for a .0015% machine-related error rate for 3 years. What do you think?"

"Well, we are not prepared to talk about specifics yet. . . . It's, ah, very important for us to get to know our suppliers . . . " Young replied.

"I'm sure we can do that later," Norman answered, "but we just can't waste very much time. We've got quite a few deals to negotiate after this one, so we need to hurry."

Young became quite worried that something was wrong with his approach to the Americans. He laughed nervously. "I'm sorry—maybe I wasn't clear. We'd like to think of a possible relationship with your firm as a long-term one, so we all need to carefully consider what might happen."

Mr. Norman sat silently, listening to this exchange. The Koreans apparently didn't want to talk business after all. But then why did they agree to meet? "Look," he said, "the numbers speak for themselves. Has anyone made you a better offer?"

"Uh, frankly, no, yours is the best offer. But there are other things to consider . . . " Young began.

"Well, then, what else is there to consider?" Norman interrupted with a laugh. "I'm missing the Superbowl for this!"

"Well, for one thing, we must consult with our superiors before finalizing arrangements—but that is even further down the line. We really should think of making our final decision in a week or so. I hope you understand," Young said with a frown, "we just want to get to know you a little tonight." The Americans seemed very impatient, and he was beginning to think they were rude.

Smith was beginning to lose patience. The airline's in-flight dinner he had eaten 3 hours earlier wasn't digesting properly, either. "A *week*?! What I *understand* is that we are very busy and you, Mr. Young, appear to be avoiding the important issues. If you don't want to do business, why don't you just say so? What's the problem?"

Mr. Young turned to his colleagues. They spoke quietly among themselves. In unison they gathered their belongings and stood. "We understand that you two probably need a good night's rest, so we beg your permission to leave. We will meet you again tomorrow morning. Please accept our apology for the misunderstanding," Mr. Young said, doing his best to hide his discomfort. The three Koreans offered their hands to the Americans, who shook them in disbelief. And the three Koreans left.

"Sheesh!" Norman exclaimed. "What do these people *want*?"

"Let's see if the Superbowl game is on TV somewhere," Smith suggested.

Review the table. Write on a separate sheet of paper which specific attributes of collectivists and individualists from the table might be contributing to the difficulties described above.

Case 2: The Meeting That Wasn't

Gregory Jones, a 25-year-old MIT graduate, was the president of the small company he founded just 1 year ago with no prior business experience. The firm had started and blossomed literally overnight when Jones had discovered a new way to fabricate superconductive semiconductors. The firm specialized in the development and manufacture of superconductive hardware of many types, and it was famous for its small, family-type climate that emphasized informality and creativity—an extension of Mr. Jones's personality. Mr. Jones had just arrived in Tokyo to discuss the possible sale of his firm's products to a large Japanese corporation. The Japanese firm, a large contractor chosen for installing fiberoptic telecommunication service in a major Japanese prefecture, was interested in the American company's new superconducting capacitors for ultra-high-speed relays used in fiberoptic network switching. Mr. Jones came to Tokyo by himself—everyone else at his firm had other work to do, leaving him the only available person for travel. He was dressed casually in slacks and a polo shirt.

His counterpart was Goto Yasuhira, the 60-year-old president of a well-established and highly respected contracting firm. He dressed impeccably; his gray hair and dignified manner commanded respect from all of his *kohai* (subordinates). Although he had never met foreign businesspeople personally, Goto was quite surprised that the president of an American company would come to discuss a possible sale. His curiosity got the better of him—particularly because he knew nothing of his American counterpart, despite research done by his staff. This man was an unknown. But surely he would find it easy to discuss business with the president of another company! He brought two subordinates with him: 40-year-old assistant operations director Honda and 35-year-old engineering supervisor Maeda.

Jones was already sitting at a table in the restaurant at which everyone had agreed to meet when Goto and his two assistants arrived.

The Japanese were directed to the American's table and were shocked to see a youthful American man, casually dressed, drinking a beer. Jones stood up and faced the three Japanese. "Hey—glad to meet you gentlemen. Can I buy you a beer or something?" Goto quickly glanced at his assistants and laughed nervously. "Is President Jones not here?"

"Oh, I'm Greg Jones . . . believe it or not!" Jones held out his hand to Goto with a wide smile. The older man seemed very nice but slightly confused.

Goto hesitantly shook Jones's hand and shook his head in disbelief. Could this young man possibly be the president of a cutting edge manufacturing company? How could he talk to such an obviously inexperienced and immature-looking person? There must have been some mistake. The man acted like a college student! And no *meishi* (business card)! *What businessman doesn't know how to properly greet people with respect?* Goto asked himself.

Meanwhile, Jones had cordially introduced himself to the other two Japanese. After repeated urging by Jones, the three sat down at the table.

No one said anything. For several long moments, the Japanese assistants followed their president's lead and looked at the table at which they sat.

Jones could not take any more. This was a strange situation. He remembered his cardinal rule in dealing with people: When in doubt, crack a silly joke and make everyone laugh. It always worked back home. "What—did we all forget our lines? Where's the script?!" He followed with a boisterous laugh—but the Japanese gazed at him with apparently great concern for his sanity.

Goto spoke quickly and quietly in Japanese to Maeda, the youngest of the Japanese at the table. Maeda shifted in his chair and spoke to Jones.

"Mr. Jones . . . you are *President* Jones?" "That's right," Jones answered. "Is there a problem?"

"Excuse me," Maeda said, turning to Goto; another hurried but quiet conversation in Japanese ensued.

To Jones's surprise, Goto stood while talking in Japanese to his subordinates. "Mr. Jones," Goto said, bowing slightly, "I have some more pressing matters to deal with. Honda and Maeda will be happy to discuss things. It was very, ah, interesting to meet you. Please exchange business cards with Maeda-kun."

And with that the elder Japanese left the restaurant.

Jones sat in disbelieving silence. *Mr. Goto seemed nice enough at the beginning, but he really flaked out!* he thought. *What did I say? What kind of people am I dealing with here?*

Review the table. Write on a separate sheet of paper which specific attributes of collectivists and individualists from the table might be contributing to the difficulties described above.

Behavioral Patterns of Horizontal and Vertical Individualism and Collectivism

MICHELE J. GELFAND
KAREN M. HOLCOMBE

Concepts

Individualism and collectivism are often treated as two distinct cultural patterns. An alternative view, offered by Triandis (1995), is that individualism and collectivism are polythetic constructs. As in zoology, where, for instance, a "bird" is defined by two attributes (e.g., feathers and wings) and hundreds of species of birds are defined by other attributes, so individualism and collectivism may be defined by four attributes (see Chapter 9 in this volume), and different species of these constructs (e.g., Korean and Japanese collectivism) can be defined by additional attributes.

One important attribute or distinction that should be taken into account when examining effects of individualism and collectivism is whether the culture is horizontal (emphasizing equality) or vertical (emphasizing hierarchy). Generally speaking, horizontal patterns assume that one self is more or less like every other self. By contrast, vertical patterns consist of hierarchies, and one self is rather different from other selves. The ways in which these relative

SOURCE: H. C. Triandis & M. J. Gelfand. (in press). Converging evidence of horizontal and vertical individualism and collectivism, *Journal of Personality and Social Psychology*; and T. M. Singelis, H. C. Triandis, D. S. Bhawuk, & M. J. Gelfand. (1995). Horizontal and vertical dimensions of individualism and collectivism: A theoretical and measurement refinement. *Cross-Cultural Research, 29*, 240-275.

emphases combine with individualism and collectivism produce four distinct patterns: horizontal individualism (HI), vertical individualism (VI), horizontal collectivism (HC), and vertical collectivism (VC) (Singelis, Triandis, Bhawuk, & Gelfand, 1995; Triandis & Gelfand, in press).

More specifically, in HI, people want to be unique and distinct from groups. They are likely to say, "I want to do my own thing" and are high in self-reliance, but they are not especially interested in becoming distinguished or in having high status. This pattern is likely to be found in many Scandinavian cultures, such as Norway and Sweden, and has been found among student populations in the United States. In VI, people want to become distinguished and acquire status, and they do this in individual competitions with others. They are likely to say, "I want to be the best." This pattern may be frequent in the United States, the United Kingdom, and in southern Europe. In HC, people see themselves as similar to others, emphasize common goals with others, interdependence and sociability, but they do not submit easily to authorities. This pattern is likely to be found, for instance, in the Israeli kibbutz. In VC, people emphasize the integrity of the in-group, are willing to sacrifice their personal goals for the sake of in-group goals, and support competitions of their in-groups with out-groups. This pattern is likely to be found in many East Asian cultures.

This four-way typology articulates exceptionally well with some of the literature that has examined varieties of cultural patterns. For instance, VC corresponds to Fiske's (1992) notion of communal sharing and authority ranking; VI corresponds to his notion of market pricing and authority ranking; HI corresponds to market pricing and equality matching; and HC corresponds to his notion of communal sharing and equality matching.

The typology also is consistent with Rokeach's (1973) analysis of political systems. He discussed political systems that highly value both "equality and freedom," which correspond to HI (social democracy; e.g., Australia, Sweden). Systems that he discussed as valuing "equality" but not "freedom" correspond to our conceptualization of HC (e.g., the Israeli kibbutz). Those systems that value "freedom" but not "equality" correspond to our notion of VI (e.g., competitive capitalism and market economies such as in the United States). Last, those societies that neither value "equality" nor "freedom" correspond to VC (e.g., fascism or the communalism of traditional societies with strong leaders).

Although people in a particular culture are likely to have a dominant response (e.g., HI, HC, VI, VC), there is also variation across situations within cultures. Thus, it is more productive to think of profiles of these patterns for people within cultures. For instance, a person in Sweden may choose HI 70% of the time, HC 15% of the time, VI 8% of the time, and VC 7% of the time. This exercise affords participants the opportunity to discern their profiles of HI and VI and of HC and VC across a wide range of situations through scenarios that have been validated (Triandis & Gelfand, in press).

Time

Twenty minutes are needed to do the exercises, plus time for discussion.

Requirements

This exercise does not require any additional equipment, other than the handouts included at the end of the chapter. An overhead projector would be helpful, but if not available, the instructor can easily read answers aloud. It is important that participants have a basic understanding of the individualism and collectivism constructs before engaging in this exercise.

Instructions

This exercise should be given after a discussion of the constructs of individualism and collectivism has been given, and preferably, one exercise on individualism and collectivism. Then, participants can be introduced to the ways in which individualist and collectivist cultures vary, namely, the vertical-horizontal distinction. The instructor can start the exercise by saying,

> You should now have a good understanding of the differences between individualistic cultures and collectivist cultures. Now let me ask you a question: Do you think all individualistic cultures are alike? Are all collectivist cultures alike? What other dimensions could further differentiate these cultures? For instance, how many people feel that although the United States and Norway are individualistic cultures, there are many other differences between them? I'd like to now discuss one major distinction that is important.

The instructor can proceed to define the distinction and give examples as described in the Concepts section above. Then the instructor should ask the students to complete the exercise individually.

When the participants have finished, the instructor should hand out the scoring/profile computation sheet and explain that the participants will compute their own profiles of HC, HI, VC, and VI. The instructor should then explain that the key to the exercise illustrates which responses reflect which constructs (HC, HI, VC, and VI) for all of the scenarios. For instance, the responses to Scenario 1 show that the response "a" reflects the HC construct, "b" reflects VI, "c" reflects VC, and "d" reflects HI. The participants should place a circle around their chosen response for the scenario under the appropriate construct. This should be repeated for all of the scenarios. The participants should then count the number of times they have responded to each construct on their profile computation sheet, which will produce their profiles.

Variations

As in some of the other exercises, this exercise can be used with both homogeneous groups and heterogeneous groups. In homogeneous groups, the instructor may want to compute a group profile as well and communicate this orally or on an overhead or chalkboard. In heterogeneous groups, the instructor may want to divide the group into cultural groups (e.g., East Asian, Scandinavian, U.S.) to illustrate possible differences in profiles across the groups.

If the participants are not university students, the few scenarios that are written for this population can be taken out.

Discussion Suggestions

The discussion can start with the notion that cultural differences should be considered as patterns, not as only one response to all situations. Participants can be asked if their dominant pattern reflects what they expected of themselves before the exercise. Participants can also be asked to do an analysis of their profile by the type of situation (e.g., political situations, economic situations, social situations) to see if there is any variation. Another option is to have participants speculate on the reasons for their least preferred pattern in the profile. Volunteers can be asked to give this information to the class. Then the instructor can ask the class if anyone had this as their most preferred pattern, and to provide their own rationale as to why they think the pattern is functional. This will create a dialogue between participants regarding the responses, with the hope that they begin to understand that no pattern is right or wrong.

References and Further Reading

Fiske, A. (1992). Four elementary forms of sociality: Framework for a unified theory of social relations. *Psychological Review, 99,* 689-723.

Hofstede, G. (1980). *Culture's consequences.* Beverly Hills, CA: Sage.

Kim, U., Triandis, H. C., Kagitcibasi, C., Choi, S.-C., & Yoon, G. (1994). *Individualism and collectivism: Theory, method, and applications.* Thousand Oaks, CA: Sage.

Rokeach, M. (1973). *The nature of human values.* New York: Free Press.

Schwartz, S. H. (1992). Universals in the content and structure of values: Theoretical advances and empirical tests in 20 countries. In M. Zanna (Ed.), *Advances in experimental social psychology* (Vol. 25, pp. 1-66). New York: Academic Press.

Schwartz, S. H. (1994). Beyond individualism and collectivism: New cultural dimensions of values. In U. Kim, H. C. Triandis, C. Kagitcibasi, S.-C. Choi, & G. Yoon (Eds.), *Individualism and collectivism: Theory, method, and applications* (pp. 85-22). Thousand Oaks, CA: Sage.

Singelis, T. M., Triandis, H. C., Bhawuk, D. S., & Gelfand, M. J. (1995). Horizontal and vertical dimensions of individualism and collectivism: A theoretical and measurement refinement. *Cross-Cultural Research, 29,* 240-275.

Triandis, H. C. (1995). *Individualism and collectivism.* Boulder, CO: Westview.

Triandis, H. C., & Gelfand, M. J. (in press), Converging evidence of horizontal and vertical individualism and collectivism, *Journal of Personality and Social Psychology.*

HORIZONTAL AND VERTICAL INDIVIDUALISM AND COLLECTIVISM EXERCISE

The following is a set of scenarios. Each scenario is followed by four options. Please imagine yourself in those situations, and place an X next to the option you consider the best. Remember, there are no "correct" answers, only your opinion of the most right or appropriate for you. There are a total of 34 situations.

1. You and your friends decided spontaneously to go out to dinner at a restaurant. What do you think is the best way to handle the bill?
   ___ a. Split it equally, without regard to who ordered what
   ___ b. Split it accordingly to how much each person makes
   ___ c. The group leader pays the bill or decides how to split it
   ___ d. Compute each person's charge, according to what the person ordered

2. A big event is taking place in your community, and you have received four requests from people to stay with you overnight while they are in town. You only have space for one guest. Which one will you invite?
   ___ a. A relative
   ___ b. A high-status member of your profession
   ___ c. The one person who is most fun to have around
   ___ d. Someone well connected in political circles

3. You have received four invitations for social events for the same night, and the events are sufficiently far from each other that you can accept only one invitation. Which invitation will you accept?
   ___ a. From a high-status member of one of your groups (e.g., sports, philosophical, religious)
   ___ b. From the one person who is known to be good company
   ___ c. From a relative
   ___ d. From a person who is well connected nationally

4. You are buying a piece of art for your office. Which one factor is most important in deciding whether to buy it?
   ___ a. It is a good investment
   ___ b. Your co-workers will like it
   ___ c. You just like it
   ___ d. Your supervisor will approve of it

5. You are deciding whom to vote for, for an important political job. Which is the most important consideration in deciding how to vote? The candidate is, other things being equal,
   ___ a. A high-status member of your community
   ___ b. Powerful (influences national policy)
   ___ c. A relative
   ___ d. Someone who appeals to you personally

6. You are buying a used car. What is the most important consideration when buying it?
   ___ a. The seller is a relative
   ___ b. The price makes it "an excellent buy" (i.e., others paid much more for the same car)
   ___ c. An expert mechanic, who is one of your long-time friends, recommended it
   ___ d. It is beautiful; it rides like a dream

7. A controversy has developed in your workplace, and you need to take a position. Which is your most likely course of action?
   ___ a. You assemble all the facts and make up your mind
   ___ b. You discuss it with your boss, and support his or her position
   ___ c. You discuss it with your peers, and take their views into account
   ___ d. You consider which position will most likely benefit you in the future.

8. Which factor is most important when hiring an employee? The applicant
   ___ a. Is easy to get along with
   ___ b. Has been an especially valued employee by a competitor
   ___ c. Is a relative
   ___ d. Is a respected member of your community

9. Suppose you had to use one word to describe yourself. Which one would you use?
   ___ a. Unique
   ___ b. Competitive
   ___ c. Cooperative
   ___ d. Dutiful

10. You are considering joining a club. Which one factor is most important in deciding which club to join?
    ___ a. The one where the people have the most fun
    ___ b. The one that is most prestigious
    ___ c. Some of your family members are already members of that club
    ___ d. The one suggested by your parents

11. You are buying some new clothing. Which is the most important factor that you will consider in choosing the style? The style that is
    ___ a. Most suitable for your unique personality
    ___ b. Most impressive in social situations
    ___ c. Worn by your friends
    ___ d. Recommended by your parents

12. You are starting a new business, and you are looking for a partner. Which is the most important factor in choosing a partner?
___ a. Someone with the same business interests
___ b. Someone who has been successful in previous business ventures
___ c. A close friend
___ d. A senior, successful, experienced member of the community

13. The meaning of life can be best understood
___ a. By paying attention to the views of parents
___ b. Through discussions with friends
___ c. Through individual meditation
___ d. Through individual exposure to the views of wise people

14. Happiness is attained by
___ a. Gaining a lot of status in your community
___ b. Linking with a lot of friendly people
___ c. Keeping one's privacy
___ d. By winning in competitions

15. You are planning to take a major trip that is likely to inconvenience a lot of people at your place of work during your absence. With whom will you discuss it, before deciding whether or not to take it? I will discuss it with
___ a. No one
___ b. My parents
___ c. My spouse or close friend
___ d. Experts about the place I plan to travel to, so I can decide if I want to go

16. A famous photographer has offered you a very reasonable price for having a picture taken. Which picture would you choose? You with
___ a. Your three best friends
___ b. A very important person (a person who is bound to get into the history books)
___ c. No one else
___ d. Many members of the community, whom you are helping; it shows that you are sacrificing yourself for them

17. Which one of these four books appears to you to be the most interesting?
___ a. How to make friends
___ b. How to succeed in business
___ c. How to enjoy yourself inexpensively
___ d. How to make sure you are meeting your obligations

18. Which is the most important factor in an employee's promotion, assuming that all other factors such as tenure and performance are equal. Employee is or has been
___ a. Loyal to the corporation
___ b. Obedient to the instructions from management
___ c. Able to think for himself or herself
___ d. Contributed to the corporation much in the past

19. When you buy clothing for a major social event you would be most satisfied if
   ___ a. You like it
   ___ b. Your parents like it
   ___ c. Your friends like it
   ___ d. It is so elegant that it will dazzle everyone

20. Which of the following activities is likely to be most satisfying to you?
   ___ a. Thinking about yourself
   ___ b. Doing your duty, as expected of you by important groups
   ___ c. Linking with others
   ___ d. Beating your competitors

21. In your opinion, in an ideal society, budgets will be determined so that
   ___ a. All people have adequate incomes to meet basic needs
   ___ b. Some people will be rewarded for making brilliant contributions
   ___ c. There will be maximum stability, law, and order
   ___ d. People can feel unique and self-actualized

22. When I enter a room full of people,
   ___ a. I look for my closest wise friend and try to do what that person suggests is best to do
   ___ b. I want to shine and be seen as unique and distinguished by most of the people
   ___ c. I want to merge in the crowd and not be noticed, but I do feel like a unique person
   ___ d. I join my close friends and do what they do

23. In my opinion, the best society is one where
   ___ a. People get more income if they contribute more to the society
   ___ b. People have more or less equal incomes
   ___ c. People can do their own thing without being noticed
   ___ d. People do their duty and enjoy it

24. When people ask me about myself, I talk about
   ___ a. My ancestors and their traditions
   ___ b. My friends and what we like to do
   ___ c. My accomplishments
   ___ d. What makes me unique

25. Suppose your fiancee and your parents do not get along very well. What would you do?
   ___ a. Nothing
   ___ b. Tell my fiancee that I need my parents' financial support and that he or she should learn to handle the politics
   ___ c. Tell my fiancee that he or she should make a greater effort to "fit in" with the family
   ___ d. Remind my fiancee that my parents and family are very important to me and he or she should submit to their wishes

26. How do you prefer to handle difficult class assignments?
    ___ a. Work alone
    ___ b. Work with a group
    ___ c. Discuss the assignment with the professor to get ahead of the others who did not do that
    ___ d. Take charge of a group; parcel out tasks to make each person's job easier and the completion of the assignment successful

27. Suppose you have two job offers to choose between. Which are the most important factors in making your decision?
    ___ a. Location of the job in relation to my family and friends
    ___ b. The position that will result in the greatest job satisfaction
    ___ c. The ability to move up quickly in that organization
    ___ d. My family will gain more status in the community

28. Teams of five people entered a science project contest. Your team won first place and a prize of $100. You and another person did 95% of the work on this project. How should the money be distributed?
    ___ a. Split it equally, without regard to who did what
    ___ b. The other person and I get 95% of the money, and the rest goes to the group
    ___ c. The group leader decides how to split the money
    ___ d. Divide the money in the way that gives me the most personal satisfaction

29. Imagine you are selecting a band for a fundraising event given by your organization. Which are the most important factors in making your decision?
    ___ a. I really like the band
    ___ b. My friends approve of this band
    ___ c. The administration of my organization approves of the band
    ___ d. I would select the band that is most likely to draw a large crowd

30. You need to choose one more class for the next semester. Which one will you select?
    ___ a. The one that will help me get ahead of everyone else
    ___ b. The one my parents said to take
    ___ c. The one my friends plan to take
    ___ d. The one that seems most interesting to me

31. You want to become more involved with a campus organization. Which one will you select?
    ___ a. The one that will look best on my resume
    ___ b. The one that people in my dorm are in
    ___ c. The one my parents recommend
    ___ d. The one I like best

32. Spring break is right around the corner and you need to make plans. Which option will you select?
    ___ a. Go home and see my family; they want me there
    ___ b. Go to Florida; I love the sunshine
    ___ c. Spend time studying to give myself a competitive edge
    ___ d. Want to do what everyone else is doing

33. Which candidate will you vote for in the election for president of the Student Government?
    ___ a. The one your friends are voting for
    ___ b. The one I like best
    ___ c. The one who will reward me personally
    ___ d. The one who is a member of an organization important to me—the status of that organization will improve if that candidate is elected

34. You are away at school and have time to write a letter. Whom will you write to?
    ___ a. My boss at work—it will help me get ahead
    ___ b. My parents
    ___ c. The person I feel happy writing to
    ___ d. My brother or sister

Scoring and Profile Sheet

Circle the letter that you selected for each item. Then add the number of circles in each column to determine your score on each dimension.

Item	Horizontal collectivism	Vertical collectivism	Horizontal individualism	Vertical individualism
1.	a	c	d	b
2.	a	b	c	d
3.	c	a	b	d
4.	b	d	c	a
5.	c	a	d	b
6.	a	c	d	b
7.	c	b	a	d
8.	c	d	a	b
9.	c	d	a	b
10.	c	d	a	b
11.	c	d	a	b
12.	c	d	a	b
13.	b	a	c	d
14.	b	a	c	d
15.	c	b	a	d
16.	a	d	c	b
17.	a	d	c	b
18.	a	b	c	d
19.	c	b	a	d
20.	c	b	a	d
21.	a	c	d	b
22.	d	a	c	b
23.	b	d	c	a
24.	b	a	d	c
25.	c	d	a	b
26.	b	d	a	c
27.	a	d	b	c
28.	a	c	d	b
29.	b	c	a	d
30.	c	b	d	a
31.	b	c	d	a
32.	d	a	b	c
33.	a	d	b	c
34.	d	b	c	a

Total

The Barnyard

THOMAS CONNELL
JAMES E. JACOB

Concepts

Culture shock is a broad concept that refers to the cognitive and emotional responses to living, working, or traveling in an unfamiliar environment. Among the common symptoms of culture shock are feelings of frustration, confusion, anger, disorientation, depression, isolation, and fear (Bock, 1970; Furnham & Bochner, 1986; Oberg, 1960). Finding one's self in an unfamiliar culture, as Brislin (1993) notes, one may experience "shock" at the inability to make one's self understood or to figure out why others are behaving as they do.

Culture shock is often triggered by exposure to unfamiliar aspects of another culture and reinforced by the sense of loss or homesickness that one experiences when cut off from familiar habits, places, and things. Among the factors that may trigger culture shock are being confronted by different language, food, environment, nonverbal style, and/or uncomfortable personal space or body distance. One of the most important factors that leads to culture shock is isolation from one's friends, family, and familiar support networks (Smith & Bond, 1993). It is in this way that tourists on even short trips overseas will gravitate to the familiar, such as McDonalds in Paris, or seek out other Americans, for example, in a museum line and exclaim, as if the bond was a special one: "I can't believe you're from Ohio!" This need to bond with others of our group is an effort to treat the anxiety that immersion in a foreign culture often provokes inside us. For families going to live overseas for longer

SOURCE: This exercise was presented by Daniel Yalowitz, Executive Director of Project Play, Inc., at the 1990 conference of the Society for Intercultural Education, Training and Research (SIETAR) held in Jamaica. Used with permission.

periods of time, the need to immerse one's self in a new culture may pose an intense and emotional challenge. At best, it involves the excitement and adventure of adapting to new experiences and making new friends. At its most extreme, it may involve the shock of settling in a new cultural setting with norms of behavior quite different from the familiar. The essence of culture shock is that "the familiar ways of behaving, learned during their socialization, do not work in the other culture" (Brislin, 1993, p. 209). In this scenario, every aspect of one's daily life becomes a potential trigger for culture shock: exposure to different foods, a different language that may be baffling and mysterious, different gender roles and expectations, and cultural practices and customs that appear unfathomable. Ironically, for many people living abroad for an extended period of time, the return to one's culture may provoke, in turn, a "re-entry shock" among people now caught between cultures.

It is important to understand that culture shock is a natural and normal part of adaptation to a new cultural setting. In fact, it should be of more concern if an individual does not experience culture shock at some time in his or her stay overseas. Failing to experience culture shock may be an indication that the individual is not engaging the new culture, either through physical distancing (remaining geographically isolated with members of one's own cultural group) or mental distancing (remaining emotionally apart from the host culture) (Brislin, 1993).

The exercise in this chapter is intended to demonstrate through experience the stress and complex set of feelings experienced when one is suddenly removed from the safety and familiarity of one's own group. Each aspect of the exercise is intended to demonstrate how culture shock acts on the individual. The use of a blindfold serves as a means of distancing the individual from a familiar environment and distorts his or her ability to trust the senses. The choice of an animal sound is both familiar but odd, and when played out in a group of other such sounds, produces the sense of confusion, isolation, and anxiety one might experience in a crowded place in another culture. The goal of reunion with one's own group—even nearly complete strangers—demonstrates the degree to which we seek our own kind and seek to find a familiar refuge from the unfamiliar and uncomfortable.

The nature of this exercise is to provide a safe environment in which to experience a surprisingly intense feeling of isolation and cultural anxiety. By denying participants their sense of sight, a dynamic component enters the equation and greatly exacerbates the growing level of anxiety of the participants. It is here that the participant's "world" shrinks and now only includes that which can be felt, heard, or imagined. Our past experience in leading this exercise over a number of years demonstrates that once the participants begin to feel embarrassed over not locating their group easily, their self-image suffers and their frustration rises as no matter what they do they still seem unable to locate their group. Moreover, once the participant perceives that everyone else seems to be doing fine (though they're not), his or her frustration level rises again—especially toward the end of the exercise as other groups shout and exclaim their happiness over being reunited. However, as the individual connects and eventually reunites with his or her own group the camaraderie and bonding that now surfaces is a powerful force that often remains with the group for the duration of the seminar. It is not surprising to hear exercise participants "quack," "whinny," or "cluck" by way of greeting to each other as they encounter one another days after participating in the exercise.

Time

Approximately 45-60 minutes are needed.

Requirements

There is no ideal class makeup or equipment necessary for this exercise. Ideally, a large room, free of clutter and obstructions, is best suited for the event. In an ordinary classroom, chairs should be pushed against the wall, clearing a safe, open space in the center of the room. Especially useful, but not required, is an ample supply of slip-on eye masks with the eye holes taped over, or strips of cloth that can be used as blindfolds. The purpose of the mask or blindfold is to prevent participants from identifying other members of their cultural group by sight, and thus forcing them to use their hearing as their primary sense. A dimmer switch is also useful for light control, although this is not a critical requirement.

Instructions

Begin in a large room free of obstacles, and with all tables and chairs, and so forth, moved safely to the corners of the room. Have the class stand in the center of the room and await further instructions from the instructor.

Step 1. For a larger group (approximately 50 or more), pick out 10 "volunteers" to serve as safety monitors, and have them join the instructor at the front of the room. These individuals will not be participating in the exercise. Rather, they will assist the instructor during the exercise. The instructor will then take them outside the room for a 5-minute discussion of the event to take place, explaining their responsibilities as safety monitors before returning to the room with them.

Step 2. The instructor will then ask the group to form small groups of 5 to 12 participants each. The instructor must ensure a mix of male and females in each group and will move students around until this is achieved. The group should know how many members it has because this will be important during the exercise.

Step 3. The instructor then directs groups to pick out a particular barnyard animal and decide on a proper noise for their animal (pigs "oink," chickens "cluck," cows "moo," owls "hoot," etc.). Once each group has gathered together and chosen an appropriate animal and sound (the instructor should be the final arbiter of the choices), the instructor now explains the rules/details of the exercise:

Step 4. The instructor advises all of the purpose of the exercise and adds that to demonstrate how profound an effect this is, he or she and the monitors will soon move participants out of their groups and mix them up in the room. Now the masks are handed out by the monitors as the instructor explains that they will be wearing masks and that they are to locate and reunite with the other members of their group by listening for and calling out the sounds of their barnyard animal. Participants are told that on locating another member of their barnyard group, they are to (somehow) join hands and shout out, for example, if you are chickens, "Cluck, cluck One!" to which the other responds, "Cluck, cluck Two." Now holding hands, the two chickens begin to cluck more loudly and in earnest as they try to attract other members of their group. As other group members link up, they, too, respond, "Cluck, cluck Three," and so forth. The purpose of counting out numbers is to enable the group to know when all group members have been located without peeking. Only when all group members are rejoined may they take off the blindfolds or masks and watch the other "animals" try to locate their groups.

Step 5. Participants put on eye covers, lights are turned down, and monitors now move participants around the classroom, turning the participants around a couple of times to enhance the disorientation process. Once all are in place, instruct participants to try and regroup by making and listening for their group's barnyard sound.

Step 6. When all group members are reunited, the instructor will make closing comments centering on the nature of culture shock and the feelings it engenders inside the individual. See Discussion Suggestions below.

Tip: There will be some participants who cannot handle being blindfolded and left in a darkened room "clucking" while trying to find their group. Instead of forcing them to participate, these participants are best used as safety monitors during the exercise.

Tip: Understand that participants are entrusting their safety to the instructor and monitors. Ensure that the monitors are carefully watching the group, preventing participants from endangering themselves by walking into walls or furniture.

Trick: To prolong the "learning experience" for some group members, facilitators might consider pretending they are a group member and make the appropriate noises to prevent members from reuniting. This is especially effective when there is only one group left searching for their other members while the rest of the class observes the event.

Discussion Suggestions

Group Versus Individual

How did you feel when you were cut off from your group?

What emotions surprised you?

How did you feel when you were reunited your group?

How does this relate to culture shock?

Who do you think would be most affected by this exercise: someone from an individual-oriented or someone from a group-oriented culture?

The instructor should discuss the issue of culture shock and its effect on the individual. How did being disoriented and in a new environment make the participants feel? Could you imagine being in another culture and feeling as disoriented as this? Can you imagine how people from other cultures might feel when exposed to the nature of your culture? Describe how natural and normal it is for people to feel culture shock, including feelings of anxiety, being lost, frustration, embarrassment, feeling like you're standing out, and so on. Did you feel like your anxiety to reconnect with your group overwhelmed your thought process and prevented you from functioning successfully?

References and Further Reading

Boch, P. (Ed.). (1970). *Culture shock: A reader in modern cultural anthropology.* New York: Knopf.

Brislin, R. (1993). *Understanding culture's influence on behavior.* Fort Worth, TX: Harcourt Brace Jovanovich.

Furnham, A., & Bochner, S. (1986). *Culture shock: Psychological reactions to unfamiliar environments.* London: Methuen.

Oberg, K. (1958). *Culture shock and the problems of adjustment to new cultural environments.* Washington, DC: Department of State, Foreign Service Institute.

Smith, P. B., & Bond, M. H. (1993). *Social psychology across cultures.* Needham Heights, MA: Allyn & Bacon.

PART 3

Multidimensional Identification

ANN-MARIE YAMADA[1]

Concepts

The need for recognition of diversity within the classroom is widely discussed, yet there are few suggestions for defining cultural groups and insufficient attention to diversity within cultural and ethnic groups (Ellemers, 1983). Students are divided into cultural groups in an inconsistent manner; grouping is often according to surname, racial or physiological characteristics, or by asking students to report their ethnic/racial heritage. Little attention has been paid to students of multiple ethnic group heritage or to students who identify with a cultural group other than that of their heritage or appearance (Brislin & Horvath, 1997). More attention to diversity related to ethnic self-identification, generational status, ethnic pride and values, and participation in culturally related behaviors/activities would ensure that the diversity within the classroom is accurately represented throughout the learning process (see Banks, 1988; Bennett, 1993; Branch, 1994).

People self-identify to varying degrees with one or more of many different cultures, and there are many different words to describe their ethnic backgrounds or cultural groups. These descriptions are based on ancestry (heri-

SOURCE: A.-M. Horvath (1997). Ethnocultural identification and the complexities of ethnicity. In K. Cushner & R. Brislin (Eds.), *Improving intercultural interactions: Vol. 2. Modules for cross-cultural training programs* (pp. 165-183). Thousand Oaks, CA: Sage; and A. J. Marsella & A.-M. Horvath (1993). *The Multi-Index Ethnocultural Identity Scale.* Unpublished manuscript, University of Hawai'i at Manoa.

1. Formerly Ann-Marie Horvath.

tage) or come from personal choice often related to cultural exposure. Some labels are specific ethnic groups (e.g., Mexican, Chinese American), whereas others are broad racial labels (e.g., black, Caucasian) or panethnicities (e.g., Hispanic, Asian American). *Ethnic identity* refers to the extent to which one identifies with a particular ethnic group(s); the ethnic group tends to be one in which the individual claims heritage (Phinney, 1996).

Every person is born into an ethnic group, or sometimes multiple groups, but people differ on how important their ethnicity is to them, how they feel about it, and how much their behavior and values are affected by it. In addition to ethnic groups, identity is composed of other facets of social/cultural background. These aspects include language preference, sexual orientation, age, gender, religion, social class, generation, and so on. It is important to consider these aspects when determining an individual's identity as a multifaceted human being; these characteristics are referred to as one's *cultural or social identity.* At times, people even identify with groups or members of groups to which they do not belong. Groups to which one aspires to belong are known as *reference groups* (Sherif & Sherif, 1969) and often shape a certain number of our beliefs and behaviors. For instance, professional groups (e.g., teachers, executives, salespeople) may serve as role models for behaviors and values we aspire to in seeking to join the group. Identity with such a group is a legitimate substitution for persons for whom ethnicity is not salient. Ethnic groups may also serve as a reference group, especially when members of the desirable group hold power and prestige within society.

The exercise in this chapter is designed to introduce some of the major components of cultural identity by asking participants to think about their own identity. The aim of this exercise is to provide a foundation as participants expand their understanding of the various aspects of cultural or ethnic identity and are introduced to the concepts of ethnic identity, social/cultural identity, and reference group. To date, the exercise has been shown to (a) engage participants (students and trainers) in a fruitful exploration of their ethnic and cultural identity, (b) introduce and clarify these concepts, and (c) provide an alternative means for teachers and trainers to discover the extent of diversity within their classrooms or programs.

Time

This exercise requires 25 to 60 minutes, depending on the extent of discussion and age level of participants. For younger participants, a selection of items may be used in lieu of the entire set of items.

Requirements

Other than the handout included in this chapter, there are no requirements for this exercise. It is helpful for the facilitator to be prepared to handle participants for whom ethnicity is not meaningful. Knowledge and examples of a range of potential social reference groups would then be useful. A version tailored for elementary school students is available on request.

Instructions

Facilitators should introduce the concepts of ethnic identity, culture/social identity, and reference group identity. Then some version of the following instructions is suggested:

> This is an exercise that demonstrates one method of assessing degree of identification with ethnic or cultural groups (including reference groups). This exercise is designed to allow you to explore your own sense of identity, pride, and participation in the activities or traditions associated with a specific group you identify with. By completing the index and then discussing your responses with each other, you will better understand the extent of your feelings toward and behaviors associated with the group you selected.

After the participants complete the items, they may discuss them with partners, small groups, or with the entire group. The questions provided in the discussion section and the variations described below require consideration in planning follow-up discussions.

Variations

1. We recognize that many people have a diverse ethnic background. Persons identifying with multiple groups may wish to complete the questions separately for each group. Instructions would be something like this: "For this exercise, if you feel you strongly identify with more than one group, choose the group you overall identify with or choose one of the groups and record it on this page. You may wish to complete this exercise separately for each group you identify with." One group chosen could be that of the mainstream culture (e.g., European American), and participants could compare their level of identity with each group to assess their acculturation level within the larger societal culture. A reference group may be substituted for an ethnic group with participants marking N/A (not applicable) for inappropriate items.

2. These items are meant to be used to examine the behavioral variations within and among ethnocultural groups. Although the items are meant to capture variation within individuals' personal identity, the items may be summed and the total scores compared among individuals identifying with the same group or across groups. The number of behaviors/activities available to a group should be considered before comparisons are made among groups.

3. To introduce the concept of a reference group identity, participants may be asked to complete the questions for a group other than their chosen ethnic groups. Participants would be encouraged to think of cultural groups that they are members of (e.g., clubs, neighborhoods, hobby-related such as surfers, chess players, religions) while responding to the item. N/A may be used for items not suitable for the chosen group.. This task is particularly useful

in classrooms with little ethnic diversity, or when ethnicity is not a salient feature of identity.

Discussion Suggestions

Participants may discuss their answers with others. This exercise is useful to demonstrate differences in identity within a cultural group as well as among different groups. Participants should be assured that various aspects of their identity may not be congruent as this demonstrates the multifaceted nature of identification.

These questions may be asked to encourage further discussion regarding the behavioral items. It may be helpful to ask participants to jot down a few of their thoughts as they answer the questions. When they have completed this, participants may select a partner and discuss their responses.

Questions to be answered first individually and then in pairs or small groups are

1. Which of these behaviors/practices/activities do you engage in that you believe are central or highly salient to your identification with the group?
2. Which of the items do you feel are irrelevant to your identification with your group?
3. Are the values or beliefs that underlie these behaviors specific to your group or universal? Can you identify any of the values behind the behaviors?
4. What are some of the influences on the behaviors you endorsed? Are these practices you learned from your family or members of your groups?
5. Do you engage in these behaviors because you choose to do so or because you have been socialized or encouraged to do so by members of your group? Give examples.

References and Further Reading

Banks, J. A. (1988). *Multiethnic education: Theory and practice* (2nd ed.). Boston: Allyn & Bacon.

Bennett, M. J. (1993). Cultural marginality: Identity issues in intercultural training. In R. M. Paige (Ed.), *Education for the intercultural experience* (pp. 109-136). Yarmouth, ME: Intercultural.

Branch, C. W. (1994). Ethnic identity as a variable in the learning equation. In E. R. Hollinss, J. E. King, & W. C. Hayman (Eds.), *Teaching diverse populations: Formulating a knowledge base* (pp. 207-223). Albany: State University of New York Press.

Brislin, R. W., & Horvath, A.-M. (1997). Multicultural training and education. In M. Segal, J. W. Berry, & P. Dasen, (Eds.), *Handbook of cross-cultural psychology* (2nd ed., Vol. 3). Needham Heights, MA: Allyn & Bacon.

Ellemers, J. E. (1983). The study of ethnicity: The need for a differential approach. In L. v. d. Berg-Eldering, F. J. M. de Rijcke, & L. V. Zuck (Eds.), *Multicultural education: A challenge for teachers* (pp. 19-26). Dordrecht, The Netherlands: Foris.

Horvath, A.-M. (1997). Ethnocultural identification and the complexities of ethnicity. In K. Cushner & R. Brislin (Eds.), *Improving intercultural interactions: Vol. 2. Modules for cross-cultural training programs* (pp. 165-183). Thousand Oaks, CA: Sage.

Marsella, A. J., & Horvath, A.-M. (1993). *The Multi-Index Ethnocultural Identity Scale.* Unpublished manuscript, University of Hawai'i at Manoa.

Phinney, J. (1992). The Multigroup Ethnic Identity Measure: A new scale for use with diverse groups. *Journal of Adolescent Research, 7*, 156-176.

Phinney, J. S. (1996). When we talk about American ethnic groups, what do we mean? *American Psychologist, 51*, 918-927.

Sherif, M., & Sherif, C. (1969). *Social psychology.* New York: Harper & Row.

Sodowsky, G., Kwan, K., & Pannu, R. (1995). Ethnic identity of Asians in the United States. In J. Ponterotto, M. Casas, L. Suzuki, & C. Alexander (Eds.), *Handbook of multicultural counseling* (pp. 123-154). Thousand Oaks, CA: Sage.

MULTIDIMENSIONAL IDENTIFICATION EXERCISE

The Multi-Index Ethnocultural Identity Scale

Ethnocultural Identity Behavioral Index

Write in the name of the ethnocultural group you feel *most strongly identified with,* and then write the number corresponding to the strength of your identification with this group. Next, please answer each item according to how much you participate in the following activities or customs of the specific ethnocultural group you chose *at the present time* (e.g., Mexican American, Japanese American, Chinese American, Irish American).

A. Name of group _____

B. To what extent do you identify with the ethnic background you selected above (i.e., how strong is your identification with this group)?

Very little	1	2	3	4	5	6	7	Very much

Please respond to the following questions according to this scale.

Never	Sometimes	Often	Very Often	Always
1	2	3	4	5

____ A. Eat the food specific to the group (e.g., Korean kimchi, Mexican tamales, German bratwurst)

____ B. Watch movies (films, VCR) that use the language of the group or that depict the cultural group

____ C. Watch TV programs that use the language of the group or that depict the cultural group

____ D. Shop at stores that feature products of the group (e.g., Chinese market, kosher deli)

____ E. Speak the language of the group with my family or close friends

____ F. Dress in the clothes of the group (e.g., Japanese kimono, Scottish kilt, Indian sari)

_____ G. Listen to the music of the group (e.g., traditional or popular music of the culture)

_____ H. Read newspapers/magazines of the group (in English or in the ethnic language)

_____ I. Am active in a political movement or ideology of the group

_____ J. Have some of the artwork of the group (e.g., decorations, artifacts in the house)

_____ K. Date members of the group (or am married to a member of the group)

_____ L. Learn the dances and music of the group (e.g., Japanese *bon* dance, Polish polka)

_____ M. Use the traditional medicines or treatments of the group (e.g., herbal medicines, acupuncture)

_____ N. Listen to or hear others speaking the language of the group (even if you do not understand)

_____ O. Attend the traditional religious or spiritual services of the group (e.g., Buddhist services, a Catholic mass, Greek Orthodox services)

_____ P. Go to physicians, hair stylists, lawyers, or other professionals who are from the group

_____ Q. Spend time talking, gossiping, or chatting with members of the group

_____ R. Spend time studying the history or culture of the group (on my own or in voluntary courses)

_____ S. Follow the political and other current events of the group (locally or in the home country/region)

_____ T. Work in an organization that is owned by members of the group or in which group members are frequently seen

_____ U. Since having the opportunity, belong to at least one cultural organization (e.g., Americans of Japanese Ancestry)

_____ V. Interact frequently at informal gatherings with members of the group (e.g. parties, potlucks)

_____ W. Participate in hobbies that are popular only within the group (e.g., origami, traditional musical instrument)

_____ X. Interact with close friends from the group

_____ Y. Participate in sports popular within the group (e.g., boccie ball, cricket, curling)

_____ Z. Vote or would definitely vote for candidates from the group

_____ AA. Observe the holidays and celebrations of the group (e.g., *Cinco de Mayo*, Octoberfest, Boys' Day)

Additional Items from the
Multi-Index Ethnocultural Identity Scale

Please fill in or check the spaces for the following items:

1. Please *write in all the ethnic groups* that you and other members of your family (e.g., biological mother, biological father) are genetically a part of: Please keep in mind the percentage of ethnicity (blood quantum) for each person so that each person is 100% identified. You may write in any specific groups where applicable (e.g., Native American—Navajo; South American—Brazilian). You do not need to write in the percentages, but please try to be as specific as possible.

   Biological mother _____

   Biological father _____

   Yourself _____

2. In terms of ethnic groups and labels, when referring to myself, I consider myself to be _____

3. What ethnocultural group would other people classify you in based on your physical appearance? _____

4. Is there a discrepancy between the group(s) you identify yourself as and the group that others place you in?

   Most of the time ____ Some of the time ____ Usually not ____
   Never ____

5. How currently active are you in learning more about and becoming more attached to your ethnocultural roots and traditions?

   Avoid being active ____ No interest ____
   Interested but not active ____ A little active ____
   Moderately active ____ Very active ____

   6. How much pride do you have in your own ethnocultural heritage and traditions?

   Example: Sara doesn't think about her ethnic heritage very much but her grandparents live with her and her family celebrates all of their ethnic holidays. She is happy to share in these cultural celebrations though she ordinarily doesn't think about her ethnicity. Sara would answer that she has *a little pride* in her ethnocultural heritage. Now please rate yourself.

   A lot of pride ____ Some pride ____ A little pride ____
   No pride ____ Dislike ____

7. Are you or would you (if possible) teach your children about their ethnic group(s) and their cultural heritage?

   Probably not ____ I haven't thought about it ____
   I will if they ask ____ I probably will teach them select things
   ____
   I will definitely teach them as much as I can ____

8. Some people are born into an ethnic or cultural group(s) and then later choose to identify with other groups in addition to or even in place of their original group. If your cultural identity has changed, please write down what caused the change (example: immigrated to Germany or married a Chinese woman):

_____

_____

_____

_____

SOURCE: A. J. Marsella & A.-M. Horvath. (1993). *The Multi-Index Ethnocultural Identity Scale.* Unpublished manuscript, University of Hawai'i at Manoa.

Asian Americans and the Model Minority Myth

SHARON G. GOTO
JENNIFER ABE-KIM

Concepts

Asian Americans have been touted as the "model minority" group. High levels of educational attainment and a strong work ethic contribute to the upward mobility of many members of this racial group. In addition, it is commonly perceived that other cultural values help Asian Americans adjust and assimilate to American society with ease. They are perceived as an economic and social success in American society. Yet the levels of success attained by many members of this group are not shared by all Asian Americans. Despite the diversity in experience, stereotypes about success are extended to all Asian Americans. They are perpetuated in the *model minority myth*.

The Asian American population is quite diverse culturally, educationally, and economically. The term *Asian American* encompasses over 25 different cultural groups, including Cambodian, Chinese, Filipino, Hmong, Japanese, Korean, Lao, Mien, Asian Indian, Guamanian, Indonesian, Samoan, and Thai (Uba, 1994). Different immigration patterns also contribute to the diversity in culture (see Takaki, 1989). Although foreign-born individuals made up about 63% of all Asian Americans according to the 1990 census, this figure varied from 33% for Japanese Americans to 80% for Vietnamese Americans (Min,

SOURCE: The following exercise has been adapted from "The Label Game" (in J. G. Ponterotto & P. B. Pederson, 1993, *Preventing Prejudice: A Guide for Counselors and Educators*, Newbury Park, CA: Sage) to help dissipate the model minority myth.

1995). English-language proficiency is often problematic for many new immigrants, affecting the opportunities available to them in the workplace and in education. Consequently, many immigrants, although well educated and professional in their homeland, find themselves underemployed in the United States. Other Asian Americans are political refugees whose past migration experiences have led to severe stress disorders. Asian Americans are also educationally and economically diverse. For every Asian American family earning about $75,000 annually, there is one earning less than $10,000 (Ong & Hee, 1994). With respect to education, the tendency for most research and media attention to be paid to the overall academic achievement of Asian Americans results in the masking of the educational needs of particular groups (Escueta & O'Brien, 1991). For instance, although a proportion of Asian Americans have attained a high level of academic achievement, a significant proportion of some Asian American groups are also represented at the lowest ends of the educational spectrum. According to the 1990 census, whereas 2.6% of whites had completed less than 5 years of education, 10.3% of Chinese and Vietnamese and 7.0% of Filipinos had completed less than 5 years of school (Wong, 1990). In addition, many doctorates held by Asians are, at closer look, earned by foreign-born Asians, not Asians who have grown up in American society.

The model minority perceptions of Asian Americans are a relatively recent phenomenon. Indeed, when tracing the perceptions of Asian Americans through time, negative stereotypes were extremely pervasive from the years of early immigration through the 1950s (Sue & Kitano, 1973). So where does the model minority myth come from? If statistics and population diversity suggest that many Asian Americans are less successful than perceived, why does the myth persist?

The model minority myth stems from a variety of sources. Cultural values that place an emphasis on the public image, "the upholding of a scrupulous public facade at all times" (Crystal, 1989, p. 407), can mask Asian American problems. In troubled times, the downplay of problems is seen as a sign of strength. There are also societal roots. Asian Americans are often contrasted with other ethnic minority groups (e.g., African Americans, Hispanic Americans) who share a subordinate status. Like Asian Americans, these other ethnic minority groups are physically distinguishable from the majority group (i.e., European Americans). Despite common subordinate status, Asian Americans are touted as having achieved an unmatched success. An implication of the model minority myth is that institutional and psychological barriers such as prejudice are minimized and seen as "workable." If Asian Americans can succeed, the reasoning goes, so can other minority groups (Kim, 1986).

The model minority myth also carries negative implications for Asian Americans. Asian Americans who believe in the model minority myth may face frustration and disappointment. Indeed, the pursuit of educational, occupational, and social upward mobility is a desirable pursuit for most individuals. However, excessive stress may persist if an Asian American fails to live up to the standards expected of him or her based on the model minority myth (Lee, 1994). Furthermore, believing in the myth may preclude the acknowledgment of institutional barriers. An Asian American may erroneously internalize failures that are due to prejudice and discrimination. The persistence of the model minority myth is perhaps most detrimental with respect to Asian American public policy (Sue, 1993). As a group, Asian Americans have not received equitable or adequate social and mental health aid. Thus, while the model minority stereotype has been used to maintain notions of meritocracy by pitting ethnic minority groups against each other, the needs of many Asian American groups have gone unrecognized and ignored (Lee, 1996).

The model minority myth stereotypes all Asian Americans as an educational, occupational, and social success. As described, the Asian American experience is extremely diverse. Yet stereotypes are by their very nature persistent despite evidence to the contrary. Unless efforts are made to dispel the model minority myth, its many negative consequences will only continue.

The following exercise has been adapted from "The Label Game" (Ponterotto & Pederson, 1993) to help dissipate the model minority myth.

Time

Thirty to 50 minutes are required, depending on group size and discussion. Approximately 15 minutes should be allowed for the participants to "discover" their roles and to gather into three groups.

Requirements

The exercise is suitable for a group of about 30 participants. If the group is larger, some individuals may gain valuable insight as observers of the exercise. The room should be large enough so that people can mingle with ease. Also needed are the cards with labels. You may photocopy the handout or use index cards (one index card for each assigned role; see handout), and three colors of dots (we've used orange, blue, and purple). You will also need tape (e.g., transparent tape).

Instructions

1. Prepare the cards.

2. Assign a card to each participant, and place the card on each participant's back so that the contents are visible to others, but not the "cardholder." The contents of the card should remain unknown to the cardholder at this point.

3. Have the cardholders interact with each other with the intent of discovering their "role." For example, the "airhead" might be treated as such by others. Participants may not directly ask what their role is, but can gain information by inference.

4. At this point, the roles are not yet confirmed, although participants may have a suspicion about them. Have them form three groups by joining with others who have the same color dot on the card.

5. Once in color groups, members can disclose their roles.

6. Ask each color group what ethnic group (e.g., African American) others might label them as, given the roles or attributes in their group. Be careful not to place responsibility on them to stereotype the groups, but rather emphasize "what might others say?"

Variations

This exercise may easily be adapted to help dispel stereotypes associated with other groups (e.g., Hispanic Americans or gays). To do this, the associated roles need to be modified, and the specific discussion adapted according to the stereotyped group. However, conversations about the general notion of stereotyping can remain similar to what is currently outlined.

Discussion Suggestions

One strategy might be to start by discussing the availability of stereotypes. Ask participants how easily stereotypes emerged from the roles. Were they surprised with how easily stereotypes emerged? Were they surprised with how easily ethnic group stereotypes could be identified?

Then, start the discussion about the model minority myth by focusing on the positive nature of Asian American stereotypes and whether these "positive" stereotypes have negative consequences. One could say something like, "Asian Americans have been stereotyped as the model minority. The stereotypes are called the model minority myth. Stereotypes about Asian Americans are made up of generally positive content. Can positive stereotypes be good?" Participants should eventually conclude that stereotypes whether positive or negative can be damaging to the stereotyped group. Also, questions can be asked to emphasize the diversity of Asian American experience. For example, how many different Asian ethnic groups can you identify? Are all groups portrayed on TV as being successful?

The discussion might conclude with a discussion of the implications of the model minority myth. Some implications are that because Asian Americans are assumed to have no problems, they are expected to succeed and therefore may experience excessive pressures to fulfill the stereotype. Also, adequate funding is not available for Asian American programs because they are perceived as having no needs.

References and Further Reading

Crystal, D. (1989). Asian Americans and the myth of the model minority. *Journal of Contemporary Social Work*, pp. 405-413.

Escueta, E., & O'Brien, E. (1991). Asian Americans in higher education: Trends and issues. *Research Briefs, 2*(4), 1-11.

Kim, E. (1986). Asian Americans and American popular culture. In H. C. Kim (Ed.), *Dictionary of Asian American history* (pp. 99-114). New York: Greenwood.

Lee, S. J. (1994). Behind the model-minority stereotype: Voices of high- and low-achieving Asian American students. *Anthropology and Education Quarterly, 25*, 413-429.

Lee, S. J. (1996). *Unraveling the "model minority" stereotype: Listening to Asian American youth.* New York: Teachers College Press.

Min, P. G. (1995). An overview of Asian Americans. In P. G. Min (Ed.), *Asian Americans: Contemporary trends and issues* (pp. 10-37). Thousand Oaks, CA: Sage.

Ong, P., & Hee, S. J. (1994). Economic diversity. In P. Ong (Ed.), *The state of Asian Pacific America: Economic diversity, issues and policies* (pp. 141-152). Los Angeles: LEAP Asian Pacific American Public Policy Institute and UCLA Asian American Studies Center.

Ponterotto, J. G., & Pedersen, P. B. (1993). *Preventing prejudice: A guide for counselors and educators.* Newbury Park, CA: Sage.

Sue, S. (1993). The changing Asian American population: Mental health policy. In *The state of Asian Pacific America: Policy issues to the year 2020.* Los Angeles: LEAP Asian Pacific American Public Policy Institute and UCLA Asian American Studies Center.

Sue, S., & Kitano, H. H. L. (1973). Stereotypes as a measure of success. *Journal of Social Issues, 29*(2), 83-97.

Takaki, R. (1989). *Strangers from a different shore.* New York: Penguin.

Uba, L. (1994). *Asian Americans: Personality patterns, identity, and mental health.* New York: Guilford.

Wong, M. G. (1990). The education of white, Chinese, Filipino, and Japanese students: A look at "high school and beyond." *Sociological Perspectives, 33*, 355-374.

CARDS FOR MODEL
MINORITY MYTH EXERCISE

blue successful in school	blue computer person
blue pianist	orange football player
orange disc jockey	orange church soloist
orange campus activist	orange basketball star
orange student body representative	orange successful in school
purple computer person	purple pianist
purple football player	purple disc jockey
purple church soloist	purple flower child
purple campus activist	purple party animal
purple student body representative	purple softball/baseball player

purple	purple
aspiring actor	cheerleader
purple	purple
future lawyer	pre-med student
purple	purple
undecided major	airhead
purple	purple
car fanatic	student body president
purple	purple
person who is perpetually "high"	most popular person on campus

Creating Nationalisms

MEHROO NORTHOVER

riters on ethnicity and nationalism are prolific—these are two themes of great concern in the current state of small, isolated conflicts that nevertheless have devastating physical and economic effects in such countries as Northern Ireland, Bosnia, Afghanistan, and elsewhere. Seminal thinkers in this area are Deutsch (1966), Kedourie (1966), Fishman (Fishman, Gertner, Lowy, & Milan (1985), and Weinreich (1985), to name a few.

There are many forms of nationalism: organic/political, democratic/ authoritarian, rational/irrational, and so on (Fishman et al., 1985). Although the term implies a nation state, it may also stand for ethnicity because the term *nation* is often synonymous with an ethnic group (e.g., Jews, Arabs, the nation of Islam). Moreover, irredentists wishing to reclaim a territory for themselves (e.g., Serbs in former Yugoslavia) or those desiring to form an independent state within a state (e.g., Quebecois in Canada) make their case on the basis of ethnicity. Ethnicity has been variously defined. It may be identified with physical features, a common language, religion, shared ancestry, and history. De Vos (1983) describes it as "subjective continuity in the minds of men." Wallman (1979) claims that "ethnicity is the process by which 'their' difference is used to enhance the sense of 'us' for purposes of organization or identification" (p. 3). Weinreich (1991) says that attachment to one's ethnicity is irrational in the sense that it encompasses strong affective ties, but that rational dialogue within a community "is concentrated on protecting the integrity of its ethnicity (its religion, *rites de passages*, customs, folklore, judiciary, etc.)" (p. 24). In his view, it is therefore necessary to investigate the irrational bases for ethnic identity (Weinreich, 1985), which Fishman and others describe as "primordial" ties as opposed to civic loyalties to the wider interests of society.

It can be argued that when these affective ties to language, religion, culture, or folk mythology exist, politicians often seize them to exploit the nascent sense of ethnic or national identity for the purpose of unifying "us" against "them." For example, Northover and Donnelly (1996) have argued this to be the case for the movement for an English-Irish bilingual state in Northern Ireland, whereas a number of empirically based, rational counterarguments can be offered against its promotion.

Socialization processes may also be exploited by political leaders. Extreme nationalists sometimes argue for a negative nationalism, which calls on ethnic prejudice, stereotyping, and increasing awareness of distinctiveness (color, religion, or language) from other groups (Tajfel, 1981), to gain favorable self-esteem for their own group, and this leads to intergroup conflict. Dollard, Doob, Miller, Mowrer, and Sears (1939) have identified frustration and anger against legitimate targets (such as against inept governments) being displaced in aggression against a scapegoat group. Political leaders such as Hitler have used such methods to turn a population against a minority of Jews in its midst. Socialization of children by authoritarian parents may also result in a personality type (Adorno, Frenkel-Brunswick, Levinson, & Sanford, 1950) that is hostile toward people of inferior status and servile toward those of higher status.

Thus, divisiveness and outright conflict can be promoted by exploitation of affective or primordial ties to one's ethnicity or of cultural and personality traits.

Such extreme nationalism as arguments for an ethnically cleansed state and that denies the legitimacy of plural societies can be answered by arguing for the benefits that a nation state might bring to its citizens.

Although nationalists might make claims for a nation on the basis of ethnicity or culture, some economists and political scientists make claims for nationality on the grounds of economic or political benefits. The case for an evolving or organic nation was made by Deutsch (1966) equating nationality with people pressing to acquire a measure of effective control over the behavior of its members, to equip itself with power. In turn, power is used by the elites to strengthen and elaborate the social channels of communication, behavior preferences, and political and economic alignments that together make up nationality.

Fishman et al. (1985), on the other hand, propose that in addition to elements in Deutsch's theory of economic interests (material modernization) and change agents such as elites and dislocation through industrialization, one should add ethnic consciousness. It is ethnic consciousness and revivals that demonstrate that nationalism is a cultural and ideological innovation (p. 497).

Time

One hour to complete the exercise with a recommended additional half-hour of discussion is needed. This should be led by a teacher or group leaders pointing out the constituent arguments used by leaders who exploit the folk mythology of ethnic purity and monocultural states to promote extreme nationalism.

Requirements

No special requirements for equipment other than the handouts, and pen and paper. Students should receive an introduction from a teacher or group leaders conversant with the underlying concepts of categorization, stereotypes, social identity theory, and notions of ethnicity and nationalism to better understand the aims of the exercise.

Instructions

Students are divided into groups of five or six. Half the groups are given the Create a Global Nation handout on creating an extremist nationalistic ideology by exploiting notions of categorization, ethnicity, and its coincidence with the nation state, for example, as in Serbia. This group's task is to exploit values of extreme nationalism to create a global nation against the alien invaders. The remaining groups are given the Embrace Integration and Plurality handout and asked to devise strategies to appeal to the population's liberal principles and to plead for integration of the aliens who would enrich national cultures and increase plurality.

Variations

The initial exercise can be followed up by a second hour-long session of analyzing any current or ongoing conflict in the world designed to create a separate nation state such as in Canada between Francophones and Anglophones, or in Bosnia among Bosnian Serbs and Muslims, using arguments based in the concepts outlined above. Half the groups could argue for the benefits of a nation state based on ideologies of ethnicity, culture, or religion. The rest could argue for a continuation of nation states on grounds of economic and defense protection provided by the state or on grounds that a healthy, democratic, plural society can only exist within the bounds of a nation and give their reasons for this argument.

A second variation to raise consciousness of the pervasiveness of the nationalist or "group" ideology is to ask students to bring in copies of various newspapers of that day (include both quality and more sensational, tabloid papers). In pairs, students can analyze first the selection of news items and then the language of reportage to discern ways in which the newspapers present such ideologies in almost banal ways (see Billig, 1995).

Discussion Suggestions

The object of the exercise is to raise the students' consciousness about pervasive but little understood constructs of ethnicity, race, and nationalism. Such ignorance of the roots of the ideologies can give rise to jingoism or persecution of minorities at worst, or an ongoing prejudice against certain groups in society at best. At the conclusion of the brainstorming session, each group is asked to present its arguments for adopting a particular strategy and to detail the methods by which this strategy would be implemented. The teacher or group leader should give examples from current or historical events to confirm or invalidate the arguments.

The first variation serves to make students aware that at present levels of political and ideological development, there is no feasible alternative to the concept of the nation and we should use it for the benefit and advantage of all groups within the nation.

The second variation alerts students to the promotion of these ideologies by politicians and religious and community leaders in both subtle and more assertive forms in speeches and in the media.

References and Further Reading

Adorno, T. W., Frenkel-Brunswick, E., Levinson, D. J., & Sanford, R. N. (1950). *The authoritarian personality*. New York: Harper.

Billig, M. (1995). *Banal nationalism*. London: Sage.

Deutsch, K. (1966). *Nationalism and social communication*. New York: Academic Press.

De Vos, (1983). Ethnic identity and minority status: Some psychocultural considerations. In A. Jacobson-Widding (Ed.), *Identity: Personal and sociocultural: Symposium*. Uppsala, Sweden: Almquist & Wiksell.

Dollard, J., Doob, L. W., Miller, N. E., Mowrer, O. H., & Sears, R. R. (1939). *Frustration and aggression*. New Haven, CT: Yale University Press.

Fishman, J., Gertner, M. H., Lowy, E. G., & Milan, W. G. (1985). *The rise and fall of the ethnic revival*. Berlin: Mouton.

Gellner, E. (1983). *Nations and nationalism*. Oxford, UK: Blackwell.

Kedourie, E. (1966). *Nationalism*. London: Hutchinson.

Northover, M., & Donnelly, S. (1996). A future for Irish in Northern Ireland? *Journal of Multilingual and Multicultural Development, 17*(1), 33-48.

Tajfel, H. (1981). *Human groups and social categories*. Cambridge, UK: Cambridge University Press.

Wallman, S. (1979). *Ethnicity at work*. London: Macmillan.

Weinreich, P. (1985). Rationality and irrationality in racial and ethnic relations: A metatheoretical framework. *Ethnic and Racial Studies, 8,* 500-515.

CREATE A GLOBAL NATION

You are warned on radio and television that strange alien creatures, dubbed "Outspies" by the media, have been seen and are suspected to be from outer space. They are not especially noticeable in crowds but in face-to-face encounters, certain peculiarities have come to light. They may be recognized by their ears, which are lobeless and have pointed tips; they have flattish noses and their skins are grayish on close examination but can pass for any color, taking on the coloration of the majority in any group or of the interlocutor in a face-to-face encounter.

Given these almost human characteristics, politicians and leaders across the world and their ambassadors at the United Nations are urging citizens of all the member nations to forget international disputes, internal conflicts, and persecution of religious and minority groups within their own borders and concentrate on strategies to identify the aliens. Once identified, policies are to be instituted depending on the will of the majority of the UN members.

The leaders are asking you who have the qualifications and understanding of how nations are born to devise strategies for mobilizing world public opinion against the Outspies. To do this, you must create a new sense of being one gigantic nation of Earthlings covering the entire planet Earth. If we don't form a global nation seeing ourselves as one great unity, Us against Them, we shall lose our sovereignty as "Earthies." The Outspies have outstanding intelligence and powers to become nearly unidentifiable when they choose, and they will use these powers to enslave us.

This is to be a long-term strategy making the citizens of nations see themselves first and foremost as Earthies and only then as members of subethnicities demanding secondary loyalties.

Your group has agreed to the point of view that all current differences between nations must be put aside to create one global state aimed at eliminating the aliens. To create a sense of nationality, discuss and list policies and strategies for creating a single global nation based on the philosophy of us against them. Your discussion will be informed by what you know of stereotyping, prejudice, scapegoating of the out-groups, and the preservation of ethnicity as Earthies in order to create greater identification with your own group and distinctiveness from the aliens.

EMBRACE INTEGRATION AND PLURALITY

You have heard on radio and television that strange alien creatures, dubbed "Outspies" by the media, have been seen and are suspected to be from outer space. Your liberal principles are outraged at the attitudes of national governments and the United Nations toward these aliens, who appear to offer no threat to Earthlings and have a greater intelligence than humans. You see the media as spearheading a global nationalism of the worst type as it arouses irrational fears of diversity of cultures that could lead to out-group persecution and global conflict, and you reject the strategy called on by the United Nations.

You are determined to argue forcefully in national and world forums, such as the United Nations, against the strategies of extreme nationalism albeit on a global scale. Use examples of the harmful effects of extreme nationalism (e.g., Nazi Germany), and your knowledge of how the opposition group will exploit concepts of ethnicity, nationalism, and group identity, to make your case. You should also advance arguments for the benefits resulting from the integration of the Outspies into existing nation states on the grounds of enrichment of societies through diversity of cultures, talents, and customs. List your arguments for allowing the Outspies to form communities and integrate peaceably into existing nation states, then formulate strategies for spreading your own views.

Ethnic Identity Development

CHRISTINE JEAN YEH

CHRISTINE JEAN YEH

Concepts

For many individuals from diverse backgrounds, questions arise as to how they develop an integrated sense of self that is inclusive of both their cultural background and mainstream culture. Since an integrated ethnic identity is believed to precede bicultural competence (Zuniga, 1988), understanding the process and components of ethnic identification is valuable and may also help prevent numerous psychological dysfunctions related to identity confusion (Sommers, 1960; Wong-Rieger & Taylor, 1981). This chapter introduces and describes an interactive exercise that facilitates student exploration and examination of their own and others' ethnic identity development.

Phinney and Alipuria (1987) define ethnic identity as "an individual's sense of self as a member of an ethnic group and the attitudes and behaviors associated with that sense" (p. 36). They further state that ethnic identity development is "the process of development from an unexamined ethnic identity through a period of exploration, to arrive at an achieved ethnic identity" (p. 38). According to Sotomayor (1977), ethnic identification refers to identification or feeling of membership with others regarding the character, the spirit of a culture, or the cultural ethos based on a sense of commonality of origin, beliefs, values, customs, or practices of a specific group of people.

SOURCE: C. J. Yeh & K. Huang (1996). The collectivistic nature of ethnic identity development among Asian-American college students. *Adolescence, 31*, 646-661.

Thus, unlike the concept of race, which pertains to specific physical traits, the concept of ethnicity connotes cultural group membership.

Ethnic identity has been a construct under considerable scrutiny in recent decades. In her literature review of ethnic identity, Phinney (1990) describes three theoretical frameworks of research: *identity formation*, *social identity*, and *acculturation*. Although these frameworks overlap in their general conceptualizations of ethnic identity, they differ with regard to which specific aspects of ethnic identity they emphasize. As a result, the range of inquiry and focus has been broad, including self-identification, group membership, attitudes toward one's ethnic group, ethnic involvement, and cultural values and beliefs (Phinney, 1990).

Acculturation theorists focus on how an individual relates to the dominant or host society, arguing that a unified ethnic identity results from the individual's commitment to, or separation from, his or her ethnic ties (Makabe, 1979; Ullah, 1985). Such research typically investigates the extent to which ethnic identity persists over time within a dominant majority group context.

Social identity theory asserts that ethnic identity is influenced by the social context and that the ethnic individual develops an identity from his or her own group as well as from the "countergroup" (White & Burke, 1987). The majority of ethnic identity studies in this framework investigate how ethnic group membership contributes to self-hatred or self-concept, as well as the solutions that "minority group" members employ to improve their social status (e.g., "passing" as a dominant group member, establishing a bicultural identity).

Identity Formation Theory

Theories of ethnic identity development have primarily followed developmental models and attempt to explain this process according to a sequence of conflicts that must be resolved before the next stage is achieved (Atkinson, Morten, & Sue, 1983; Gay, 1985; Phinney, 1990). Atkinson et al. (1983) propose that minority identity development follows five distinct stages:

1. Conformity—preference for values of the dominant culture instead of one's own cultural group
2. Dissonance—confusion and conflict regarding the dominant culture's system and one's own group's cultural system
3. Resistance and immersion—active rejection of the dominant system and acceptance of one's own cultural group's traditions and customs
4. Introspection—questioning the values of both the minority and majority cultures
5. Synergistic articulation and awareness—resolution of conflicts in previous stage and developing a cultural identity that selects elements from both the dominant and minority cultural group's values

Likewise, Phinney (1990) views the process of ethnic identity development as a progression through four separate phases:

1. Diffuse—ethnic identity is not yet explored

2. Foreclosure—commitment is based on parental values and not made independently
3. Moratorium—the individual is exploring his or her ethnic identity but has not yet settled on or committed to one yet
4. Achieved—the individual has explored his or her identity and is firmly committed

Similarly, Gay (1985) argues that ethnic identity progresses through three stages: preencounter, encounter, and postencounter. During the preencounter stage, ethnic individuals have little sense of ethnic identity. In the encounter stage, they immerse themselves in their ethnic culture and reject all that is Euro-American. Finally, in the postencounter stage, identity conflicts are resolved and they make a commitment to ending racism.

Although stage models of ethnic identity development provide heuristic benefits, they may be inappropriate in describing the collectivistic nature of ethnic identity for many reasons. First, stage theories imply that ethnic identity is a final and fixed outcome resulting from a unidirectional progression through the various stages. Ethnic identity is described in deterministic, all-or-nothing terms. The authors perceive ethnic identity to be a multifaceted, evolving (Phinney, 1990), diverse, and dynamic (Jeffres, 1983) phenomenon not contingent on a particular linear progression. Ethnic identity may change during one's life due to factors of social contexts, family interactions, geographic location, and psychological proximity to ethnic political movements (Hayano, 1981). Finally, stage theories imply that progression through the stages is both desirable and highly valued, a goal that many may neither desire nor be able to achieve.

Many stage theories fail to capture the complexity and uniqueness of the ethnic minority experience. The stage model for minority identity development proposed by Atkinson et al. (1983) has received scrutiny and criticism from the psychology field. Jones (1990) argues that this model is too linear; there is no explanation of what factors contribute to or promote progression on to the next stage. This model also does not acknowledge the possibility of an individual being in more than one stage at a time. Second, this model does not fully acknowledge the dominant society's role in the continuing cycle of racism in the United States (Helms, 1986).

Furthermore, Jones (1990) argues that the model of ethnic identity development proposed by Atkinson et al. (1983) places the blame of racism on the victim—suggesting and encouraging change in the ethnic group—and not on the majority group's attitudes and behaviors. A final criticism of ethnic identity development models is that there are few majority group identity models, thus placing emphasis on minority group differences. Because U.S. society includes various cultural groups and influences, theories should emphasize cultural similarities as well as differences.

The ethnic identity development exercise (EIDE) is a projective exercise that obtains detailed and descriptive information about ethnic identity development. Individuals are instructed to describe (write, draw) the process of their ethnic identity development. They are asked to include anything that they believe to be relevant or significant in this process. The instructions were developed to provide individuals the freedom to explore and describe their ethnic identity development in a way that is meaningful to them.

Research in developmental psychology and projective techniques indicates that the use of drawings (visual representations) in psychological assessment is a valuable and effective means of soliciting information about various intrapsychic structures, such as wishes and fantasies, behaviors and emotions (Koppitz, 1968), body image concerns, interpersonal relationships, personality characteristics, and identity conflict (Ellis, 1989). Historically, drawings have been used to identify personality factors and intellectual capacities (Hammer, 1958; Koppitz, 1968). This method is particularly relevant for children and adolescents, who may not yet have the vocabulary or verbal skills required for adequate self-expression.

The drawing process has also been used in psychological research, because its indirect and task-oriented nature often provides a nonthreatening, anxiety-reducing means of expressing feelings and potential distress for adolescents (Kelley, 1984). Therefore, exercises using methodologies that encourage projective self-expression (e.g., the drawing process) may be successful in uncovering descriptive factors, processes, and conflicts related to ethnic identity development.

Time

Total time needed will be approximately 90 minutes. This includes time for background information and instructions, 15 minutes; activity time, 30-45 minutes; and discussion time, 30 minutes.

Requirements

Materials: the EIDE handout, markers, crayons, blank white paper, colored paper, and large sheets of paper.

Room: tables or flat surfaces for writing and drawing.

Participant requirements: No prior knowledge about ethnic identity is necessary because this exercise is meant to help students (in high school, college, or graduate school) explore and consider their own ethnic identity development. Students can be of any ethnic background (including those of European American descent).

Instructions

The EIDE is most effective when integrated with course material (readings or lectures) about ethnic identity development.

Readings

Reading assignments may be more appropriate for college-age students. Student may be asked to read several articles before the class during which the activity is introduced (see References and Further Reading section).

Lecture

a. Review the important concepts—what is ethnic identity?

b. Review main theories about ethnic identity development, that is, identity formation theory, and Phinney's and Gay's theory of ethnic identity development.

c. Review criticisms of the theories:

— The malleable and relational nature of self is not recognized.
— Between- and within-group differences are overlooked.
— Implied progression through the stages is highly valued.
— There is a linear, unidirectional progression.
— No explanation of factors contributing to progression is given.
— The theories place blame and problems on the minority group.
— There are no majority group models.

d. Introduce the EIDE and explain instructions. Sample verbal instructions are as follows:

Now that we have discussed different theories and ideas that people have about ethnic identity, I am interested in seeing how each of you describes your own ethnic identity development. You will each engage in an exercise that examines what influences helped you shape your sense of ethnic identity. On a piece of plain paper, I'd like each of you to write/draw the different factors (e.g., people, events, activities, media, literature, organizations) that have helped to shape how you feel and think about yourself as part of a particular ethnic group. Include anything you feel has been relevant in your own life. Take about 30 minutes in this exercise and use whatever materials (markers, paper, etc.) you feel can help you make this description more complete.

e. After students complete the exercise, break into small groups of three or four persons. In these small groups, each student will take a turn describing his or her EIDE paying special attention to the developmental process. Group members are encouraged to ask each other questions during this part of the exercise.

f. After students present their EIDEs to the group, display the EIDEs or pass them around. The visual representations are quite powerful and validating when viewed individually. This exercise allows class members to explore, contrast, and compare their own, as well as their classmates', experiences. Students frequently feel more bonded to one another, despite ethnic differences, after completing the exercise. In addition, students typically report that the concepts and literature concerning ethnic identity are made more meaningful following the EIDE. End the class by having the students form one discussion group (see list of questions in the Discussion Suggestions section).

Variations

For college students and graduate students

— Add a list of articles for them to read before the exercise. Suggested readings are included in the References and Further Reading section.
— Ask students, while in the small groups, to develop their own theory of ethnic identity development based on their groups' EIDEs. Here, they can use large sheets of paper to describe this theory and display it to others.

For high school students

— To help them understand the concept of ethnic identity, ask them to discuss, as a group, what it means to be African American, Asian American, American Indian, Mexican American, European American, and so on. Ask them what these different identities mean to them.

For classes with several ethnically diverse groups represented

— After the class completes the EIDE, divide the groups according to ethnic background and see the within- and across-group differences in the classroom. Ask each group what it felt was important to consider in its particular models of ethnic identity development.

For European American students

— Often, when completing this exercise, European American students may feel alienated, or report that they do not have an ethnic identity. They may report that they have a hard time connecting their experiences and relationships to a particular ethnic group because their ethnicity wasn't discussed at home and was not a concern in their social life. A possible way to address this issue is to broaden the exercise to include various types of identity. Ask students to list and rank different groups they identify with (as women, college students, athletes, etc.). After ranking these identities according to importance, they can focus on situations where ethnicity (Anglo American) becomes an issue (in college admissions, attending a social event that is predominantly Asian American, etc.).

Discussion Suggestions

After the class finishes the exercise, have them form small groups. Each student will have the opportunity to describe his or her EIDE to the rest of the group. Have each group focus on the following themes and questions:

— How did you decide what to draw?
— How would you describe your EIDE in your own words and images?
— What feelings, thoughts, reactions do you have in response to other EIDEs in your small group?

Large group discussion questions

After the small groups finish meeting, have the class join all together and discuss the following questions:

— What sorts of themes emerged from doing this exercise?
— How was it, completing this exercise? Was it difficult? Why or why not?
— What reactions do you have from your small group meetings?
— Are there within- and across-group differences and similarities in the EIDEs?
— What common influences, people, events were typically involved in this developmental process?
— What role does identity conflict play in this developmental process?
— How do different students' experiences compare or contrast?
— What else would you have liked to include in this exercise?
— How might doing this exercise influence your ideas about ethnic identity development theories?
— How can ethnic identity development theories be more inclusive of the issues, themes, and concerns we addressed today?

References and Further Reading

Arce, C. (1981). A reconsideration of Chicano culture and identity. *Daedalus, 110,* 177-192.

Atkinson, D. R., Morten, G., & Sue, D. W. (1983). *Counseling American minorities: A cross-cultural perspective.* Dubuque, IA: William C. Brown.

Betancourt, H., & Lopez, S. R. (1992). The study of culture, ethnicity, and race in American psychology. *American Psychologist, 48,* 629-637.

Ellis, M. L. (1989). Women: The mirage of the perfect image. *Arts in Psychotherapy, 16,* 263-276.

Gay, G. (1985). Implications of the selected models of ethnic identity development for educators. *Journal of Negro Education, 54,* 43-55.

Hammer, E. (1958). *The clinical applications of projective drawings.* Springfield, IL: Charles C Thomas.

Hayano, D. (1981). Ethnic identification and disidentification: Japanese-American views of Chinese-Americans. *Ethnic Groups, 3,* 157-171.

Helms, J. E. (1986). Expanding racial identity theory to cover counseling process. *Journal of Counseling Psychology, 33,* 62-64.

Jeffres, L. W. (1983). Communication, social class, and culture. *Communication Research, 10,* 220-246.

Jones, W. T. (1990) Perspectives in ethnicity. In L. Moore (Ed.), *Evolving theoretical perspectives on students* (pp. 59-72). New Directions for Student Services No. 51. San Francisco: Jossey-Bass.

Kelley, S. J. (1984). The use of art therapy for sexually abused children. *Journal of Psychosocial Nursing, 22*(12), 12-18.

Koppitz, E. M. (1968). *Psychological evaluation of children's human figure drawings.* New York: Grune & Stratton.

LaFramboise, T., Coleman, H. L. K., & Gerton, J. (1993). Psychological impact of biculturalism: Evidence and theory. *Psychological Bulletin, 114,* 395-412.

Makabe, T. (1979). Ethnic identity scale and social mobility: The case of Nisei in Toronto. *Canadian Review of Sociology and Anthropology, 16,* 136-145.

Markus, H., & Kitayama, S. (1991). Culture and self: Implications for cognition, emotion, and motivation. *Psychological Review, 98,* 224-253.

Markus, H., & Kunda, Z. (1986). Stability and malleability of the self-concept. *Journal of Personality and Social Psychology, 51,* 858-866.

Phinney, J. S. (1990). Ethnic identity in adolescents and adults: Review of research. *Psychological Bulletin, 108,* 499-514.

Phinney, J. S. (1996). When we talk about American ethnic groups, what do we mean? *American Psychologist, 51,* 918-927.

Phinney, J., & Alipuria, L. (1987). *Ethnic identity in older adolescents from four ethnic groups.* Paper presented at the biennial meeting of the Society for Research in Child Development, Baltimore. (ERIC Document Reproduction Service No. ED 283 058)

Sommers, V. S. (1960). Identity conflict and acculturation problems in oriental-Americans. *Journal of Orthopsychiatry, 30,* 638-644.

Sotomayor, M. (1977). Language, culture, and ethnicity in developing self-concept. *Social Casework, 58,* 195-203.

Triandis, H. C. (1989). The self and social behavior in differing cultural contexts. *Psychological Review, 96,* 506-520.

Ullah, P. (1985). Second generation Irish youth: Identity and ethnicity. *New Community, 12,* 310-320.

White, C., & Burke, P. (1987). Ethnic role identity among black and white college students: An interactionist approach. *Sociological Perspectives, 30,* 310-331.

Wong-Rieger, D., & Taylor, D. M. (1981). Multiple group membership and self-identity. *Journal of Cross-Cultural Psychology, 12*(4), 61-79.

Yeh, C. J., & Huang, K. (1996). The collectivistic nature of ethnic identity development among Asian-American college students. *Adolescence, 31,* 646-661.

Zinn, M. (1980). Gender and ethnic identity among Chicanos. *Frontiers, 5,* 18-24.

Zuniga, M. E. (1988). Assessment issues with Chicanas: Practice implications. *Psychotherapy, 25,* 288-293.

ETHNIC IDENTITY
DEVELOPMENT EXERCISE (EIDE)

We are interested in how individuals develop a sense of ethnic identity. We would like for you to create a visual representation of how you developed a sense of yourself as part of a particular ethnic group. We are interested in your past and present thoughts and feelings, and the types of choices and decisions you have made that were related to the formation of your ethnic identity. On the back of this sheet of paper, write or draw any experiences that may have influenced your ethnic identity development (e.g., important relationships, critical events, activities, organizations, classes, travels, literature, art, religious activities, and personal, spiritual, and educational activities).

SOURCE: Developed by Christine Yeh, Ph.D., and Karen Huang, Ph.D., 1996.

Accuracy of
Interpersonal Perception

KENNETH N. CISSNA

Concepts

It is no great trick to predict accurately how others are going to respond when we are communicating with people who are pretty much like us. The well-known process of *projection*—assuming that our own attitudes, beliefs, values, feelings, and behaviors are also typical of the other—will seem to serve us well. We project our attributes onto the other. This is a common enough process, and it works reasonably well in circumstances where people are fairly similar to each other. For example, if we share the same cultural heritage, grew up in the same community, and have gone to the same schools and churches, we may be able to predict accurately many characteristics of one another with a reasonably high degree of success. Unfortunately, this doesn't require any real ability in interpersonal perception; it requires only that we be fairly similar to the other and that we project, often unwittingly, our own qualities onto the other.

Projection, however, will not be at all useful in situations in which there is much diversity among people. For example, in many communities, this means that dealings between governmental officials and the public are often intercultural; most classrooms evidence cultural differences both among the students and between instructors and students; increasingly, business transactions and negotiations involve intercultural encounters; and some have argued even that differences between men and women can constitute distinct cultures. If we assume that others are pretty much like we are, and we then project our own characteristics onto the other, important services may not be

175

provided, learning will be inhibited, economic opportunities will be lost, and relationships will suffer.

The exercise in this chapter is intended to help participants realize (a) how often we tend to assume (sometimes correctly, sometimes incorrectly) that others are pretty much like ourselves and to project our own qualities onto others, and (b) how difficult it can be to recognize accurately differences between others and ourselves.

This position finds its significance in Gerald Miller's (Miller, 1975; Miller & Steinberg, 1975) view that accurately recognizing something of the uniqueness of an other is at the heart of what could be called truly interpersonal communication. Miller's view assumes that people communicate to influence the events going on around them, which requires that we be able to make fairly accurate predictions about how other people are likely to respond to us. We have, Miller argued, three general kinds of data about other people on which we can base these predictions. First, we can use cultural data, which involves understanding how a person is likely to behave because he or she is a member of a particular society and participates in a particular culture. Second, one can rely on sociological data. Information about other people regarding their reference and membership groups as well as the social categories into which they can be placed also allows for considerable accuracy in interpersonal prediction under many circumstances. Finally, one can predict how others are likely to respond by using psychological information about the other as a unique and special person—perhaps different from one's self and different from others.

Recognizing differences between specific people is commonly known as "differential accuracy" and recognizing similarities among groups of people "stereotyped accuracy" (Cronbach, 1955; Hinton, 1993; Hobart & Fahlberg, 1965; Jones, 1990; Kenny, 1994; Larson, Backlund, Redmond, & Barbour, 1978; Miller, 1975). Of course, both can be useful, but psychological information is at the heart of being able to recognize differences between and among ourselves and others. And for Miller, it is only when we are using psychological information about the other that we are engaged in interpersonal communication.

Although in reality there may be many possible positions on any issue, we can bring the process of interpersonal perception into focus under circumstances in which our choices are dichotomous, so we are either similar to the other or dissimilar, and we are either accurate in our prediction or inaccurate. In this circumstance, one person (judge) is attempting to predict something about another (target). Judge and target can—with regard to any particular trait—be either similar or dissimilar. We are interested in distinguishing between accuracy due to projection and accuracy due to a real knowing of the other as a person. If judge and target are similar, and the judge is correct in predicting something about the other, we cannot be sure why that is—perhaps it is projection, perhaps it is an indication of more complex (and to that extent more interesting and even desirable) cognitive processes. Hobart and Fahlberg (1965) call this outcome "compounded." If judge and target are similar and the judge incorrect, we have "unrecognized similarity," which happens in situations where people, for whatever reason, believe they are even more different than they actually are.

Where judge and target are different, however, we get even more insight into interpersonal perception. In this circumstance, projection is the most likely explanation of inaccurate predictions. The judge thought the target was similar to the judge but the target actually had a different response. Correct predictions when the judge and target are different reflects the ability to recognize difference. Hobart and Fahlberg call this empathy; others have called it role taking, *accuracy in interpersonal perception*, sensitivity, or decentering (Dance & Larson, 1976; Hinton, 1993; Jones, 1990; Kenny, 1994; Larson et al., 1978; Tagiuri & Petrullo, 1958). It would seem to be an absolutely crucial process in the world in which we are going to live.

Time

This exercise requires 60 to 90 minutes, depending on number of questions, number of participants, and depth of discussion.

Requirements

Little is required other than the handouts. A chalkboard, overhead projector, flip chart, or other method of displaying information is useful. The exercise is probably better if the dyads who do this exercise together have had some experience with each other that would provide some basis for them knowing something about each other.

I have not done the exercise with any highly homogeneous or highly heterogeneous groups, though I believe it should work with both.

Instructions

I have usually used this exercise in a class in which the students had a partner with whom they had been doing a series of exercises for several weeks, and with whom they then did this one. If the participants do have ongoing partners, the partners of people who are absent are paired together. If you have an odd number of participants, you can easily serve as a partner as you facilitate.

1. Each participant needs to be paired with a partner. After partners are identified, ask that partners move away from each other so they are not sitting in close proximity. If this isn't possible, ask them to turn their backs toward each other or somehow separate themselves so they aren't tempted to talk about the questions or their answers (or later, to peek at the other's answers).

2. Each participant should be given the Own Answers answer sheet (see Handout 1) and the adapted list of questions (for an example, see Handout 2—I don't put a title on it, but if I did I'd probably call it "Cissna's Questions" rather than "Questions for the Interpersonal Perception Intercultural Encounter Exercise"). Have each participant indicate on the answer sheet how he or

she thinks or feels (agree or disagree) in relation to each question. Someone will undoubtedly want to argue with you about an item—claiming he or she doesn't or can't simply agree or disagree with it. Ask the participants to answer by indicating whether on balance they tend to agree a little more or to disagree a little more. For the purpose of completing this exercise, you don't want to engage in a discussion of the items, first, because it will take time you may not have, and second, because such a discussion could reveal participants' answers to their partners.

3. Each participant then completes the Partner's Answers answer sheet (see Handout 3), where they indicate how they think their partner answered the items.

4. Then give each participant a copy of Handout 4, Calculating Accuracy.

5. Participants—still working alone—should first compare their own Own Answers and Partner's Answers answer sheets to determine how often they thought they and their partner would agree (i.e., answer the same way). To do this, they should place the two answer sheets alongside each other and simply count the number of times they have given the same answer on both sheets. They should write that number in the "assumed similarity" spot on Handout 4.

6. Next, the partners should move their seats so they are sitting close together, and place their Own Answers answer sheets next to their partner's Own Answers answer sheet. The partners then mark in the margin of their Own Answers answer sheets *S* if they both gave the same answer (i.e., they agreed) or *D* if they have different answers.

7. They should then copy the column of *S*s and *D*s onto the other partner's Own Answers answer sheet.

8. They should count the numbers of same and different answers (*S*s and *D*s) and write those numbers in the appropriate places on Handout 4. The partners should have identical numbers written on their sheets, and the numbers should add up to the total number of questions (e.g., 20).

9. All participants then give their Own Answers answer sheets to their partners. Participant should now be in possession of their own Partner's Answers answer sheet (their predictions about how their partner answered) and their partner's Own Answers answer sheet (how their partner actually answered).

10. Working separately, each participant aligns these two sheets, and in the margin of the partner's Own Answers answer sheet, right next to the column of *S*s and *D*s, they make another column consisting of *C* if their predictions were correct (and the answers match) and *I* if incorrect (i.e., the predictions about the partner do not match what the partner actually said).

11. They should now count the numbers of correct and incorrect answers (*C*s and *I*s), and write those numbers in the appropriate spots on Handout 4. A

few partners may have the same numbers of correct and incorrect answers, but most won't, but in each case the correct and incorrect numbers should again add up to the total number of questions.

12. Participants should count the numbers of same correct, same incorrect, different correct, and different incorrect answers (*SCs, SIs, DCs,* and *DIs*), and write those numbers in the appropriate places on Handout 4. These four numbers should also add up to 20 or whatever number of questions you are using. I suggest that you ask participants to do this check because it lets you and them know that they have done it properly.

13. Ask each participant to read to you, one at a time, how many different correct answers (*DCs*) and how many different answers (*Ds*) they have. Write these numbers on the board (or on overhead or a large tablet) in two columns—one for the different correct numbers (*DCs*) and the other one for the total number of different numbers (*Ds*). After you have recorded everyone's numbers, get someone to add the columns, and compute the percentage that different correct is of different (i.e., divide the *DC* total for the whole group by the *D* value for the whole group). Typically, that number is between 40% and 50%.

14. Although that seems a pretty good batting average, ask them how good a predictor they think a coin would be (take it out and flip it a few times). Of course, over enough trials a coin will average 50%, which is usually better than the participants do. (This isn't quite true, of course, because the coin doesn't project or assume similarity, so most groups of participants will do far better than the coin on those items where they have the same answers—but that isn't the point of the activity).

15. Then you should explain why we are especially interested in the times when they had different answers. Theoretically, identifying differences from oneself and others and between various others is at the heart of Miller's conception of interpersonal communication. Methodologically, there is no way to know the mechanism they used to make correct predictions when they had the same answers. Both accurate role taking and projection will yield accurate answers. But only role taking will produce accuracy when their answers are different. And recognizing differences is going to be increasingly crucial in our increasingly diverse society and in any intercultural situation. Students have been able to see this distinction, and to see that they had far higher scores for same correct as a percentage of same than they did different correct as percentage of different.

16. Toward the end, I think it important to debrief the students by being sure they understand two things this exercise is not. First, this activity is not a measure of how well they know their partner, which would require far more items over a far broader range of issues. Even less is it a measure of their overall role-taking ability, which would require not only more questions and more issues but also far more people. This is an exercise designed to illustrate a particular process in interpersonal relationships, which is especially problematic in intercultural situations.

Variations

The questions that participants respond to can and should be adapted to the group. The questions should be ones that participants will not all answer in the same way. In addition, unless you want to spend time dealing with the questions themselves, they should be relatively straightforward attitudinal and value items that are answerable by all participants. I recommend using a relatively small number of questions, and I think it is probably easier if you have a nice round number of questions (such as 20). I like to include some items for which participants are likely to know one another's answers, items that won't embarrass or call attention to any participant, and ones that the participants can respond to quite reasonably with either agree or disagree.

An interesting variation might be to arrange pairs so that some of them would be presumed to be more homogeneous (similar to one another) and others more heterogeneous (dissimilar to one another). Besides comparing overall accuracy rates, assumed similarities between pair types could be compared, revealing stereotypes while acknowledging group differences.

Discussion Suggestions

The exercise itself is intended as the starting point for a discussion. Usually, participants are a bit subdued when they realize that—as a group—a coin would have better predicted their partner's differences from them than they were able to themselves. Participants might usefully explore together how they went about making predictions, accurate and not. Another topic for discussion might involve considering the how and when participants used projection, when they recognized real differences, and even when they may have—which will happen more often in diverse situations—made predictions based on assumed dissimilarity. Correct predictions based on this strategy are not distinguishable from accurate role taking; incorrect predictions following from assumed dissimilarity are actually unrecognized similarity, which may also be a useful area for discussion, especially in situations where there are intergroup tensions and people may believe the "others" to be even more unlike themselves than they are. (In fact, in this situation, if the dominant tendency is to assume dissimilarity rather than similarity—projection—and if the participants are indeed more similar than they think, then the relevant measure of accuracy is recognition of similarity rather than of difference.)

Another possible area of discussion might involve the extent to which self-presentation and participants' desires to maintain desirable self-images influenced their own answers (the direct perspective). This exercise assumes that people are both able and inclined to answer as honestly as they can, but some questions may involve issues that are out of one's awareness, and in those cases others' perception are sometimes more "accurate" than one's self-perception.

References and Further Reading

Cronbach, L. J. (1955). Processes affecting scores on "understanding of others" and "assumed similarity." *Psychological Bulletin, 52,* 177-193.

Dance, F. E. X., & Larson, C. E. (1976). An elaboration of the mentation function. In F. E. X. Dance & C. E. Larson, *The functions of human communication* (pp. 116-127). New York: Holt, Rinehart & Winston.

Hinton, P. R. (1993). *The psychology of interpersonal perception.* London: Routledge.

Hobart, C. W., & Fahlberg, N. (1965). The measurement of empathy. *American Journal of Sociology, 70,* 595-603.

Jones, E. E. (1990). *Interpersonal perception.* New York: Freeman.

Kenny, D. A. (1994). *Interpersonal perception: A social relations analysis.* New York: Guilford.

Larson, C. E., Backlund, P., Redmond, M., & Barbour, A. (1978). Empathic ability. In C. E. Larson, P. Backlund, M. Redmond, & A. Barbour, *Assessing functional communication* (pp. 77-84). Urbana, IL: ERIC Clearinghouse on Reading and Communication Skills, and Falls Church, VA: Speech Communication Association.

Miller, G. R. (1975). Interpersonal communication: A conceptual approach. *Communication, 2,* 93-105.

Miller, G. R., & Steinberg, M. (1975). *Between people: A new analysis of interpersonal communication.* Chicago: Science Research Associates.

Tagiuri, R., & Petrullo, L. (Eds.). (1958). *Person perception and interpersonal behavior.* Stanford, CA: Stanford University Press.

HANDOUT 1:
OWN ANSWERS

Name_____

Write *A* for agree and *D* for disagree in the blank spaces corresponding to each statement. We are interested in what *you think* about each of these issues.

1. _____

2. _____

3. _____

4. _____

5. _____

6. _____

7. _____

8. _____

9. _____

10. _____

11. _____

12. _____

13. _____

14. _____

15. _____

16. _____

17. _____

18. _____

19. _____

20. _____

HANDOUT 2

1. I read quite a few novels.

2. I am a well-organized person.

3. I'm pretty easy to get to know.

4. I see myself as more warm-hearted than firm-minded.

5. I often feel that my body is more unattractive than attractive.

6. My home life and personal relationships are more important to me than my work.

7. People should not live together until after they are married.

8. My earliest educational experiences were quite positive.

9. Swearing bothers me.

10. I like to study.

11. Money is an important part of my idea of what makes a good life.

12. I'm not upset by interracial dating and marriage.

13. I think watching television is a waste of my time.

14. I have more male friends than female friends.

15. I would never lie about a serious matter to either parent.

16. I enjoy staying out all night.

17. Keeping in shape is important to me.

18. Sex is as important as it is made out to be.

19. Listening to music is a good way to spend time.

20. I'm smarter than most people think I am.

HANDOUT 3:
PARTNER'S ANSWERS

Name _____ Partner's name _____

Write *A* for agree and *D* for disagree in the blank spaces corresponding to each statement according to how you think your partner answered. This time, we are interested in what *you think your partner thinks* about each of these issues.

1. _____
2. _____
3. _____
4. _____
5. _____
6. _____
7. _____
8. _____
9. _____
10. _____
11. _____
12. _____
13. _____
14. _____
15. _____
16. _____
17. _____
18. _____
19. _____
20. _____

HANDOUT 4:
CALCULATING ACCURACY

Assumed similarity _____

	SAME	DIFFERENT	
CORRECT	_____ Same correct (SC) *Unknown*	_____ Different Correct (DC) *Role taking*	_____ Correct (C)
INCORRECT	_____ Same Incorrect (SI) *Unrecognized similarity*	_____ Different Incorrect (DI) *Projection*	_____ Incorrect (I)
	_____ Same (S)	_____ Different (D)	

$$\text{Accuracy} = \frac{\text{Different Correct (DC)}}{\text{Different (D)}} = \frac{\rule{2cm}{0.4pt}}{\rule{2cm}{0.4pt}} = \underline{\hspace{2cm}} \%$$

The Wheel of Influence

A Training Exercise in Client-Centered Multiculturalism

DAVID R. CLEMONS

J. COLEMAN HECKMAN

SUZETTE LAMB

Concepts

The concept of difference is undoubtedly central to the multiculturalism movement that has taken place in recent decades (Sue, Arredondo, & McDavis, 1992). Multicultural counseling, for example, is commonly defined as "counseling that takes place between or among individuals from different cultural backgrounds" (Jackson, 1995, p. 3). Speight, Myers, Cox, and Highlen (1991) consider the central question of multicultural training to be, "How can two people who differ from each other effectively work together?"

Sue et al. (1992) outlined the importance of both self-awareness and understanding of the worldview of the culturally different client to the competent provision of services within a multicultural context. However, counselor self-awareness often takes a back seat to learning about culturally different clients in many training programs. Richardson and Molinaro (1996), therefore, along with other authors in recent multicultural training literature, highlight the importance of developing awareness among individuals from the dominant white culture to the role of culture in their experience (e.g., Preli & Bernard, 1993; Sabnani, Ponterotto, & Borodovsky, 1991; Speight et al., 1991).

Client-centered multiculturalism is a term we have developed to empha-size the need for recognition of the uniqueness of our individual experiences and perceptions of relative influences. Hence, client-centered means the cli-ent is the "expert" on his or her own multiculturalism (Gonzalez, Biever, & Gardner, 1994). It is not for us, the "other," to determine what and to what extent cultural factors influence those we work with, but it is our responsi-bility to identify and explore those factors. In doing so, it is imperative that we are aware of our own multiculturalism. Then, we are able to look at both our and others' "wheels of influence" to get a sense of our similarities, differ-ences, and ranges of experience. It is a tool for self-discovery, discussion, and an indicator of potential trouble spots in interactions.

For the basic use of the exercise in this chapter, it is helpful to include a sample of defined terms to emphasize the importance of a mutual under-standing of the identified concepts. However, the flexible nature of this exer-cise allows for the use of any terms that are pertinent given the context.

Racial identification. Race is a socially constructed term that has relatively little basis in terms of genetic differences. However, it does have significant meaning within our society. We include the term here as a distinction of the physical characteristics that are often viewed as differences between groups; the most common being skin color. To what degree do the participants think race has influenced their lives? Have they experienced racism, and if so how?

Ethnicity. In this exercise, we distinguish ethnicity as the sense of common-ality that is transmitted through family traditions and rituals (McGoldrick, Pearce, & Giordano, 1982). To what degree do the participants identify with ethnicity? Do they see themselves as ethnically neutral?

Socioeconomic status. What are the participants' perceptions of the influence of socioeconomic status on their view of themselves and the world? Do they view themselves as economically deprived or economically privileged? Or, does the relative influence of economic and social status seem irrelevant?

Gender. To what extent do the participants view gender as an influence on their worldview? Do they perceive privileges afforded to them on this basis, or do they feel disadvantaged?

Sexual orientation. The dominant heterosexual community might not iden-tify with the influence of sexual orientation. However, this may be an ex-tremely important category regarding the life experiences of gay men and lesbians. To what extent do the participants think that their sexual orientation has influenced their attitudes and beliefs?

Education. What is the level of education of the participants' parents? What is their current educational status? To what degree do they attribute their educational achievement to their parents' achievements? Is there a link between their educational status and background and their socioeconomic status?

Age. To what extent do the participants view age as a factor in their ability to find opportunities? Have they ever been subject to discrimination on the basis of their age? What influence has the time of their birth played in their world-view? Which generation do they identify with, and how is this important?

Religion. Were they acculturated into a religion? Did their parents have two different religions? Was their family nonreligious? Were they agnostic or atheist?

Time

This exercise requires 30 to 60 minutes, depending on the number of participants and discussion time.

Requirements

Participants will need a blank pie graph on which to overlay their identified terms and to visually illustrate how much each makes up their cultural experience. A chalkboard, wipe board, or individual handouts can be used to display the results.

Instructions

After presenting an overview of the basic premise of client-centered multiculturalism, each participant should be asked to draw on a board or handout what cultural factors they believe influence his or her daily life and to what extent. It is suggested that the number of factors be kept at eight or less. The factors that are agreed on should be listed, mutually defined, and then each participant should assign a percentage to each of the factors. This percentage denotes the weight each factor carries in their lives. The allotted percentage may speak to past or present influence. Participants should be asked not to discuss their "wheel of influence" during the self-assessment phase of this exercise. After everyone has completed their wheel, discussion can commence. The course of the discussion will depend on the context within which this exercise is being used.

Variations

This exercise can be used in a number of different settings. Therapists in training and professionals who work with multicultural populations could compare their wheels with wheels of clients to highlight areas that may impede the helping process, not due to bias/prejudice, but due simply to a lack of awareness of critical cultural differences. Professionals in organizational settings can use this as a team-building exercise to allow participants to recognize what they "bring to the table" and how this conflicts or merges with others in their work settings. Educators may apply this in the classroom to gap cultural differences between students and/or to delineate differences between seemingly homogeneous groups for increased cultural sensitivity. In individual supervision, a supervisee and supervisor might both construct their wheels and compare to locate differences that may be potential stumbling blocks in the challenging process of supervision. In group supervision, each member could construct his or her wheel and simply share it with the group in the form of an oral narrative. The group could also choose one or more cultural factors for discussion.

In therapy, the wheel can serve as a graphic for discussion of any differences encountered in working with clients of diverse backgrounds and experiences. In couples, family, and group therapy settings, the wheel can be a neutral way for clients to represent themselves and a common vehicle for discussing differences in a nonthreatening, nonblaming format.

Discussion Suggestions

Discussions about the wheel of influence can occur at multiple levels. One starting point could be what factors should be included in the exercise and why and how each of those factors is defined. Once the inclusive factors have been determined and defined, participants could be asked to give oral narratives of their wheels to include past and/or present experiences and examples. Additionally, discussion could commence around the similarities and/or differences of each of their wheels and how they think these might affect their relationships. Problem solving, creativity, and willingness to share and listen should be emphasized. Participants could be put into pairs and asked to attempt to guess their partner's percentages of influence and then discuss their right and wrong impressions. Finally, participants can be asked to reflect and comment on what they may have learned about themselves and others by completing this exercise.

References and Further Reading

Gonzalez, R. C., Biever, J. L., & Gardner, G. T. (1994). The multicultural perspective in therapy: A social constructionist approach. *Psychotherapy, 31,* 515-523.

Jackson, M. L. (1995). Multicultural counseling: Historical perspectives. In J. G. Ponterotto, J. M. Casas, L. A. Suzuki, & C. M. Alexander (Eds.), *Handbook of multicultural counseling* (pp. 3-33). Thousand Oaks, CA: Sage.

McGoldrick, M., Pearce, J. K., & Giordano, J. (1982). *Ethnicity and family therapy.* New York: Guilford.

Preli, R., & Bernard, J. M. (1993). Making multiculturalism relevant for majority culture graduate students. *Journal of Marital and Family Therapy, 19,* 5-16.

Richardson, T. Q., & Molinaro, K. L. (1996). White counselor self-awareness: A prerequisite for developing multicultural competence. *Journal of Counseling and Development, 74,* 238-242.

Sabnani, H. B., Ponterotto, J. G., & Borodovsky, L. G. (1991). White racial identity development and cross-cultural counselor training: A stage model. *The Counseling Psychologist, 19,* 76-102.

Speight, S. L., Myers, L. J., Cox, C. I., & Highlen, P. S. (1991). A redefinition of multicultural counseling. *Journal of Counseling and Development, 70,* 29-36.

Sue, D. W., Arredondo, P., & McDavis, R. J. (1992). Multicultural counseling competencies and standards: A call to the profession. *Journal of Counseling and Development, 70,* 477-486.

Beyond Political Correctness

POONAM SHARMA
DENISE LUCERO-MILLER

Concepts

In today's "politically correct" society, increased attention is being given to the issue of diversity. Undoubtedly, any attempt to increase sensitivity to individual differences and to combat prejudiced attitudes and behaviors is a positive step forward in America's struggle to move from the traditional "melting pot" philosophy to a more culturally sensitive "salad bowl" paradigm (O'Mara, 1994). Although well intended, efforts to enhance awareness of diversity issues often fail due to the lack of recognition of the insidious nature of subtle prejudice. In promoting cultural sensitivity, it is not enough to simply focus on the overt and obvious behaviors that are discriminatory in nature. Personal biases that exist at a deeper, more covert level must be examined as well to promote genuine, respectful relationships with individuals from America's numerous subcultures. Diversity must also be defined in ways that are inclusive of the variety of dimensions along which people may differ. Diversity is not confined solely to ethnic differences, but includes differences of sexual orientation, religion, socioeconomic status, and physical ability as well.

SOURCE: This is an original exercise adapted from items found in the Social Distance Scale (in E. S. Bogardus, 1967, *A forty-year racial distance study*. Los Angeles: University of Southern California).

As Cole (1996) indicates, early environmental influences often contribute to the development of stereotypical thinking in children. When left unchallenged, such thinking becomes automatically activated, making it difficult for newly acquired ideas established through later learning to be integrated at a deeper level. As a result of this process, it becomes possible for an individual to exhibit unintentionally prejudiced behavior, despite believing that he or she actually maintains a nonprejudicial belief system. Cole refers to this conflict between "early learning" and "later learning" as *unintentional prejudice.* Unintentional prejudice results in greater personal discomfort as the discrepancy between early and later learning increases. Devine, Monteith, Zuwerink, and Elliot (1991) found that low- and moderately prejudiced individuals who exhibited differences in their belief systems and actual behaviors toward African Americans and homosexual men experienced guilt and self-criticism. Using only homosexual men as the stereotyped group, Monteith, Devine, and Zuwerink (1993) report similar results. These authors conclude that well-learned, automatic stereotypes may result in prejudicial responses that conflict with nonprejudicial value systems. Gaertner and Dovidio (1986) use the term *aversive racism* to describe the discrepancy "between feelings and beliefs associated with a sincerely egalitarian value system and unacknowledged negative feelings and beliefs about Blacks" (p. 62).

As indicated above, the disavowal of prejudicial beliefs does not necessarily translate into nonprejudicial responses and behaviors. Consequently, individuals who strive to practice culturally sensitive behaviors may continue to exhibit unintentional, subtle biases toward culturally different groups. Unless such biases are brought into personal awareness, they cannot be changed. Actively attending to unexpected emotional reactions such as discomfort and guilt is crucial in heightening awareness. Unfortunately, increased sensitivity is often difficult to achieve because individuals have a tendency to avoid deeper exploration of negative emotional responses (Cole, 1996).

The purpose of the exercise in this chapter is to encourage individuals to explore automatic, unintentional biases. This objective will be achieved by asking individuals to indicate their comfort level in situations that require close personal contact with persons encompassing a variety of personal characteristics along the dimensions of ethnicity, sexual orientation, and physical ability. The underlying premise of this exercise is that although an individual may maintain the belief that he or she is relatively prejudice free, such attitudes may be challenged when one is faced with the prospect of interacting with culturally diverse groups on a more intimate level (Bogardus, 1968). Emotional reactions can serve as a road map to areas of unacknowledged, subtle bias because early learning is often encoded at an affective, rather than intellectual, level. Although this exercise can be used with individuals who vary in their degree of sensitivity to individual differences, it may be particularly enlightening for those who, despite their commitment to eliminating overt racism, may be unaware of their own unresolved issues in this area.

Time

This exercise requires 30 to 45 minutes, depending on the length of discussion.

Requirements

There are no special requirements for this exercise. All you need are the handout and pencils.

Instructions

Present the concept of unintentional bias and the importance of looking beyond a surface level when evaluating one's personal biases to understand the insidious nature of early learning. The exercise can then be introduced as a tool for exploring some of these subtle biases. Pass out the handout and ask people to respond to the questions as honestly as possible, relying on automatic, emotional reactions rather than their intellect to guide their answers. Tell participants that they should not put any identifying information on the questionnaires. Also inform them that although answers will be discussed in a general way, they will not be required to reveal their personal answers unless they are comfortable doing so. After the questionnaires have been completed, break people into small groups for a discussion. Handouts can be gathered up at the end of the activity, mixed up, and redistributed so that people do not have their own questionnaire. The facilitator can then ask for a show of hands and tally on the board the various rankings for each of the scenarios, as well as those individuals who are marked "unacceptable."

Variations

New scenarios modeled on the present questionnaire can be used to address the issue of unintentional bias toward a variety of subgroups. For example, scenarios can be developed to address the impact of differences in socioeconomic status and religious differences on level of prejudice.

Discussion Suggestions

A discussion of the exercise is essential in addressing the issue of unintentional bias. To promote a sense of safety, questions should be more general in nature. Answers to specific questions on the questionnaire should be solicited only on a voluntary basis. A nice icebreaker is to ask, "Was anyone surprised by their answers?" This can follow with a general discussion of the types of situations that might be easiest for the general American public to accept and that would cause the most discomfort. Levels of acceptance of different groups (e.g., Hispanic, physically challenged) by the dominant culture should also be examined. The discussion can conclude with an exploration of the sources of learning about attitudes toward various cultural groups. Examples or responses solicited during the discussion can be used to reinforce the ideas described in the initial presentation on unintentional bias.

References and Further Reading

Bogardus, E. S. (1967). *A forty-year racial distance study.* Los Angeles: University of Southern California.

Bogardus, E. S. (1968). Comparing racial distance in Ethiopia, South Africa, and the United States. *Sociology and Social Research, 52,* 149-156.

Cole, J. (1996). *Beyond prejudice* [On-line]. Available: www.eburg.com/beyond.prejudice

Devine, P. G. (1989). Stereotypes and prejudice: Their automatic and controlled components. *Journal of Personality and Social Psychology, 56,* 5-18.

Devine, P. G., Monteith, M. J., Zuwerink, J. R., & Elliot, A. J. (1991). Prejudice with and without compunction. *Journal of Personality and Social Psychology, 60,* 817-830.

Essed, P. (1991). *Understanding everyday racism.* Newbury Park, CA: Sage.

Gaertner, S. L., & Dovidio, J. F. (1986). The aversive form of racism. In J. F. Dovidio & S. L. Gaertner (Eds.), *Prejudice, discrimination, and racism* (pp. 61-89). San Diego, CA: Academic Press.

Monteith, M. J., Devine, P. G., & Zuwerink, J. R. (1993). Self-directed versus other-directed affect as a consequence of prejudice-related discrepancies. *Journal of Personality and Social Psychology, 64,* 198-210.

O'Mara, J. (1994). *Diversity activities and training designs.* San Diego, CA: Pfeiffer.

Pederson, P. B. (1978). Four dimensions of cross-cultural skill in counseling training. *Personnel and Guidance Journal, 56,* 480-484.

Ridley, C. R. (1995). *Overcoming unintentional racism in counseling and therapy: A practitioner's guide to intentional intervention.* Thousand Oaks, CA: Sage.

Swim, J. K., Aikin, K. J., Hall, W. S., & Hunter, B. A. (1995). Sexism and racism: Old fashioned and modern prejudices. *Journal of Personality and Social Psychology, 2,* 199-214.

Wade, P., & Bernstein, B. (1991). Culture sensitivity training and counselor's race: Effect on black female clients' perceptions and attrition. *Journal of Counseling Psychology, 38,* 9-15.

QUESTIONS FOR BEYOND
POLITICAL CORRECTNESS EXERCISE

1. a. Your 19-year-old daughter calls you from college to let you know she is moving out of her dorm room into an apartment with someone. Rank in order of preference (1 = most preferred) which of the following people you would find acceptable as your daughter's roommate. Place an *X* by any person you would find completely unacceptable.

   ___ Caucasian female

   ___ Physically challenged female with paraplegia

   ___ Asian female

   ___ Homosexual female

   b. How might your response(s) change if this scenario were about the roommate of a co-worker's daughter?

2. a. You and your spouse have been asked to attend an important dinner for your boss. You did not have much notice and cannot find a family member or friend to baby-sit your 5-year-old child. You decide to call a reputable child care agency for a state-certified child care worker. Rank in order of preference (1 = most preferred) which of the following people you would find acceptable as a sitter for your child. Place an *X* by any person you would find completely unacceptable.

   ___ Hispanic female

   ___ Caucasian female

   ___ Homosexual female

   ___ Physically challenged female with an amputated arm

   b. How might your response(s) change if this scenario were about a sitter for the child of an acquaintance?

3. a. An apartment in the building next to yours has just been rented. Rank in order of preference (1 = most preferred) which of the following people you would find acceptable as neighbors. Place an *X* by any couple you would find completely unacceptable.

   ___ Hispanic couple

   ___ Homosexual couple

   ___ Caucasian couple

   ___ African American couple

   b. How might your response(s) change if this scenario were about neighbors moving in next door to a house in which you intended to stay for a long time?

4. a. You have just installed a new hot tub on your deck and decide to have a hot tub party. You invite a few of your closest friends to come over and soak in the hot tub and tell them they may bring a guest. Rank in order of preference (1 = most preferred) which of the following people you would find acceptable as a guest. Place an *X* by any person you would find completely unacceptable.

____ Homosexual male
____ African American male
____ Physically challenged male with cerebral palsy
____ Caucasian male

   b. How might your response(s) change if this scenario were about a guest invited to a birthday party?

5. a. Your sister calls you to tell you one of her friends is visiting the city in which you live. She asks you if you would mind letting her friend stay at your place over the weekend. Rank in order of preference (1 = most preferred) which of the following people you would find acceptable as a weekend guest. Place an *X* by any person you would find completely unacceptable.

____ Caucasian female
____ Physically challenged female who is deaf
____ Native American female
____ Homosexual female

   b. How might your response(s) change if this scenario were about a weekend guest at a neighbor's house?

6. a. Your son tells you he is in a committed relationship with someone and would like to bring this person home at Thanksgiving to meet the family. Rank in order of preference (1 = most preferred) which of the following people you would find acceptable as your son's partner. Place an *X* by any person you would find completely unacceptable.

____ Physically challenged female who is blind
____ African American female
____ Homosexual male
____ Caucasian female

   b. How might your response(s) change if this scenario were about the partner of your boss's son?

PART 4

Cognitive Site Mapping

Placing Yourself in (Con)Text

ELIZABETH RENFRO
SUSAN WILEY HARDWICK

Concepts

Contemporary scholars—and poets since humankind's beginning—have recognized that we humans socially construct certain foundational Truths (Belyea, 1992; Garfinkle, 1967; Geertz, 1973) through which we interpret everything in our world. Much current social and educational theory has drawn from this a discouraging picture of dominant systems of belief and practice that stifle, silence, and disempower alternative visions and meaning-making systems. Many recent social constructivist theories, however, challenge the standard binary model of power and culture interactions (oppressor/oppressed; insider/outsider) that denies agency to those outside the dominant group (Minh-Ha, 1991; Taylor, 1991). They instead call attention to the dialectical relationship that occurs when diverse beliefs and practices come into contact. Although not denying the oppression and colonization practiced by dominating cultures, this approach stresses the ways in which the oppressed and the oppressor educate, influence, and change one another.

This approach can be an empowering one to apply within the classroom, if we can find ways to foreground the cultural production going on within each individual and in the group as a whole as a result of the classroom interactions. One way to begin this is to locate, examine, and discuss our individual subject positions (note the spatial metaphor). In so doing, we can "complicate" and "interrogate" complex issues, rather than approaching them through the simplifying blinders of unexamined personal situatedness.

The tricky part, of course, is that most humans are completely unaware of themselves as socially constructed beings. The ability to be self conscious, to analyze the foundations of our perceptions, is not only hard to do oneself but is also extremely challenging to teach. After all, it's threatening, this looking with a critical eye at the subtexts of belief, the Truths from which our thinking—our everyday lives—derive. And how do we help students (and ourselves) leap the self-protections we've all developed to shield our value-laden thinking processes? We would like to suggest a tool that can provide a way into such risky critical thinking and self-critique: *cognitive site mapping.*

Also termed *mental maps,* cognitive site mapping was developed in the social sciences and applies a social constructivist theoretical approach to meaning making. It recognizes that a human reads physical or spatial environment(s) based on individual experiences and cultural backgrounds, producing in his or her mind's eye a "cognitive site map," that is, an "organized representation of part of the spatial environment" (Downs & Stea, 1977), which is filtered through the individual's experience-based values, biases, interests, and sense of self. Thus, an individual's mental map of a particular site reveals much about that person's internalized understandings of culture(s) and power relations.

In the classroom, cognitive site mapping can take the form of helping students recreate their mental maps on paper, either in actual, spatial map form or in narrative descriptions. This activity grounds—literally and figuratively—each student's subject position, that is, the complex web of personal experiences, feelings, and attitudes that in turn directly and indirectly affect the way that person perceives and "understands" that with which he or she comes into contact.

When a group, first individually and then communally, maps a particular place (a place everyone in the class has been, the site of a historical event, a story scene, even the classroom itself), the range of individual interpretations—their overlaps, similarities, and differences—becomes more immediate and concrete. Students (and teachers) can see and discuss specific examples of how a group of individuals can come to such a wide variety of understandings or interpretations of an experience, a piece of literature, or anything else that they have all "read." By tracing commonalities among the maps everyone has drawn, the community can also see and then begin to analyze its shared perceptions. Furthermore, as the group analyzes what its visual representations of a place reveal, students then also begin to engage in metacognition, tracing *how* they have come to think what they think.

Time

This exercise requires 45 to 60 minutes (up to several class sessions, depending on follow-up activities).

Requirements

We like using an overhead projector to show examples, share group work, and so forth. But the exercises may be done with only handouts. Students need no advance preparations, and the exercise works equally well with students of very diverse backgrounds or with a homogeneous group.

The following are suggested for use either as overhead transparencies or as handouts (please note that permission should be requested from the publishers):

- Ancient Yurok map (from *The Inland Whale*; Kroeber, 1959)
- Neighborhood map by a boy and a girl (from "Gender and Geography"; Matthews, 1988)
- Medieval conception of the universe (from *Western Civilization*; Spielvogel, 1994)
- Cognitive site maps of Los Angeles by different groups (from *Image and Environment*; Downs & Stea, 1973)

Instructions

The instructions below are for a generalized, introductory version of cognitive site mapping, focusing on drawing spatial maps. In the Variations section that follows, we describe a course-specific application that we have used in cultural geography, in which the cognitive site mapping is done via students composing narrative descriptions rather than actual spatial maps. In our own teaching, we've also adapted cognitive site mapping activities to women's studies, composition, and literature courses.

5-10 minutes	Participants draw individual maps of the local city or area. It's best to choose a site with which the students have a fair degree of familiarity (e.g., the town itself, or the neighborhood, if in a large city).
10-15 minutes	Share in pairs or small groups. Make list of commonalities and (fairly) unique items on individual maps. Speculate on what differences and similarities mean vis-à-vis backgrounds of group members.
15 minutes	Teacher shares two or more culture-specific maps with whole class to illustrate the connections between place and culture (including cultural values, biases, etc.). We've used maps from medieval Europe, Yurok Indian maps, maps drawn by people of different ethnic groups in Los Angeles, and gender-specific maps for comparing and contrasting.

Discussion questions: Note the shared and distinct features among the maps. What do they reveal about the way different individuals construct the "reality" of the same place? What might the maps indicate about cultural lifeways, values, and concerns of the cultural group(s) to which each individual belongs? What are some of the dangers inherent in drawing such cultural inferences?

15 minutes   Back to teams or whole class: Discuss what you think your maps reveal about the people who created them. Consider cultural lifeways, values, concerns, power interplays, and so on.

Variations

Cultural Geography Course

The student-centered activity described below offers a menu of ideas for using cognitive site mapping theory in an introductory geography class. Suggested activities may be used in sequence for an entire class period or may be used selectively depending on time constraints. This geography activity moves students from an explicit use of cognitive site mapping to a more implicit use of this theory by accessing their mental map knowledge through the use of in-class speculative writing.

Step 1. Students select their favorite and least favorite places on a blank map of the United States by marking a plus for their top five most preferred locations and a zero for their five least desirable places.

Step 2. Instructor presents a mini-lecture on concepts and themes central to understanding cognitive site mapping theory, perception, and the importance of mental maps as important theoretical background for expanding geographic knowledge of the "real world."

Step 3. Have a large group discussion of prior research on mental maps and how these findings compare with student perceptions (as shown on their own maps of the United States).

Step 4. Students view a postcard of their local landscape and write brief speculative essay describing what they see.

Step 5. Students then receive a small piece of paper for a second short writing—a description of the postcard view. This time, each student is asked to write about the perception of place based on his or her estimation of what the person listed on the piece of paper might see and feel when viewing this same scene.

Step 6. Students then work in pairs to compare and contrast differing perceptions of place as expressed in their writing.

Step 7. Wrap up: Have a large group discussion on the importance of understanding our own mental maps, cognition, perception, and sense of place as a measurement of prior knowledge and attitudes about each person's socially constructed personal geography.

Discussion Suggestions

Observation and Analysis

Discussion can range over a variety of areas with these exercises, though we have found that the most fruitful discussion arises as we try to discover/ uncover possible reasons for the similarities and differences in each of our individual maps. Such reasons grow out of our various family values; our individual life experiences, including degrees of exposure to various media; and our cultural values (and it's important to remember that we all belong to a number of overlapping culture groups, including those based on ethnicity/ties, class, religion, gender). Also to be considered are the dynamics of the current situation in which the maps were drawn (i.e., the classroom, if the maps were produced in class).

The kinds and level of questions the instructor might ask depend on the sophistication and experience of the students with thinking about issues of cultural difference. The key, though, is always to focus on observing and then analyzing specific features of the maps, for example, natural physical features (rivers, mountains, etc.); human-designed navigation elements (streets, cardinal directions); individual and/or personal features (Mary's house, the market where my dad shops). It is also useful to draw attention to elements that seem common or "natural" for inclusion (e.g., the school itself, the town's main street) and those that seem unexpected or idiosyncratic (my grandfather's house).

After making these general observations, the next step is to lead into analysis, to try to uncover what these maps show us about ourselves and others' perceptions of the world. Thus, we might ask such basic questions as "Why do you think so many people included the mall on their maps?" followed by asking individuals their own reasons for this. Common responses might be, "I love to shop," "It's the only place I can go at night to wander around without being afraid of being attacked," and "I like to pretend I get to buy a whole new wardrobe." Teachers can then move discussion from the personal to the more generalized by asking what this commonly drawn landmark indicates is significant or valued by many people. Discussion can move further into exploration of what personal, familial, and cultural values may account for the map drawers' valuation of this feature (the mall), that is, could it be consumerism, socializing, safety for females, or something else? What personal experiences might affect this?

A more advanced discussion question along the same tack might be, "What do you think it means that some of the maps have lots of humanmade landmarks, but some have mostly natural landmarks?" or "Why do you think some of the maps illustrate a small area and some a very large area?" followed by asking individuals to discuss what they see as their own reasons for including what they did on their maps. Students who have already looked at and discussed the ways in which our cultures (including our upbringing) affect our views of our world (including our immediate surroundings) will not find this difficult. If such discussion hasn't yet arisen, you might begin with questions like "If maps have mostly humanmade landmarks, what do you think that says about the interests of the map makers?" or "Why would the natural landmarks be important to people?" The ensuing discussion can be guided in ways to help students see and value both the commonly held personal, familial, and cultural values they share, plus the unique viewpoints and values each person's individual experiences may have nurtured.

The Classroom Experience

We have also used the activity periodically during the course to monitor the perceptions each student has about the class or the classroom experience. Looking at student responses to such questions as "Compare the classroom map you've just drawn [in the 10th week of class] to the one you drew in the first week of class. What similarities and differences do you see? What do you think the similarities and differences indicate about your feelings about the class, the classroom, and your classmates and instructor?" It's interesting to note shifts in tone, comfort levels, and power relations in the class. These often show up in the form of which people (or their labeled desks) appear on most maps, where the teacher is sited, and so on).

Role Play

One somewhat risky—but effective—approach can be to have students role play, giving them personas very different from their own from which to draw a spatial or a narrative map of a particular place. The risk, as well as the advantage, is that these representations reveal a great deal about the stereotypes each of us holds regarding what people different from us think, feel, and value. Thus, class discussion needs to address how, for example, a middle-class male student presents the views of his assigned persona, a 35-year-old rural mother visiting his neighborhood in Los Angeles for the first time. You might ask such questions as "What values, biases, concerns is he assuming his character would hold that would cause her to describe North Hollywood in this particular way? What might be the sources of his assumptions?" You can also assign the same persona to two different students, and then compare the ways in which each has constructed her or his character's map. What personal experiences, beliefs, and assumptions that each student holds might account for differences in the maps?

Follow-Up

Follow-up work can be done throughout the school year/term by applying this activity to any of the texts and subjects being studied (e.g., settings in literature, history, political science).

References and Further Reading

Beaty, W. W., & Troster, A. I. (1987). Gender differences in geographic knowledge. *Sex Roles, 16,* 565-590.

Belyea, B. (1992). Images of power: Derrida/Foucault/Harley. *Cartographica, 29*(2), 1-9.

Chioco, J. J. (1993). Mental maps: Preservice teachers' awareness of the world. *Journal of Geography, 92,* 110-115.

Danzer, G. A. (1991). World maps, worldviews, and world history. *Social Education, 55,* 301-303.

Downs, R. M., & Stea, D. (1973). *Image and environment.* New York: Aldine.

Downs, R. M., & Stea, D. (1977). *Maps in minds: Reflections on cognitive mapping.* New York: Harper and Row.

Garfinkle, H. (1967). *Studies in ethnomethodology.* Englewood Cliffs, NJ: Prentice Hall.

Geertz, C. (1973). *The interpretation of cultures.* New York: Basic Books.

Hall, S. S. (1992). *Mapping the new millennium: The discovery of new geographies.* New York: Random House.

Harley, J. B. (1990). Cartography, ethics and social theory. *Cartographica, 27*(2), 1-23.

Jackson, P. (1994). *Maps of meaning.* London: Routledge.

Kroeber, T. (1959). *The inland whale.* Berkeley: University of California Press.

Matthews, H. (1988). Gender and geography. *The Geographical Magazine, 60,* 47-49.

Minh-Ha, T. T. (1991). *When the moon waxes red: Representation, gender, and cultural politics.* New York: Routledge.

Monmonier, M. (1991). *How to live with maps.* Chicago: University of Chicago Press.

Sibley, D. (1995). *Geographies of exclusion.* New York: Routledge.

Spielvogel, J. J. (1994). *Western civilization.* St. Paul, MN: West Educational.

Taylor, D. (1991). Transculturating transculturation. B. Marranca & G. Dasgupta (Eds.), *Writings from PAJ* (pp. 60-74). New York: PAJ.

Color My World

ALISON GOURVÈS-HAYWARD

The physical properties of color can be defined using three variables (Armstrong, 1991). First is hue, the pure colors that can be seen in a rainbow or in the electromagnetic spectrum by passing white light through a prism and can be measured in wavelengths (Lindsay & Norman, 1972). Color can also be classified by luminosity or brightness; for example, a range of pale pink to dark red would constitute a brightness scale. The third variable is that of intensity or saturation, that is, the degree of freedom from white; for example, pink would have lower saturation than red because of the larger amount of white in it, whereas dark red would have high saturation. All three criteria are used to define color in modern Western societies, but this is not necessarily the case in other societies.

Although these physical properties would appear to be universal, different conventions are used by different cultures to express this physical reality. For a hundred years, researchers have been aware that there are great differences in the number of color terms in a given language, with the earlier stages of European languages and the more primitive contemporary languages containing fewer color terms than the modern European languages. The first observations on color definition (Geiger, 1880; Gladstone, 1858) assumed that relative paucity of color terms meant limited perception. Gradually, it became accepted that perceptual abilities and naming behavior may be independent (Allen, 1879; Magnus, 1880) although some researchers maintain that a limited number of terms available limits the degree of discrimination (Anglin, 1995; Kay & Kempton, 1984).

In 1969, Berlin and Kay carried out an extensive study of color terms in 98 languages that produced some surprising results. This study took place within the context of the theories of extreme cultural relativism (Boas, 1911/1966; Whorf, 1956) and of what has become known as the Sapir-Whorf hypothesis, the "strong" form of which being that speakers of different languages live in "distinct worlds, not merely the same world with different labels attached" (Sapir, 1929). The classic "proof" of this theory is that of the "Eskimo words for snow" example, which, as Laura Martin (1986) points out in her detailed analysis of the phenomenon, has been quoted, misquoted, and exaggerated from Boas's original statement that Eskimos had four separate lexically unrelated words for snow (Boas, 1911/1966). Although originally intended to illustrate the noncomparability of language structures, the example has been used to show that Eskimo people and English speakers see snow differently or that people create more labels for things when they are needed (Brown, 1958).

Berlin and Kay's (1969) assumption was that there would be considerable intercultural differences in "basic color terms," but in fact, their findings showed that there was a great deal of agreement on the colors judged to be the best examples of basic color terms and that there also seemed to be a universal order in the way these terms developed. The 98 languages tested could be divided into 22 linguistic groups, according to which terms they used, group one having only black and white and the last group the 11 colors of the rainbow (Munsell Color Company, 1966). The distribution was organized as shown in Table 25.1, but modified in 1975 to include languages that use the same word for blue and green, like Breton. The acquisition of these languages goes from left to right on the table, that is, if a language has a term for blue, then it also has all the terms to the left of blue on the table. On the other hand, some languages have green without yellow, or purple without pink, orange, and gray, hence the 22 groups.

The American psychologist Eleanor Rosch (Heider), in her research on prototypes and natural categories, comes to a similar conclusion, focal colors being consistently chosen as the "best example" of a color. There would be, for example, a universal representation of focal red, with all other shades of red belonging to a greater or lesser extent to the category red. The boundaries separating different colors would be different, however, according to the number of terms available; for example, red would also cover the other warm shades such as orange and yellow for languages where there were only three basic terms, the central red remaining the same (Heider, 1972; Mervis, Catlin, & Rosch, 1975; Rosch, 1975).

Even if we accept that there are such universals and that the paucity of certain terms does not necessarily mean a limited perception, the fact that a language contains a limited or a vast number of terms in a particular area is, to a certain extent, a reflection of a cultural reality. Colors have different associations within different cultures, for example the Navaho color system is connected to the use of objects and colors in ceremonials (McNeill, 1972), whereas the three basic terms *white*, *black*, and *red* in certain African languages correspond to such fundamentals as *white* for mother's milk, *black* for the earth, and *red* for blood. It is true that Western cultures tend to be extremely color oriented, note the large number of color expressions in the English language and that in a nonindustrial society, the need for color differen-

TABLE 25.1 Hierarchical Organization of Basic Color Terms

					Purple
White	Red	Green	Blue	Brown	Pink
Black		Yellow			Orange
					Gray

SOURCE: Berlin and Kay (1969).

tiation between large numbers of synthetic dyes or color coding for electric wires or traffic lights does not make itself felt. To maintain a balanced view, it should be pointed out, however, that in other areas, such as that of kinship, English has far fewer terms than some African and Asian languages, in which there are specific terms for many relationships such as one's younger or older brother, one's father's or mother's sister, or one's child's parent-in-law.

The main aim of the exercise in this chapter is to provide firsthand experience of using a far more limited number of categories than those available in English to define color so that students will be encouraged to see a different point of view, from a different cultural perspective. It also hopes to provoke discussion of the following question: To what extent does language "color" the world around us and to what extent does our perception of the world "color" our language?

Time

Thirty minutes to 1 hour is needed, depending on warm-up activities and amount of discussion.

Requirements

This activity is best in a group of 10-20 persons, small enough for discussion, but big enough to have differing opinions. It can be carried out in a mixed or monoculture group. The exercise is ideally done singly and then in small groups of two or three before discussion with the whole class, but if there are not enough color chips, it can be carried out initially in groups. For each student, the handouts and a set of color chips used for paint samples, with as wide a range of colors as possible, are needed. These can be found anywhere house paint is sold, such as hardware stores. Alternatively, paints or colored crayons could be used. The color chips will be numbered by the manufacturer; cover the name of the color that's printed on the chip with tape while the students are classifying the colors. (The number of the color should be showing.) The tape can be removed when the students compare their findings. It is essential that the colors themselves be used, with the names taped over, because the color names could evoke different things for different people. Each student does not have to have the same colors in his or her set, although this would make comparison more simple, but they should all have examples of the 11 Berlin and Kay "basic colors" and also some very pale and some very dark shades. Some easily ambiguous colors like turquoise should also be included.

Instructions

Initially, the students will be asked to classify their color chips into groups containing the 11 basic colors (see Color My World Exercise 1 handout). A choice of colors could be, as well as the 11 basic colors: ruby, scarlet, crimson, maroon, bright pink, pale pink, dusky pink, peach, apricot, several shades of turquoise, lime green, jade, bottle green, sky blue, navy blue, pale blue, eggshell blue, mauve, lilac, lavender, violet, lemon, cream, beige, pale beige, dark brown. The second part (Color My World Exercise 2 handout) involves classifying the same colors using the basic terms available to Gouro (one of the languages spoken in the Ivory Coast) speakers and demands quite a perceptual leap, which students usually find exciting. The colors above would be classified as follows by a Gouro speaker, although there would not be complete agreement between individuals. All very dark colors and *all* blues and greens unless almost nonchromatic would be considered black, or *ti*; all warm colors, reds, oranges, yellows, pinks except extremely dark or almost white shades would be red, or *son*; and all very pale colors would be white, or *fou*. Colors are defined either by brightness (light or dark—ti or fou) or by intensity (son).

Discussion Suggestions

A warm-up session in which students are told about the physical aspects of color, with, if possible, a picture of the spectrum, followed by some information on cultural differences in color categorization and of the relative importance of color terms in Western civilizations would be useful. Students could also be asked to write down as many color expressions as possible, then discuss the connotations of these.

Color My World Exercise 1 should bring out some individual differences in the group, usually around green and blue, and provoke discussion about how decisions were come to, whether a prototype was chosen to build the color group (this is usually the case), which chip represented the "real" red, or whether we all see the same things even if we use different labels. Color My World Exercise 2 can build on this, with discussion on how the color space has been divided and of the implications of these limited categories for everyday life. Students can be asked how they would manage if they wanted a Gouro friend to send them some blue and green material, for example. Again, it is also interesting to see how choices were made and how much resistance the students felt to this change. A follow-up exercise could be to take an extract from literature or from a newspaper article where a lot of color terms are used and replace the colors by these three terms or to describe a common scene or color photograph using these three terms. Depending on the level of the group, there could be more in-depth discussion of perceptual differences. Do Gouro speakers discriminate between colors as we do? To what extent does our culture influence our perception?

References and Further Reading

Allen, G. (1879). *The colour sense*. London: Turner.

Anglin, J. M. (1995). Classifying the world through language: Functional relevance, cultural significance and category name learning. *International Journal of Intercultural Relations, 19*, 161-181.

Armstrong, T. (1991). *Colour perception*. Stradbroke, Diss, UK: Tarquin.

Berlin, B., & Kay, P. (1969). *Basic color terms: Their universality and evolution*. Berkeley: University of California Press.

Boas, F. (1966). *Introduction to the handbook of North American Indians*. Lincoln: University of Nebraska Press. (Original work published 1911 in the *Smithsonian Institution Bulletin, 40*, Pt. 1)

Brown, R. W. (1958). *Words and things*. New York: Free Press.

Fantini, A. E. (1995). Language, culture and world view: Exploring the nexus. *International Journal of Intercultural Relations, 19*, 143-153.

Geiger, L. (1880). *Contributions to the history of the development of the human race*. London: Turner.

Gladstone, W. E. (1858). *Studies on Homer and the Homeric Age*. London: Oxford University Press.

Gourvès-Hayward, A. M. (1992). L'acquisition de l'anglais par les Elèves Africains à Télécom Bretagne [The acquisition of English by Francophone Africans at Telecom Bretagne]. *Actes de la Troisième Journée E.R.L.A. G.L.A.T.* (Applied Lexical Research Group, University of Brest and the Applied Linguistics for Telecommunications Group, Ecole Nationale Supérieure des Télécommunications de Bretagne). Brest, France: Ecole Nationale Supérieure des Télécommunications de Bretagne.

Heider, E. R. (1972). Universals in color naming and memory. *Journal of Experimental Psychology, 93*, 10-20.

Kay, P., & Kempton, W. (1984). What is the Sapir-Whorf hypothesis? *American Anthropologist, 1*, 86.

Lindsay, P., & Norman, D. (1972). *Human information processing*. San Diego, CA: Academic Press.

Magnus, H. (1880). *Untersuchungen über den Farbensinn der Naturvölker* [Research on the color sense of primitive peoples]. Jena: Fraher.

Martin, L. (1986). "Eskimo words for snow": A case study in the genesis and decay of an anthropological example. *American Anthropologist, 88*, 418-423.

McNeill, N. B. (1972). Colour and colour terminology. *Journal of Linguistics, 8*, 21-34.

Munsell Color Company. (1966). *The Munsell book of color*. Baltimore: Munsell Color Communication Products.

Mervis, C., Catlin, J., & Rosch, E. (1975). The development of the structure of color categories. *Developmental Psychology, 11*, 54-60.

Palmer, F. R. (1976). *Semantics*. Cambridge, UK: Cambridge University Press.

Rosch, E. (1975). The nature of mental codes for color categories. *Journal of Experimental Psychology, Human Perception and Performance, 1*, 303-322.

Sapir, E. (1929). *The status of Linguistics as a science in culture, language and personality*. Berkeley: University of California Press.

Whorf, B. (1956). Language, thought and reality. In J. B. Carroll (Ed.), *Selected writings of Benjamin Lee Whorf*. Cambridge: MIT Press.

COLOR MY WORLD EXERCISE 1

Take a set of color chips and put them into the following categories:

Basic color term	Number on color chip
Black	
White	
Red	
Green	
Yellow	
Blue	
Brown	
Purple	
Pink	
Orange	
Gray	

Compare your findings with a group of other students with the same chips.

Was there any disagreement? If so, where? and why?

How did you go about the task?

Did you find it difficult? Give reasons for your answer.

How did you and other students classify colors—using hue, brightness or intensity, or a combination?

What names would you use to classify these colors? Compare them with the others in your group and then with the names given by the paint manufacturer.

What conclusions can be drawn from any differences?

COLOR MY WORLD EXERCISE 2

Speakers of Gouro, one of the languages spoken in the Ivory Coast, have three basic color terms to classify colors. They are *ti*—black, *fou*—white, and *son*—red. Take the same color chips as before and put them into these three groups.

Gouro word	Number on color chip
Ti	
Fou	
Son	

As before, compare your findings with a group of other students with the same chips.

Was there any disagreement? If so, where? and why?

How did you go about the task?

Did you find it more difficult than the last exercise? Give reasons for your answer.

How did you and other students classify colors—using hue, brightness or intensity, or a combination?

Did the number of terms available to you change the way you perceived the colors?

What difficulties might you have in your culture if you only had these three color terms?

Would another culture have the same difficulties?

Try to use only these three terms for the next few days and see to what extent your world has been colored!

Multicultural Expressions
of Religious Symbols

WILLIAM J. BROWN
BENSON P. FRASER

Concepts

Recently, two police officers in Portsmouth, Virginia, arrested two women wearing veils in front of a grocery store. The officers reported that the two women looked suspicious and conjectured that they were planning a burglary. The two women explained to the officers that they were Muslim, that their veils were part of their traditional Muslim dress, and asked that they not be touched. Despite their protests the women were body searched by the men, an offense to Muslim women, and later released from jail after the police realized they were innocent. The incident brought about tremendous public protest and needless tension between the police and the local community.

Within the diversity of culture, race, and social norms in the United States, there lies a diversity of religious expressions that people must accommodate and respond to appropriately. Several scholars discuss the importance of religious beliefs and values to the formation of a person's social identity (Bishop, 1992; Dumestre, 1991; Sullivan, 1995). For example, Bergin and Jensen (1990) found that 46% of the mental health professionals they surveyed reported that their approach to life was based on their religion (p. 102). Every cultural group has a religious or moral value system (Bishop, 1992). In the multicultural environment of the United States, the majority of Americans regard religious belief as very important in their lives (Carter, 1993; Seabury, 1982). The problem is that most Americans do not know how to discuss religious values and beliefs (Doniger, 1988). Sullivan (1995) observes, "It is ignorance, not lack of respect, that characterizes the American approach to religion" (p. 74). Dumestre (1991) believes that the antireligious nature of university education minimizes the study and discussion of religious values in American culture. Sensitivity to diverse cultural and religious values is critical to the field of counseling (Bishop, 1992), health education (Padilla & DeSnyder, 1987), higher education (Sullivan, 1995), science (Campbell & Curtis, 1996), and law and public policy (Carter, 1993).

The embarrassing situation in which a Virginia police department found itself resulted from ignorance of the clothing worn by a religious group. The display of religious faith through clothing, jewelry, pictures, books, and other artifacts may be an important means of expression in the workplace. Organizational executives and managers must be sensitive not to overregulate religious expression by prohibiting the display of religious symbols.

For example, one common means of expressing religious beliefs is through food choices. Organizations arranging food for employees or conference participants must be conscious that practicing Catholics prefer seafood on Fridays during Lent, Jewish and Islamic believers prefer nonpork entrees, and many Hindus and an increasing number of Westerners eat vegetarian for health and dietary reasons. Forcing people into difficult situations by knowingly serving objectionable food shows insensitivity to the religious beliefs of others.

There is also a need for Americans to learn how to intelligently discuss religious values within the context of a multicultural society rich in religious symbols. Unfortunately, concerns about the separation of church and state have created a social climate that discourages the free expression of religious values and beliefs. Ensuring free religious expression will help overcome what Sullivan (1995) refers to as the "rhetorical disjunction between the available public language about religion and the religious experience of Americans" (p. 72).

Acceptance of religious diversity can be enhanced by recognizing the antireligious nature of much public education and the cultural biases of our own social environment.

We recommend four productive ways of responding to religious expressions different from our own: (a) observe religious symbols respectfully while withholding judgment of the appropriateness of the expression encountered, (b) ask the person or persons to explain why a certain religious symbol is important to them, (c) ask the person or persons what they intend to communicate to others through their religious expression, and (d) ask the person if you could discuss your response to their religious expression. In this way, both the person or persons exhibiting religious symbols and those who encounter diverse religious expressions can achieve a greater mutual understanding and sensitivity to one another.

Time

This exercise requires 20 to 30 minutes, depending on the discussion time and size of small groups.

Requirements

The handout, a pen, and a blank sheet of paper are needed.

Instructions

After discussing the cultural differences of how religious values are expressed in a multicultural society, the instructor will ask the participants to take part in a 20- to 30-minute exercise. First, the instructor will ask the participants to read on their own a short business meeting scenario and to complete a set of four questions at the end of the scenario. Next, participants will be divided into groups of 4-5 people by the instructor to read and discuss their answers. Finally, the instructor will discuss the authors' recommended answers to the four questions with the participants.

Variations

Have each person in each group assume the role of one of the meeting participants. Then ask group members to answer the following questions: How would you answer the four questions posed by the exercise? What problems do you anticipate in regard to the diversity of religious beliefs among the group members? How could you diffuse potential problems that you anticipate from your perspective?

Discussion Suggestions

After the instructor determines that the participants have had enough time discussing their answers to the four questions, he or she will read and discuss with the entire group of participants the four answers recommended by the authors of the exercise. These are provided below.

Authors' Recommended Answers to the Four Questions

1. Four air tickets should be arranged for the Bahrain firm and three air tickets for the Australian firm.

Why? A single Muslim woman should not be expected to attend such a meeting without a male chaperon, preferably her father. An air ticket should be offered for her father or for a substitute chaperon chosen by her father.

2. Four hotel rooms should be reserved
for the Bahrain firm and
three hotel rooms for the Australia firm.

Why? The father of the single Muslim woman or male chaperon would need a separate room. Although the Australian couple already lives together and they are engaged to be married soon, staying in the same room together may be offensive to the Muslims and the evangelical Christian, who likely view premarital sexual relations as immoral.

3. The assistant marketing director
should lead the meeting for the Australian firm.

Why? The Japanese marketing director would probably feel uncomfortable negotiating decisions with a woman marketing director, and the assistant director's church background would likely help him be a good substitute. Foursquare church theology promotes women leadership, the church denomination having been founded by a woman. The woman marketing director could put her assistant "out front" as leading the meeting but still be in control "behind the scenes" without worrying about her assistant infringing on her authority.

4. Social time should be structured to promote friendly
but professional social interaction,
to allow for personal prayer and devotions,
and clothing should be conservative.

Why? The religious values of several group members would cause them to be disturbed by a high degree of overt physical contact between members of the opposite sex in public places. It would be natural for the engaged couple to express physical romantic interaction, but they may not realize such romantic interchanges would make several group members very uncomfortable.

Regarding religious devotion, time should be allowed for prayer breaks for the practicing Muslims, who often pray three times per day, and personal devotion time on Sunday morning for any who may want to participate in a local place of worship.

Regarding ocean activities and dress, the participants should be asked to wear conservative beach clothing, because bikini-type swimsuits would likely be offensive to the Muslims. These simple guidelines may seem confining to some of the group participants but would be greatly appreciated by other members of the group, leading to a more productive meeting.

References and Further Reading

Bergin, A. E., & Jensen, J. P. (1990). Religiosity of psychotherapists: A national survey. *Psychotherapy, 48,* 95-105.

Bishop, D. R. (1992). Religious values in cross-cultural counseling. *Counseling and Values, 36,* 179-191.

Campbell, R. A., & Curtis, J. E. (1996). The public's views on the future of religion and science: Cross-national survey results. *Review of Religious Research, 37,* 164-171.

Carter, S. L. (1993). *The culture of disbelief: How American law and politics trivialize religious devotion.* New York: Basic Books.

Chia, E. K. F., & Jih, C. S. (1994). The effects of stereotyping on impression formation: Cross-cultural perspectives on viewing religious persons. *Journal of Psychology, 128,* 559-565.

Doniger, W. (1988). *Other people's myths: The cave of echoes.* New York: Macmillan.

Dumestre, M. J. (1991). Liberal arts education as an expression of religious education. *Religious Education, 86,* 292-306.

McLean, G. F. (Ed.). (1989). *Research on culture and values: The intersection of universities, churches, and nations.* New York: University Press of America.

Padilla, A. M., & DeSnyder, N. S. (1987). Counseling Hispanics: Strategies for effective intervention. In P. Pedersen (Ed.), *Handbook of cross-cultural counseling and therapy* (pp. 157-164). New York: Praeger.

Seabury, P. (1982). Caesar and the religious domain in America. *Teaching Political Science, 10,* 20-29.

Sullivan, W. F. (1995). Diss-ing religion: Is religion trivialized in American public discourse? *Journal of Religion, 75,* 69-79.

MULTICULTURAL EXPRESSIONS OF RELIGIOUS SYMBOLS EXERCISE

Please read the following scenario and answer the four questions at the end. Then divide into groups of 4-5 people and read and discuss your answers with other members of your group. Finally, compare your answers with the answers provided by your instructor.

Scenario

A group of marketing representatives from two marketing firms must meet to plan a joint marketing plan for a new product. One firm, located in Bahrain, has three representatives that must attend the meeting: a single Muslim woman from Bahrain whose father works in the finance department of the firm, a single Muslim man from Bahrain, and a married Japanese man from Osaka who is the executive director of the marketing division. The second firm, located in Sydney, also identifies three representatives to attend the meeting: an Australian woman with an affinity for new-age religious beliefs who serves as the marketing director; the advertising manager, a Thai national immigrant to Australia who recently became engaged to the marketing director and who currently lives together with her; and a single man actively involved in a Foursquare Christian church co-pastored by a married couple.

The six marketing representatives decide to meet at a hotel resort in Penang, Malaysia, for a 3-day meeting. They project that they will need to work about 20 hours to develop a marketing campaign. Assume that you work for the Australian firm and must set up the meeting in Penang and arrange all the travel and conference administration. Please answer the following questions (you will not actually attend the meeting yourself) and be prepared to explain the reasons for your answers:

1. How many air tickets should you purchase for each firm? Why?
2. How many hotel rooms should you reserve for each firm? Why?
3. Who should lead the meeting from the Australian firm? Why?
4. How should social time be structured and what guidelines should be provided, if any, for social interaction? Why?

Does the Squeaky Wheel Get the Grease?

Understanding Direct and Indirect Communication

AARON CASTELAN CARGILE

SUNWOLF

Concepts

As the proverb in the title of this chapter suggests, one useful approach to communicating with others involves the *direct* statement of the self's needs, desires, and experiences so that they may be recognized and addressed by others. This mode of communication expects people to be honest and up front with what they say, and not to beat around the bush. Additionally, it is a mode of communication with which most Americans are familiar because it is endorsed by mainstream American culture (see, e.g., Katriel & Philipsen, 1981). Even so, it is not the only mode of expression, and in many different cultures throughout the world (especially East Asian and Arab cultures), it is not the preferred mode.

A second, and opposite, mode of expression involves *indirect* communication. According to Searle (1969), indirect communication takes place when the speaker expresses to the hearer more than he or she actually says by referring to some mutually shared background information and by depending on the hearer's powers of inference. For example, a simple word such as Chicago may evoke memories of a particular experience between friends and be sufficient for communicating an idea related to their experience. In addition to verbal references, indirect communication also relies greatly on nonverbal means of expression. Instead of encoding one's ideas clearly, or even vaguely, in words, those ideas may be wrapped up in a gesture or a particular "look." For example, Lebra (1976) describes one Japanese wife who expressed her discord with her mother-in-law to her husband through slight irregularities in her flower arrangements. Here again, the speaker depends on the hearer's powers of inference for the idea to be successfully communicated. According to Hall (1976), such examples of indirect expression are part of high-context communication systems: "HC [high context] transactions feature pre-programmed information that is in the receiver and in the setting, with only minimal information in the transmitted [verbal] message" (p. 101).

Although indirect communication is not emphasized in American culture, or in many other Western European cultures, this is not to say that members of these cultures are completely unfamiliar with, or unpracticed in, this mode of expression. For example, there are occasions that are recognized to require *tact* and *discretion*—code words for indirect communication. If guests overstay their welcome, most Americans would be quick to acknowledge that saying, "Well, I've got to get to work early tomorrow morning" is more appropriate than saying, "Well, I wish you would go now," when communicating one's desire for guests to leave. This is because a concern for politeness undergirds indirect communication (Brown & Levinson, 1978). Expressing thoughts in an indirect rather than a direct manner is a means to being polite. More specifically, Kim (1994) suggests that three different concerns relate to the politeness of indirect language: (a) the concern for avoiding hurting the hearer's feelings, (b) the concern for minimizing imposition, and (c) the concern for avoiding negative evaluations by the hearer. If a speaker is obtuse with his or her vague manner, he or she can reduce the perception of imposing on the hearer. Last, if a speaker's (negative) message is ambiguous, he or she can minimize the hearer's dislike of him or her. In these manners, indirect communication is a much more socially sensitive and relationally appropriate means of expression than direct communication (Yum, 1994). Direct communication, on the other hand, is a much more effective means of expression, especially when the speaker values clarity and precision above all else.

Time

This activity will take approximately 30 minutes, depending on the length of discussion.

Requirements

There is no special knowledge or background required on the part of participants for this activity. The two story handouts included at the end of this chapter are needed.

Instructions

Prepare copies of the two handouts ("The Lion's Whisker" and "The Woman Who Followed Death") for all participants. *Optional:* Make an overhead of each story, to be used during the group discussion or to be used in place of handouts. The goals of this exercise are to

- Illustrate the intercultural constructs of direct and indirect communication.

- Sensitize participants to two different but equally valid perspectives on human interaction.

- Allow participants to discover the beliefs and customs of a culture using one of its socialization tools: folklore.

- Give participants a piece of another culture that is portable, entertaining, easy to recall, and in a form (story) that can be shared with others.

1. Introduce the exercise by reading the following message about the role of folklore in society:

Folktales are actually carriers of culture, as well as forms of entertainment. Values, customs, norms, roles, and religious beliefs are often embedded within the narrative of folktales and, in this way, may be passed on from one generation to the next. The stories of a culture are usually effective tools of socialization for members, but they can also provide outsiders a glimpse of a culture with which they are not familiar.

(*Option:* You may wish to begin, instead, by asking the group: "What is a folktale? Would someone give us an example of a folktale? How many of us were told folktales as a child? Who told you those tales?" You may then read the same above message.)

2. Give Handout 1 ("The Lion's Whisker") to each participant. Let them know they will have 3-4 minutes to read the story to themselves. Suggest that while they read the story, each time they notice a cultural belief, value, custom, or role, to underline it on their handout. Challenge participants to see how many they can find in the time allowed. To keep the exercise moving, and at the same time to be fair, give a 1-minute warning before you stop the reading.

3. (If you prepared an overhead of that story, put the overhead up now.) Ask the participants to share their observations.

4. Give participants Handout 2 ("The Woman Who Followed Death" and repeat Steps 2 and 3.

5. Share with the group the material on direct and indirect communication contained at the beginning of this chapter. Ask whether they think, in the case of each story, that particular story valued direct or indirect communication. Have them explain their reasons.

6. Use the discussion suggestions following these instructions to generate further dialogue about the participants' reactions to and interpretations of the two different stories.

Variations

Variation A. Proceed as above, except that in Step 2, divide the participants into small discussion groups (4-6 members). Ask each group to generate as many observations about cultural beliefs, values, customs, or roles as they can as they read the stories. Have each group report to the class their group's observations.

Variation B. Same as Variation A, except that each group gets one of the two stories. Ask someone to volunteer to retell each story before beginning the group discussion, so all participants are now familiar with both stories.

Variation C. Same as Variation A, except that participants are asked to answer five prepared questions about each story (see Handout 3) instead of attempting to find cultural beliefs and values on their own. This option is preferred for participants less experienced with the field of intercultural communication, who might have difficulty recognizing culture on their own, and it may help instructors who wish to focus primarily on the concepts of direct and indirect communication.

Discussion Suggestions

Use the following questions to facilitate a class discussion about the stories.

1. What do you believe the story was about?
2. Did the story have a lesson or moral? Did it have more than one? Do you agree with this moral?
3. What are the advantages and disadvantages of communicating in a direct manner, as Savitri did? Can you think of times when you would, as well as times when you would not, tell someone exactly what you're thinking?
4. What are the advantages and disadvantages of letting only your actions and your gestures speak for you, as the woman in "The Lion's Whisker" did?
5. Do you believe that open and honest communication is necessarily better or worse than communication that is vague and ambiguous? Why?
6. Can you think of a folktale we may all know that is an example of direct communication? Of indirect communication? (If needed as a prompt, try "The Three Little Pigs," "Little Red Riding Hood," "Cinderella," "Beauty and the Beast.")

7. Do you believe there are regional differences in the United States concerning whether direct or indirect communication is most valued? (If needed, suggest the east coast, the south, New York, Kansas, Alaska, Texas, New England, South Dakota, or Hawaii.)

8. Do you believe there are gender differences in whether direct or indirect communication is preferred? Can you give an example?

9. In your own experience, do some organizations seem to encourage either direct or indirect communication? Can you give an example? What might be the consequences for employees who violate these expectations?

10. Is folklore itself a direct or indirect method of communication? Why? Can there be folktales that directly give a lesson or moral? (If needed, suggested *Aesop's Fables*.)

References and Further Reading

Brown, P., & Levinson, S. (1978). Universals in language usage: Politeness phenomena. In E. Goody (Ed.), *Questions and politeness* (pp. 56-289). Cambridge, UK: Cambridge University Press.

Cohen, R. (1987). Problems of intercultural communication in Egyptian-American diplomatic relations. *International Journal of Intercultural Relations, 11*, 29-47.

DeSpain, P. (1993). *Thirty-three multicultural tales to tell*. Little Rock, AR: August House.

Forest, H. (1995). *Wonder tales from around the world*. Little Rock, AR: August House.

Gudykunst, W. B., & Ting-Toomey, S. (1988). *Culture and interpersonal communication*. Newbury Park, CA: Sage.

Hall, E. T. (1976). *Beyond culture*. New York: Doubleday.

Katriel, T. (1986). *Talking straight: Dugri speech in Israeli Sabra culture*. Cambridge, UK: Cambridge University Press.

Katriel, T., & Philipsen, G. (1981). "What we need is communication": Communication as a cultural category in some American speech. *Communication Monographs, 48*, 301-317.

Kim, M. S. (1994). Cross-cultural comparisons of the perceived importance of conversational constraints. *Human Communication Research, 21*, 128-151.

Lebra, T. S. (1976). *Japanese patterns of behavior*. Honolulu: University Press of Hawai'i.

Okabe, K. (1987). Indirect speech acts of the Japanese. In D. L. Kincaid (Ed.), *Communication theory: Eastern and Western perspectives* (pp. 127-136). New York: Academic Press.

Searle, J. R. (1969). *Speech acts*. Cambridge, UK: Cambridge University Press.

Yolen, J. (Ed.). (1986). *Favorite folktales from around the world*. New York: Pantheon.

Yum, J. O. (1994). The impact of Confucianism on interpersonal relationships and communication patterns in East Asia. In L. A. Samovar & R. E. Porter (Eds.), *Intercultural communication: A reader* (7th ed., pp. 75-86). Belmont, CA: Wadsworth.

HANDOUT 1:
THE LION'S WHISKER

Once there lived a couple who was not quite content in a small village in Ethiopia. The husband showed little interest in the marriage, though they had not been married long. He usually came home late from working in the fields—and sometimes, he failed to come home at all. His wife loved him but felt so ignored by her husband, and felt such hostility from him, that she knew she needed help. She went to talk with the oldest and wisest man in the village.

The old man listened patiently to her bitter words. When he asked her what she had thought of doing, she said that she felt she should probably confront her husband with his duties and with her needs. She would demand better treatment. The wise elder smiled. "That would be one choice, of course," he said softly. "But I know of a potion that will change your husband into an obedient and loving man. If you give it to him, he will come home on time and try always to please you."

"Give it to me, I will pay anything!" she cried. For truly, she wanted to stay married.

"I lack one vital ingredient," continued the wise man. "A single whisker taken from a living lion. If you can bring me such a whisker, I will make the potion and you shall have it."

"I will get it for you," the woman said with determination.

The next day the woman began studying the nearby lions, and she watched them for many days. Finally, she was ready. One day she carried a large chunk of raw meat down to the river where one lion came to drink. Hiding in the forest, she waited quietly until the lion appeared. The woman was frightened. She wanted to run away, but she found the courage to toss the meat to the hungry beast. The lion grabbed the meat, devoured it, and walked slowly back into the jungle.

Every morning that week the woman fed the lion in this way, though her fear remained great. During the second week she came out of her hiding place and let the lion see who was bringing the meat. The third week she moved closer to the lion as he ate, though her body trembled. As time passed she moved still closer. And when five weeks had passed, she was able to sit down quietly next to the lion while he ate. And so it became possible, one day, for her to gently reach over and pluck a single whisker from his chin.

She ran to the wise man with her prize. He smiled at her in surprise and asked her to explain how she had managed to acquire it. After hearing her story, the old man shook his head. "You are brave enough to pull a single whisker from a living lion. This was a dangerous task, which required courage, cleverness, and endless patience. If you can accomplish this, then can you not use that same courage, cleverness, and endless patience to improve your marriage?"

"Take time," he suggested. "By your actions show him your love and your needs, and see what may happen then."

The woman went home and thought about this advice. She never spoke to her husband about her anger or what she had done. But slowly, through her actions and not her words, the relationship began to improve. And one day it came to pass that their marriage had grown into one of intimacy and balance, which lasted for all the years of their lives.

HANDOUT 2:
THE WOMAN WHO FOLLOWED DEATH (INDIA)

Once there lived a young woman who was so loved by her father, and whose wisdom he so respected, that he did the *unthinkable*: He gave to her the right to choose her own husband, believing only she would know who would be a worthy partner.

Savitri traveled far and listened to many people. She saw a young man with shining eyes guiding and caring for his old blind father. She heard the stories of his virtue. She knew then who should be her partner and she returned to tell her father. Her father's adviser, however, a holy man, was horrified at her choice. "This young man is indeed a person of great value," he admitted, "But it is written that he will die one year from today. Choose another." Savitri trembled, but said, "I have chosen, and whether his life be short or long, I would share it."

For nearly a year the two lived happily. However, on the eve of their anniversary, her husband suddenly dropped to ground, complaining of a severe headache. Savitri laid him in the shade of a tree, his head on her lap, and watched as her beloved husband's eyes closed and his breathing stopped. Suddenly there appeared a powerful man, his body burned like the sun, though his skin was darker than the deepest night. It was Yama, Lord of the Dead, come for the spirit of her husband. "Indeed you are full of merit if you can see me, child. Happiness awaits your husband in my kingdom," offered Yama, "He has been a man of great virtue." And with that he pulled the spirit of her husband from his body and turned to leave.

Savitri rose and ran after Yama, and though he moved swiftly, she struggled to follow. She called out, "Lord Yama, though it be your duty to take my husband, yet it is my duty to ask you for his life." The Lord of the Dead looked puzzled. "No one can ask for a life back once I have taken it. Go home." Yet Savitri followed, knowing firmly what she wanted, and knowing Yama could give it to her if he wished. After many miles Yama turned. "I will not give what you ask—still your directness pleases me. I will grant you a favor—anything but the life of your husband."

Savitri thought quickly. *"Please restore to my father-in-law his eyesight."* Yama granted this request, but still she followed. "Savitri, you have come far enough."

"Give me the life of my husband," she repeated. Yama shook his head. "No. Still, I admire your devotion and directness. I will grant you another favor—anything but the life of your husband." *"Grant many more children to my father."* Again, Yama granted her request, but still she followed, scratched and bleeding in her struggle to keep up.

"Savitri, your love must bend to fate. I forbid you to come further. Still, I admire your courage and directness. I will grant you one last favor, but this time ask something for yourself—anything but the life of your husband." Savitri paused.

"Then grant many children to me, and let them be the children of my husband whose soul you have taken!" Yama's red eyes grew wide, and a slow smile spread on his dark face. "Savitri, your wit is as strong as your directness. You have not asked for the life of your husband, yet I cannot grant this wish without returning him to you. You have won your husband's life."

And, indeed thereafter, Savitri and her husband were blessed by a long life together of great peace and harmony—and by many children.

HANDOUT 3:
PREPARED QUESTIONS FOR VARIATION C

Questions About "The Lion's Whisker"

1. In this story, the husband came home late, if at all. Do you think his behavior was appropriate?
2. Needing help, the woman went to the oldest and wisest man in the village. Do you think elderly persons in our society receive as much respect and attention as this elder did? Should they?
3. What did the woman learn by feeding the lion? What was the wise man's "potion" for helping the woman's marriage?
4. What are the advantages and disadvantages of saving the woman's marriage by using what the wise man taught her? Do you think it would work?
5. What is the "moral" of this story? Do you agree with this moral?

Questions About "The Woman Who Followed Death"

1. Why was it "unthinkable" that Savitri's father gave her the right to choose her own husband?
2. The holy man knew that Savitri's choice for a husband would die within a year. Do you believe that our future, or some features of it, may be predetermined?
3. After her husband died, what did Savitri do to get his life back? Did other people in Savitri's position ever do the same thing? (How "normal" was it?) Why or why not?
4. What were the advantages and disadvantages of Savitri's actions?
5. What is the "moral" of this story? Do you agree with this moral?

Are Emotional Expressions Universal or Culture Specific?

CAROLYN H. SIMMONS

hether emotional expressions can be easily recognized across cultures has been debated by researchers for several decades. Ekman (1992, 1993, 1994) is credited with the most extensive investigation of human emotions and their concomitant facial muscular actions and changes in autonomic nervous system activity. Since the mid-1960s, Ekman and his colleagues have amassed considerable evidence supporting the position that there is a physiological link between the experience and the expression of basic emotions, with the result that the expression of these emotions is universally recognized.

Ekman and Friesen (1975) collected data from several different cultures; their results demonstrated high agreement across cultural groups in labeling the emotions represented in facial expressions. Based on this study and subsequent research, Ekman has concluded that some emotional expressions are universal. Furthermore, he argues that "no one to date has obtained strong evidence of cross-cultural disagreement about the interpretation of fear, anger, disgust, sadness, or enjoyment expressions" (Ekman, 1993, p. 384), a position supported by others (e.g., Buck, 1988; Izard, 1994). To Ekman's list of basic emotions, Matsumoto (1992) has added the emotional expression of contempt.

Critics of this perspective have argued that the universality of emotional expression has not been—and cannot be—demonstrated persuasively. Klineberg (1938) believed that "the expression of the emotions is at least to some extent patterned by social factors" (p. 517) and illustrated this conclusion with translated examples from Chinese literature of elaborate, culture-specific expressions of such emotions as anger, sorrow, joy, surprise, and love. Josephs (1995) has proposed that emotional meanings cannot be interpreted outside their context of usage—that is, outside the culture in which they are observed.

This view is shared by Lutz and White (1986) and others, who argue that emotional expressions are social constructs learned within a specific culture and that even when the same or similar emotion is experienced in different cultures, the cultural norms for expression of emotions ("display rules") vary considerably across cultures. Wierzbicka (1995) has noted the difficulty of stimulus and language equivalence in describing emotional expressions across cultures. Russell (1991, 1994) has provided detailed criticism of the research methods used to test universal recognition of emotions from facial expressions. Turner and Ortony (1992) have concluded that basic components of emotional expression may be universal, but full emotional expressions are not, and that there are no objective, general criteria for "basic emotions."

The exercise in this chapter demonstrates that some expressions of emotion have strong experiential physiological components and are therefore well recognized across cultures. However, other displays of the same emotions are elaborated with culture-specific expressions and gestures that result either in misinterpretation or bafflement in observers who are not members of the culture in which the expressions originated.

Time

This exercise requires 20 minutes to 1 hour, depending on discussion time, number of participants, and whether the variation is used.

Requirements

The handout should be copied and given to participants. A chalkboard or overhead projector is useful for showing the results. This activity is effective as an introduction to the study of emotional expression in different cultures; no background understanding is required of the participants. However, the discussion will be more extensive when the exercise is used with advanced students who are familiar with the research literature.

Instructions

The instructor can introduce the activity by asking the question:

Are emotional expressions part of our biological makeup as humans and therefore expressed or communicated in universally recognizable ways? Or do the processes of socialization and enculturation teach us how to express emotions in ways that are recognized by other members of the same culture but not necessarily recognized, and even misinterpreted, by those from a different culture?

My experience has been that most students start this exercise with the assumption that emotional expressions are easily recognized across cultures. The handout can then be distributed to the students; the directions at the top should be read aloud to emphasize that students are being asked to select emotional expression labels from the categories provided rather than devising their own labels.

While students are working individually on the activity, the instructor can write the statements on the chalkboard or can prepare to write the results on an overhead on which the statements already have been written. Each statement is then read and a vote taken of the emotional expression that is described. Generally, there is consensus on descriptions with a strong physiological component (e.g., Descriptions 1 and 9 are widely recognized as *fear*; Description 3 as *shame*; Descriptions 6 and to a lesser extent 4 as *anger*; 11 as *sadness*; 13 as *disgust or contempt*; and 14 as *joy*). On the other hand, some emotional expressions are consistently mistaken for emotions that are expressed in a similar way in the mainstream U.S. culture (e.g., Description 8 is usually mistaken for *surprise* by U.S. students, and Description 5 as *disgust or contempt*.) Finally, some emotional expressions are very culture specific and even limited to certain historical times within a culture. Such expressions are rarely recognized by any participants (e.g., Descriptions 2, 7, 10, and 12, which Klineberg found in Chinese literature).

The key for the handout is as follows:

1 and 9 = fear
2 and 5 = surprise
3 = shame
4, 6, and 8 = anger
7, 12, and 14 = joy
10 and 11 = sadness
13 = disgust or contempt

Variations

With a culturally heterogeneous group, students can form culturally homogeneous subgroups to write descriptions of the expression of the seven emotions listed as choices at the top of the handout. Students should be cautioned *not* to use emotion words in their descriptions, for example, "her eyes narrowed to a glare" or "her face shone with happiness." In this variation, students often include descriptions of hand gestures for negative emotions such as anger, disgust or contempt, and shame. These descriptions can then be shared with the other cultural groups in the class to explore whether people from other cultural backgrounds can recognize the emotional expressions described.

Discussion Suggestions

Several disciplines have studied emotional expression across cultures, and these different disciplines provide interesting approaches for discussion. For example, a class in nonverbal communication might discuss spontaneous communication (which is innate and biologically based), symbolic communication (which is culturally learned), and communication events that contain both elements (Buck, 1988), as well as the effect of culture on affective communication (Gudykunst & Ting-Toomey, 1988). The debate between Russell (1991, 1994), Ekman (1992, 1993, 1994), and Izard (1994) as to whether there are universal emotional expressions provides lively debate for a course in social or cross-cultural psychology.

In advanced classes or for extended discussion, other topics can be addressed. For example, the instructor could raise the hypothesis that individualist cultures have fewer display rules for the expression of negative emotions than do collectivist cultures, with the result that members of individualist cultures are more frequently exposed to such expressions (Gudykunst & Ting-Toomey, 1988) and more accurate at recognizing them (Matsumoto, 1989).

References and Further Reading

Buck, R. (1988). Nonverbal communication: Spontaneous and symbolic aspects. *American Behavioral Scientist, 31,* 341-354.

Ekman, P. (1992). An argument for basic emotions. *Cognition and Emotion, 6,* 169-200.

Ekman, P. (1993). Facial expression and emotion. *American Psychologist, 48,* 384-392.

Ekman, P. (1994). Strong evidence for universals in facial expressions: A reply to Russell's mistaken critique. *Psychological Bulletin, 115,* 268-287.

Ekman, P., & Friesen, W. V. (1975). *Unmasking the face.* Englewood Cliffs, NJ: Prentice Hall.

Gudykunst, W. R., & Ting-Toomey, S. (1988). Culture and affective communication. *American Behavioral Scientist, 31,* 384-400.

Izard, C. E. (1994). Innate and universal facial expressions: Evidence from developmental and cross-cultural research. *Psychological Bulletin, 115,* 288-299.

Josephs, I. (1995). The problem of emotions from the perspective of psychological semantics. *Culture and Psychology, 1,* 279-288.

Klineberg, O. (1938). Emotional expression in Chinese literature. *Journal of Abnormal and Social Psychology, 3,* 517-520.

Lutz, C., & White, G. M. (1986). The anthropology of emotions. *Annual Review of Anthropology, 15,* 405-436.

Matsumoto, D. (1989). Cultural influences on the perception of emotion. *Journal of Cross-Cultural Psychology, 20,* 92-105.

Matsumoto, D. (1992). More evidence for the universality of a contempt expression. *Motivation and Emotion, 16,* 363-368.

Russell, J. A. (1991). Culture and the categorization of emotions. *Psychological Bulletin, 110,* 426-450.

Russell, J. A. (1994). Is there universal recognition of emotion from facial expression? A review of the cross-cultural studies. *Psychological Bulletin, 115,* 102-141.

Turner, T. J., & Ortony, A. (1992). Basic emotions: Can conflicting criteria converge? *Psychological Review, 99,* 566-571.

Wierzbicka, A. (1995). Emotion and facial expression: A semantic perspective. *Culture and Psychology, 1,* 227-258.

EMOTIONAL EXPRESSIONS EXERCISE

The following are descriptions of emotional expressions. For each one, write the emotion that is being expressed or described, selecting from the following:

anger, disgust or contempt, fear, joy, sadness, shame, surprise

1. Every one of his hairs stood on end and the pimples came out on the skin all over his body. _____

2. She drew one leg up and stood on one foot. _____

3. His face was red and he went creeping alone outside the village. _____

4. He raised one hand as high as his face and fanned his face with his sleeve. _____

5. They stretched out their tongues. _____

6. She gnashed her teeth until they were all but ground to dust. _____

7. He scratched his ears and cheeks. _____

8. Her eyes grew round and opened wide. _____

9. A cold sweat broke forth on his whole body, and he trembled without ceasing. _____

10. He moved one hand around the front of his beard and touched his head with the fingers of the other hand. _____

11. She was listless and silent. _____

12. She stretched the left arm flatly to the left and the right arm to the right. _____

13. His nose wrinkled and the corners of his mouth turned down. _____

14. Her smile widened until small wrinkles appeared at the corners of her eyes. _____

SOURCE: The first 12 descriptions are adaptations of translations from Chinese literature by Klineberg (O. Klineberg, 1938, Emotional expression in Chinese literature. *Journal of Abnormal and Social Psychology, 3,* 517-520). The last 2 descriptions are based on descriptions by Ekman and Friesen (P. Ekman & W. V. Friesen, 1975, *Unmasking the face.* Englewood Cliffs, NJ: Prentice Hall).

Index

Abe-Kim, J., 151, 245
Abraham, R.,15, 20
Abramson, L. Y., 96
Acculturation, 81-82, 166
Adorno, T. W., 160, 162
Ady, J. C., 111, 245
African American, 24, 51, 54, 78, 79, 142, 152, 154, 170,
    192, 195, 196
African culture, 4, 82, 87-88, 208-209
Aikin, K. J., 194
Akert, R. M., 83, 86
Alexander, C., 47, 50, 145, 190
Alipuria, L., 165, 172
Allocentrism, 112
    See also Collectivism; Self-construal
Alloy, L. B., 96
Allport, G. W., 43, 74, 76
Altman, I., 30, 34
Amato, P. R., 30, 34
America:
    adjustment to, 57-64
    individualism in, 67, 111
    multiculturalism in, 3-4
American:
    attitudes towards Chinese, 58
    attributions of school failure, 94
    conversational constraints, 102
    ethnocentrism and minimization, 41
    interaction with Korean, 118-119
    migration to and education, 57

    student behaviors, 58
Anderson, J. R., 9, 13
Anglin, J. M., 207, 211
Appleton, N., 76
Arab, 221
Arce, C., 171
Armstrong, T., 207, 211
Aronson, E., 83, 86
Arredondo, P., 187, 190
Asian American, 142, 151-157, 170, 195
    stereotypes of, 151-153
    See also separate groups (e.g., Japanese American)
Asian culture, 24, 67, 94, 112, 122, 209, 221
Asian Indian, 151
Assimilation, 82-91
Atkinson, D. R., 166, 167, 171
Attitudes, 83, 175, 200
Attribution, 93-99
    isomorphic, 93-94
    of success and failure, 95
Axelson, J., 74, 76

Babiker, I. E., 58, 60
Backlund, P., 176, 181
Bae, H., 94, 96
Baeyer, C., 96
Bank clock accuracy, 33, 38
Banks, J. A., 5, 141, 144
Barbour, A., 176, 181
Barker, G. P., 96

237

About the Contributors

Jennifer Abe-Kim is currently Assistant Professor of Psychology at Loyola Marymount University (LMU) in Los Angeles. She did her undergraduate work at Wheaton College in Illinois and her graduate work in clinical psychology at University of California, Los Angeles. She teaches classes in psychology and Asian Pacific American studies at LMU and is part of the research faculty for the National Research Center on Asian American Mental Health (UC Davis) and the Center for Managed Care of Psychiatric Disorders (UCLA/RAND). Her research interests include mental health service delivery to ethnic minorities in managed care contexts and the assessment and measurement of cultural variables for Asian Americans. She resides in Los Angeles with her husband and twin daughters.

Jeffrey C. Ady received his Ph.D. in communication from the University of Kansas in 1992 with specializations in intercultural and organizational communication. He teaches and researches in the two areas. Specific interests are intercultural conflict management, cross-cultural negotiation, and sojourner adjustment. He has traveled extensively in Asia and has numerous professional interests in Japan.

Dharm P. S. Bhawuk is Assistant Professor of Management, College of Business Administration, University of Hawai'i at Manoa. He received his Ph.D. in organizational behavior and human resource management from the University of Illinois at Urbana-Champaign. His research interests include cross-cultural training, intercultural sensitivity, diversity in the workplace, individualism and collectivism, quality and culture, culture and cognition, and political behavior in the workplace. He has published several empirical papers in the *International Journal of Intercultural Relations*, *International Journal of Psychology*, *Cross-Cultural Research*, and *Journal of Management*. He has also published a number of book chapters and is an editor of the book *Asian Contributions to Cross-Cultural Psychology* (Sage, 1996).

Richard W. Brislin is Director of the Ph.D. program in international management and is Professor of Management and Industrial Relations at the College of Business Administration, University of Hawai'i. He directs a yearly program for university professors planning to introduce cross-cultural studies into their courses. He is the developer of materials used in cross-cultural training programs (e.g., *Intercultural Interactions: A Practical Guide* (2nd ed., 1996) and is author of a text in cross-cultural psychology (*Understanding Culture's Influence on Behavior*, 1993). He has coedited two volumes, for Sage, of modules for training and educational programs: *Improving Intercultural Interactions: Modules for Cross-Cultural Training Programs*. One of his books, *The Art of Getting Things Done: A Practical Guide to the Use of Power*, was a Book-of-the-Month Club selection in 1992. He is frequently asked to give workshops for American and Asian managers working on international assignments, and the training materials he has prepared are widely used in various international organizations.

William J. Brown (Ph.D., University of Southern California) is Dean of the College of Communication and the Arts at Regent University. He has worked in numerous international settings and lived in Hong Kong, the Pacific Islands, and Canada for over 12 years. His research interests include the international and intercultural dimensions of social influence and the use of entertainment-education media to promote prosocial values, beliefs, and behavior.

Aaron Castelan Cargile (Ph.D., University of California, Santa Barbara) is Assistant Professor at California State University Long Beach, where he teaches courses in intercultural communication, advanced intercultural communication, and communication theory. He maintains a research interest in all forms of both intercultural and intergroup communication, and he is focused particularly on the role of accented speech in such interactions. His recent publications have appeared in *Communication Yearbook 19* and *Intercultural Communication Theory*.

Fred L. Casmir has taught for 41 years at Pepperdine University and was among the earliest pioneers in the field of intercultural and international communication in the United States. He has taught courses in intercultural and international communication, as well as a media worldwide course. He has developed both the intercultural studies minor and major, for which he serves as Coordinator, at Pepperdine University. He will be chairperson of Division V (Intercultural, International and Development Communication) of ICA beginning in 1997. He has lectured, consulted, and held various teaching positions on five continents, and he has had some of his work published on five continents. His main research and theory-building concerns center around communication-process-oriented third-culture building, communication-theory building, and the cultural impact of mass media. He recently edited *Ethics in Intercultural and International Communication*, to be published in 1997.

Kenneth N. Cissna (Ph.D., University of Denver, 1975) is Professor of Communication at the University of South Florida. He teaches undergraduate and graduate courses in interpersonal communication, group communication, and dialogue. His recent research has focused on human dialogue, especially on the implications of the 1957 public conversation between philosopher Martin Buber and psychotherapist Carl Rogers. His articles have appeared in a variety of books and journals in communication and related fields; his books include *The Reach of Dialogue* (with Rob Anderson and Ron Arnett), *Applied Communication in the 21st Century*, and *The Martin Buber-Carl Rogers Dialogue: A New Transcript With Commentary* (with Rob Anderson).

David R. Clemons earned his undergraduate degree in business administration from the University of Texas and worked for several years in banking and finance before making a career change. He has worked in the counseling arena in various capacities since 1989, when he began training as a chemical dependency counselor. He holds a master's degree in psychology with an emphasis in marriage and family therapy and is currently a doctoral student in counseling psychology at Our Lady of the Lake University in San Antonio, Texas. His current research interests include the application of postmodern theoretical ideas to psychotherapy, qualitative research methods, and the effectiveness of solution-focused therapy modalities.

Thomas Connell is Vice President of INTERLINK Consulting Services, Inc., a firm providing cross-cultural communications, regional orientation, and terrorism awareness training to organizations with international interests. A regular speaker at numerous Department of Defense organizations and consultant to U.S. businesses, he holds a B.S. in journalism, an M.S. in international human resource management, and a Ph.D. in U.S./Latin American history. He directed the only cross-cultural communications course in DOD for nearly a decade. His book *Kidnapped! The Internment and Abandonment of the Peruvian Japanese in the United States during WWII* is expected to be released next year. He is

Associate Professor of International Management Communications, International Organizational Behavior, and Latin American History at Troy State University and winner of several awards including the Silver Anvil Award, two-time winner of the Thomas Jefferson Award, and author/narrator of several award-winning radio/TV documentaries.

Estelle Disch is Associate Professor of Sociology at the University of Massachusetts Boston (UMB) where she teaches courses related to cultural diversity, gender, and human services. She has consulted to faculty and staff at many colleges and universities about curricular transformation and inclusive pedagogy. As Coordinator for Diversity Awareness at the Center for the Improvement of Teaching at UMB, she has been very involved in faculty development related to working effectively with diverse students. She is a white Anglo-Saxon former Protestant on a lifelong quest to overcome the limitations of a privileged upbringing in a white suburb. She has recently edited *Reconstructing Gender: A Multicultural Anthology* (1997). Her current research focuses on survivors of sexual exploitation by professionals.

Benson P. Fraser (Ph.D., University of Washington) is Associate Professor in the College of Communication and the Arts at Regent University. He has conducted extensive international research and is an adviser to international graduate students. His research interests include the influence of role models on culture and the impact of media across cultural boundaries.

William K. Gabrenya, Jr. is a cross-cultural psychologist at the Florida Institute of Technology where he teaches courses in cultural and social psychology. He is currently editor of the International Association for Cross-Cultural Psychology's *Cross-Cultural Psychology Bulletin*. His research focuses on culture and social interaction, values, social class, and sojourner adjustment, with an area interest in Chinese studies. He received his doctorate in social psychology at the Center for Research in Social Behavior of the University of Missouri–Columbia, was a postdoctoral research associate in the Behavioral Sciences Laboratory at Ohio State University, and has been a visiting professor at National Taiwan University. He lives a perfect, suburban American middle-class lifestyle with a wife, one boy, one girl, a dog, and a mortgage.

Harry Gardiner is Professor of Psychology at the University of Wisconsin–La Crosse where he teaches courses in child development, cross-cultural psychology, cross-cultural human development, and humor in education for teachers. His M.A. is from the University of Hawai'i and his Ph.D. from Manchester University in England. He taught in the graduate program at Chulalongkorn University in Bangkok for 2 years. He has engaged in training, teaching, and research in Europe, Asia, and the United

States. He was a charter member of the International Association for Cross-Cultural Psychology and currently serves as Secretary/Treasurer of the Society for Cross-Cultural Research as well as a consulting editor for the *Journal of Cross-Cultural Psychology* and assistant editor for *Teaching for the Cross-Cultural Psychology Bulletin.* He recently coauthored a book, *Lives Across Cultures: Cross-Cultural Human Development,* which will be published in 1998.

Michele J. Gelfand is Assistant Professor of Industrial and Organizational Psychology at the University of Maryland at College Park. She received her Ph.D. in social/organizational psychology from the University of Illinois at Urbana-Champaign in 1996. Her research focuses on incorporating dimensions of cultural variation into theories of negotiation, conflict, and organizational justice, and on the effects of diversity in work groups. Her recent publications have appeared in the *Handbook of Industrial and Organizational Psychology, Journal of Vocational Behavior, Journal of Personality and Social Psychology, European Journal of Social Psychology,* and *International Journal of Psychology.* She teaches courses in cross-cultural psychology, industrial and organizational psychology, and cognition in organizations.

Sharon G. Goto received her Ph.D. in social/organizational psychology from the University of Illinois at Urbana-Champaign. She is Assistant Professor at Pomona College and is part of the research faculty for the National Research Center on Asian American Mental Health (UC Davis). Her research focuses on cultural diversity issues. Specifically, she is interested in cross-cultural interpersonal interactions both within and beyond the workplace, and strategies that foster success for ethnic minorities. Her research has concentrated largely on Asian American populations. She is currently working on a collaborative project that looks at Asian American perceptions of racism and their effects on subjective well-being. Another project focuses on mentoring Asian Americans. Her teaching interests largely parallel her research interests. She currently teaches an Asian American psychology course and a fieldwork course for Asian American psychology, and she is developing a course looking at the Asian American experience within organizations.

Alison Gourvès-Hayward was born in the south west of England and was educated at University College, London and the University of Leicester. She taught French in England before moving to France, where she is currently Head of the English Department at the Ecole Supérieure des Télécommunications de Bretagne. She is particularly interested in the communicative approach to language teaching and has recently taken an active part in a European project on learning to learn, producing materials for both French and Portuguese teaching. Her work with Francophone Africans lead to an interest in semantics and culturally biased perceptual and sociolinguistic differences. She is at present involved in a pilot course organized between parallel classes in French and American universities. This course aims to provide students with the conceptual framework necessary to analyze cultural differences and similarities and is facilitated by electronic mail, WWW, and teleconferencing. She is married with one son, aged 11.

Susan Wiley Hardwick is Professor of Geography at Southwest Texas State University and has also served as co-coordinator of the university's Literacy and Learning Program. Her teaching and research specializations focus on geographic education, cognition and spatial learning, immigrant settlement and survival in western North America, and the regional geography of the Russian Federation. She is author of nine books and numerous articles including, most recently, *Geography for Educators: Standards, Themes, and Concepts* (1996), *Valley for Dreams: Life and Landscape in the Sacramento Valley* (1996), and *Russian Refuge* (1993). Her forthcoming book *Russia: A Regional Geography of Change and Endurance* will be published in late fall 1997. Two years ago, she was selected out of more than 21,000 faculty for the California State University Statewide Outstanding Professor Award.

J. Coleman Heckman has an interest in psychology that began during high school with the simple act of listening and giving advice to friends and family. He then decided to pursue an undergraduate degree in psychology at Boston University, and after completing his degree he realized how interested he was in working specifically with children and adolescents. He then obtained a master's degree in school psychology at Trinity University in San Antonio, Texas, where he was well trained in assessment and educational psychology. However, his underlying interest in the area of counseling and the therapeutic process led him to seek more training, and he is currently continuing his education as he enters his third year in the Psy.D. program at Our Lady of the Lake University, in counseling psychology.

Karen M. Holcombe is a graduate student at the University of Maryland at College Park, where she is pursuing a Ph.D. in industrial/organizational psychology. Her primary research interest lies in the area of cross-cultural psychology; other research interests include leadership and service quality.

James E. Jacob (Ph.D.) is Dean of the College of Behavioral and Social Sciences, and Professor of Political Science, at California State University, Chico. He received his A.B. from the University of California at Berkeley, and his M.A. and Ph.D. from Cornell University. He lived in France for 3 years, and his teaching fields include nationalism, international relations, the causes of war, European politics, and Soviet and post-Soviet foreign policy. His research interests include ethnic conflict, cross-cultural communication, and terrorism. He is coeditor with the late William R. Beer of *Language and National Unity* and author of *The Hills of Conflict: Basque Nationalism in France.*

Min-Sun Kim (Ph.D., Michigan State University, 1992) is Associate Professor in the Department of Speech at the University of Hawai'i at Manoa. Her research interests focus on the role of cognition in conversational styles of different cultural and gender orientations. She has applied the models she has developed to understand communication differences in the areas of requesting, re-requesting, and conflict styles. Her publications have appeared in a variety of journals including *Human Communication Research, Communication Monographs, International and Intercultural Communication Annual, Communication Research, Communication Quarterly, International Journal of Intercultural Relations, Howard Journal of Communication,* and *Research on Language and Social Interaction,* among others. She is currently investigating cross-cultural conflict styles involving Korea, Japan, Hawaii, and the mainland. Her most recent research, concerning self-construals and re-requesting styles, will be published in *Communication Monographs* (1997).

Randy Kluver (Ph.D., University of Southern California, 1993) is Associate Professor of Speech and Rhetoric and Director of the interdisciplinary Asian Studies program at Oklahoma City University. His research and teaching concentrates on the cultural dimensions of political communication. He previously taught at Jiangxi Normal University, Nanchang, Jiangxi Province, People's Republic of China. He is author of *Legitimating the Chinese Economic Reforms: A Rhetoric of Myth and Orthodoxy* (1996).

Suzette Lamb (LPC, M.S.) grew up in a military family, traveling all over the United States and abroad. This exposure to multiple cultures and personalities spurred her interest in people and the ways they act and interact. She received her undergraduate degree from Trinity University in San Antonio, Texas, while working with at-risk youths in a local YMCA and a tutor in a group home for boys. After graduation, she worked for the local community mental health center as a case manager for children and adolescents and their families. She then began the master's program at Our Lady of the Lake University, in counseling psychology with a specialization in marriage and family therapy and began to work for a nonprofit mental health facility where she continues to provide therapy for youths and their families. She is currently in her third year of the Psy.D. program at Our Lady of the Lake University in counseling psychology.

Robert V. Levine is Professor of Psychology at California State University, Fresno, where he teaches courses in social psychology. His research has focused on cross-cultural differences in the psychology of time and the psychology of helping behavior. He is author of the book *A Geography of Time*.

Denise Lucero-Miller is Staff Psychologist and Practicum Coordinator for Texas Woman's University Counseling Center in Denton, Texas. She also previously served as the Counseling Center's Cultural Diversity Liaison to the university community. She received her Ph.D. in counseling psychology (1995) and her M.Ed. in community counseling (1991) from the University of Oklahoma. Her predoctoral internship was completed at the University of Texas Health Sciences Center in San Antonio, Texas. Her clinical and teaching interests include women's issues, multicultural counseling, and therapist training and supervision.

Miriam Ma'at-Ka-Re Monges earned her doctorate in African American Studies at Temple University and has a master's in social work and a B.A. cum laude in education. She is author of *KUSH: The Jewel of Nubia: Reconnecting the Root System of African Civilization* (in press). She has also written an article, "Reflections of the Role of Female Deities and Queens in Ancient Kemet" in the *Journal of Black Studies* and a chapter "I've Got a Right to the Tree of Life" in the book edited by Charles Jones, *The Panthers Revisited* (in press). She is Assistant Professor of Sociology/Social Work, with major responsibility to African American Studies, at California State University, Chico. In November, she will be traveling to Norway to train social workers at Bodo College in methods of infusing multiculturalism into theory and practice.

Mehroo Northover was born in India in a minority community, which has maintained a strong sense of ethnicity over 1,500 years. Her early education was in India in an English-language school and university. As a result of a bicultural, bilingual background, she has developed an academic interest in issues of migration, ethnicity, and bilingualism, which have been the focus of her teaching. She has lived in several countries including the multicultural city state of Singapore for some years. As a result, she became interested in the successful policies adopted by the government in creating a supranational identity for its citizens. She has been a lecturer in linguistics and communication and has teaching and research interests in ethnic identity and bilingualism, second-language learning, and intercultural communication.

Pamela M. Norwood is Assistant Professor in the College of Education at the University of Houston. She teaches a course in curricular and instructional studies, as well as bilingual education. Her research interests include teacher education issues in the education of culturally diverse youths and minority at-risk female adolescents. She has conducted numerous inservice presentations for teachers serving multicultural populations.

Elizabeth Renfro has taught in the English, Honors, and Multicultural & Gender Studies Departments at California State University, Chico, for 22 years. She has also coordinated the university's Writing Across the Disciplines/Literacy & Learning Program since its inception in 1985, and she has recently developed a peer mentoring program in women's studies. Professional work includes over a hundred workshops, papers, and articles on teaching and learning; numerous articles and papers on literature, feminist criticism, and women's studies; and three books: *Basic Writing: Process and Product* (1985), *The Shasta Indians of California* (1990), and *Finding Voice, Sending Voice: Reading Diverse Voices in Literature* (in press).

Deborah Carr Saldaña is presently Assistant Professor in the Department of Urban Education at the University of Houston–Downtown. Her research interests include exemplary middle school practice and issues related to multicultural education. Presently, she is involved in several projects focusing on the improvement of teaching and learning in urban, multicultural classrooms.

Ruth Seymour is Lecturer on the journalism faculty at Wayne State University, and former Director of the Journalism Institute for Minorities. She teaches core newswriting courses as well as intercultural communication. Her research interests are in the possibilities of intercultural communication via mass media, and in the representation of social difference, especially culture and race, in those media. She has an M.A. in mass communication and anthropology from Wayne State University and a B.A. from Michigan State University. She reported lifestyle, police, general assignment, and religion for the *Detroit Free Press* (1980-1987) and also wrote for the *Detroit News* (1978-1980). Among her journalism awards is a national Gold Medallion Mass Media Award "for outstanding contributions to better human relations and the cause of brotherhood" from the National Conference of Christians and Jews (1985).

Poonam Sharma completed her doctoral degree in counseling psychology at the University of Texas at Austin in 1994. She completed a predoctoral internship and postdoctoral fellowship in clinical psychology at the U.T. Health Science Center in San Antonio, where she is currently employed. She is Assistant Professor in the Department of Rehabilitation Medicine and Staff Psychologist for the Reeves Rehabilitation Center. Her primary research interest is in the area of diversity issues and mental health, with a special focus on the Asian population. She is currently involved in teaching rehabilitation medicine residents about psychological issues in medical rehabilitation, as well as statistics and research methodology.

Jo Anne Shwayder received her B.A. in Pyschology/Anthropology from Pitzer College and her M.Ed. in Educational Psychology from the University of Hawai'i. She conducted research and taught English in Nepal, Indonesia, Hawai'i, and Southern California. She is currently a Ph.D student at UCLA in the Psychological Studies in Education department at UCLA.

Carolyn H. Simmons is Professor at the University of North Carolina at Wilmington with teaching interests in cross-cultural and social psychology and lifespan development. Her doctorate in social psychology was earned at the University of Kentucky. She has also held faculty appointments at Howard University and the University of Colorado at Denver. Current research interests include helping behavior, cross-cultural dimensions of cooperation and competition, and cultural differences in response to natural disasters.

Theodore M. Singelis received his B.A. in psychology from Yale University. After living in Korea and Japan for 5 years, he was awarded an East-West Center grant to study at the University of Hawai'i where he earned an M.A. in speech and a Ph.D. in psychology (1995). At the East-West Center, he presented original materials at workshops in developing training and course materials for cross-cultural psychology and intercultural communication. Although this is his first book, over the past 3 years he has published more than 15 journal articles and book chapters. He is a consulting editor for the *Journal of Cross-Cultural Psychology* and Treasurer of the International Association for Cross-Cultural Psychology. Currently, he is Assistant Professor in the Psychology Department at California State University, Chico, where he teaches cross-cultural psychology, research methods, and psychology of prejudice. His research interests include cultural conceptions of self, intercultural communication, and emotion.

Kyle D. Smith received his Ph.D. in social psychology from the University of Washington in 1987 and has taught in Turkey and Micronesia as well as the mainland United States. Currently, as Associate Professor of Pyschology at the University of Guam, he teaches courses in cross-cultural and social psychology with students from Guam, the Philippines, Micronesia, the Pacific Rim, and the United States. His research addresses emotion and moral concepts (including the ideal person, evil, and human rights) cross-culturally.

Sunwolf (J.D., University of Denver College of Law; M.A., University of California, Santa Barbara), a former trial attorney, is a college teacher, trial consultant, and professional storyteller who also serves on the faculties of the National Criminal Defense College, the Institute for Criminal Defense Advocacy, and the National College of Advocacy for the Association of Trial Lawyers of America. She teaches small group, interpersonal, and intercultural communication as well as storytelling, and she lectures on negotiation and contract law in France for the Paris Bar Association. Her research interests include social influence, group decision making, jury deliberations, and the persuasive effects of telling tales. She collects multicultural folktales, ghostlore, world folktales of justice, and wisdom stories.

Ann-Marie Yamada is pursing a Ph.D. in clinical psychology with a dual special emphasis in cross-cultural/intercultural mental health and clinical health psychology at the University of Hawai'i at Manoa. She is an East-West Center Degree Fellow with the Program on Education and Training and has been involved with the coordination of numerous workshops and seminars focused on intercultural topics. As a member of a military family, her intercultural experiences began at an early age through involvement with members of the international military community. Her current research projects center on ethnocultural identity and include study of the multiple dimensions that contribute to one's cultural identities and exploration of cultural identification in multiheritage and multicultural persons. She enjoys teaching cross-cultural psychology as an instructor at the University of Hawai'i.

Christine Jean Yeh received her Ph.D. in counseling psychology from Stanford University. She completed her clinical training at Counseling and Psychological Services at the University of California at Berkeley. Presently, she is Assistant Professor of Education and Psychology in the Department of Counseling and Clinical Psychology at Teachers College, Columbia University. Her research interests include cross-cultural conceptualizations of self and morality as well as Asian American ethnic identity, counseling, and mental health use. Her teaching interests are in the areas of multicultural counseling, guidance counseling for school-age children and youth, and culture and self. At the time her chapter was written, she was a postdoctoral scholar at the Stanford Center on Adolescence at Stanford University.